exploring
TRANSPORTATION

by

Stephen R. Johnson
Tech Prep Regional Coordinator
Southeastern Career Center
Versailles, Indiana

Patricia A. Farrar Hunter
Technology Education Instructor
Roswell, Georgia

Contributing Photographer

Jack Klasey
Kankakee, Illinois

South Holland, Illinois

THE GOODHEART-WILLCOX COMPANY, INC.

Publishers

Library of Congress Catalog Card Number 92-25483
International Standard Book Number 0-87006-979-9

2 3 4 5 6 7 8 9 10   93   96 95 94

Library of Congress Cataloging in Publication Data

Johnson, Stephen R.
  Exploring transportation / by Stephen R. Johnson and Patricia A. Farrar-Hunter.

    p. cm.
  Includes index.
  ISBN 0-87006-979-9
    1. Transportation. I. Farrar-Hunter, Patricia A.
II. Title.
HE151.J66   1993
388--dc19   92-25483
                                              CIP

INTRODUCTION

Our modern world is made more comfortable by the use of various technologies. These technologies involve the efficient use of tools and other resources to produce goods and structures, communicate ideas, and relocate people or goods.

This text is concerned with relocation, thus the title, **Exploring Transportation.** For you who are beginning to explore technology, it provides a thorough understanding of the systems and jobs that not only bring us the clothing, food, and other products we use daily, but stand ready to whisk us across the city or across continents to reach destinations too distant to walk.

Exploring Transportation is organized into twenty-four chapters and six sections. The first of these sections introduces the concepts of transportation, energy, and power. Then it explains the close relationship that brings these three elements together.

The next section discusses the sources of energy, how we can convert them to power sources and how power is used in transportation. In the third section you will learn about mechanical, electrical, and fluid power systems and how they operate. The fourth section deals with familiar modes of transportation: land, water, air and space.

You will be introduced to a fifth system known as intermodal (a combination of several modes). Section five discusses vehicle systems. Here you will learn how systems are combined to move, support, and control all types of vehicles. A final section will give you a glimpse of the future of transportation and how it is likely to affect you and the way you live.

Stephen R. Johnson
Patricia A. Farrar Hunter

CONTENTS

ACKNOWLEDGEMENTS

The authors would like to thank the following individuals and companies who provided photographs, drawings, and technical assistance during the development of this book.

Airbus Industrie of North America
Allied Signal Aerospace, Garrett Engine Division
America West Airlines
American Electric Power
American Gas Association
Amtrak
Autodesk, Inc.
Baldor Electric
Battery Council International
Bayliner Marine Corporation
BC Transit
Bell Helicopter Textron, Inc.
Bodine Electric
Boeing Airplane Company
Boston Gear
British Information Services
Carnival Cruise Lines
Caterpillar Inc.
Chrysler Corporation
Cleveland Gear
Coastal Corporation
Conner Prairie
CSX Creative Services
Cyprus Mineral Company
Delta Airlines
Delta Queen Steamboat Company
Edison Electric Institute
Eileen B. Johnson
Estes Industries
Eurotunnel
Eveready Battery
Fisher Controls International, Inc.
Ford Motor Company
Freightliner Corporation
French Technology Press Office
Fruehauf Corporation
GE Ocean Systems
General Dynamics
General Electric Company
General Motors Corporation
Goodyear Tire and Rubber Company
Gould
Greyhound
Grumman Corporation
Harley-Davidson International
Harvard University
Hayes-Dana, Inc.
HSST-Nevada Corporation
Jeffboat Shipyard
John B. Corns
John Deere & Company

K. Leach
Kawasaki
Kohler Company
Mark Morelli
Mark Van Manen
Martin Marietta Space Systems
McDonnell-Douglas
Miller Electric Mfg. Co.
Mobil Oil Company
Murphy/Jahn, Architects
NASA
National Park Service
Nilfisk of America, Inc.
Norfolk Southern Corporation
Nuclear Power in Canada/Canadian Nuclear Power
  Association
Outboard Marine Corporation
Panama Canal Commission
Polaris
Port of Long Beach
Pratt and Whitney, Canada
Quaker State Oil Refining Corporation
Rand McNally
St. Lawrence Seaway
Santa Fe Railway
Saturn Corporation
SI Handling Systems, Inc.
Smithsonian Institute
Standard Oil Company—Ohio
Sun Electric Corporation
Suzanne Silagi
Textron Lycoming
Thrall Car Manufacturing Company
Thunder Bay Harbor Commission
Transrapid International
United Airlines
United Parcel Service
United Technologies Corporation
U.S. Air Force
U.S. Army Corps of Engineers
U.S. Coast Guard
U.S. Navy
U.S. Postal Service
Weyerhaeuser Company
Wisconsin Department of Tourism

Special thanks to cartoonist, James Nelson for his drawings throughout this text.

The authors gratefully acknowledge the following for photographs supplied in the section pages:

Chessie System
City of Chicago, Department of Aviation
Mannesman-Demag Corp.

Radisson Hotels International
H. Smith
Theresa Magee, BC Transit

Section I
INTRODUCING TRANSPORTATION

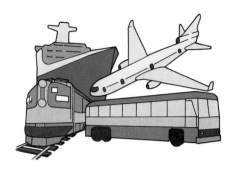

Chapter 1

WHAT IS TRANSPORTATION?

After studying this chapter, you will be able to:
☐ Define transportation.
☐ Discuss the importance of the study of transportation.
☐ Define a technological system.
☐ Describe the five elements of a technological system.
☐ List the inputs of a technological system.
☐ Describe transportation as a technological system within our society.

You walk to the mailbox to get the mail, Fig. 1-1. You reach in the refrigerator for a carton of milk. You may think of getting a letter from a good friend. You're only hoping that there will be enough milk to drink with your cookies. But have you ever wondered how these products got within your reach? They have been delivered to you by trains, trucks, planes, or maybe even bicycles, Fig. 1-2. To move products or people from one place to another place is called *transportation*. The word transportation comes from a shorter word, transport. Transport means to carry across, Fig. 1-3.

What comes to your mind first when you say the word transportation? Do you think of a car, a motorcycle, a skateboard, a train, a truck, or an elevator? This list goes on. What do all of these have in common? They all move people or products from one place to another. You may pick up your pencil and move it from one side of your desk to the other. You have just transported it. You have performed a simple form of transportation. Carrying a package on your bicycle from your house to a friend's house is also an example of transportation.

Fig. 1-1. How does your mail arrive in your mailbox?

WHY STUDY TRANSPORTATION?

Most people take transportation for granted. They usually don't think about how it affects their life. But you should understand the things you use daily. That is why it is important to study transportation. It affects the way you live. Transportation

Fig. 1-2. A truck is one method of transporting mail.

Fig. 1-3. The word "transport" means to "carry across." It is borrowed from the Latin language. "Porto" in Latin means "to carry." "Trans" means "across."

Fig. 1-4. Transportation is essential in our lives. Without it, travel and the movement of goods would not be possible.

is essential in nearly everything you do, Fig. 1-4. You need some mode (type) of transportation in order to survive. Even if it is the most simple type of transportation, such as walking.

Think of what your life would be like if you had no transportation. There would be no way to get to the movies. You could not get to your friend's house. No one could take a vacation. Can you imagine what it would be like without cars, buses, trains, bicycles, motorcycles, airplanes, and boats? Life would be rather dull. You would be very limited in where you could go and what you could do. Are you beginning to see the importance of transportation? You need to study transportation because it is one of the technological systems within our society, Fig. 1-5. This system affects your life in many ways. Therefore, you need to understand anything that impacts your life so greatly.

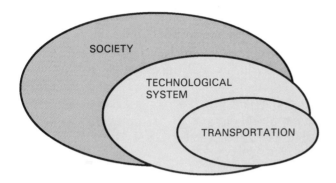

Fig. 1-5. Our society and all of our technological systems depend upon transportation.

You will study transportation in the following chapters of this book. These chapters will introduce you to energy systems, transportation systems, and vehicular systems. You will see how the world of transportation fits together.

TECHNOLOGICAL SYSTEMS

In the world around you, you are surrounded by various technological systems. *Technology* is the application of knowledge and creative thinking that changes resources to meet human needs. This usually results in an easier life-style. You live in a technical world. Life is very different for you to day than it was for your great-grandfather. See Fig. 1-6. Many changes and advancements have taken place. Part of these changes and advancements are the direct results of transportation systems.

A *system* involves a combination of parts that are related to each other. These parts work together to accomplish a desired result. A system that may be familiar to you is the circulatory system located within your body. You may also know about our system of government. Both of these systems have separate but relating parts that work together.

All systems consist of an input, a process, and an output. Within a system, we should also see a goal and some means of feedback, Fig 1-7. As a system works toward the desired goal, the environment or setting must be considered. Feedback from the system is also needed. Feedback provides information on how the system is working.

When you combine the two, technology and a system, the result is a *Technological system*, Fig. 1-8. Technological systems are those systems humans have built to make life easier. Transportation is a technological system.

System Inputs

The *inputs* of a system are those resources needed to begin the system. These resources are needed to make the system operate. For example, if you were

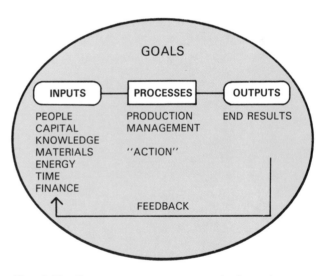

Fig. 1-7. Every system on earth has inputs, processes, outputs, and feedback.

Fig. 1-6. Technological advancement usually brings about an easier life-style.   (Conner Prairie)

Fig. 1-8. Technology and a system make up a technological system.

going to bake cookies, you need input. Your input would be the ingredients. You would need eggs, milk, sugar, etc. These ingredients would be needed to begin your system of baking cookies. See Fig. 1-9.

There are several different types of resources that must be considered for a transportation system. These resources are:

• People.
• Capital.
• Knowledge.
• Materials.
• Energy.
• Time.
• Finance.

In the following paragraphs, you will get a general knowledge of each resource.

People

Humans are a very important resource into any system. Using people in a system brings a variety of knowledge, attitudes, and skills. Having a variety of knowledge, attitudes, and skills is an advantage to any system. With such variety, a system can advance. In the transportation system people are needed to operate and manage the system. An airplane pilot, a cab driver, a ticket agent, and an auto mechanic are all examples of people in a transportation system, Fig. 1-10.

Capital

In many systems capital is needed. Capital is all the tangible (real) items that are needed and used within a transportation system. Capital is used to help perform the process. Buildings, vehicles, roads, computers, and airplanes are all examples of capital within a transportation system. See Fig. 1-11.

Knowledge

To have a successful transportation system, knowledge is needed. Knowledge is brought to the system by people. Through experience and application, people "inhale" information. Through understanding and intelligence, people "exhale" knowledge. Knowledge is essential. In order to reach the desired goal, the system must have knowledge as an input. For example, a train engineer must have the knowledge to read the instruments in order for the train to stay on schedule and function properly, Fig. 1-12.

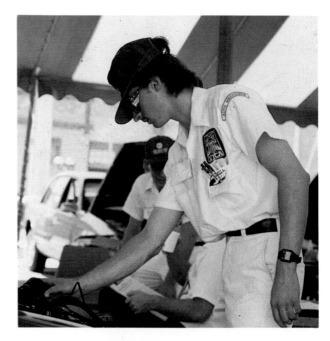

Fig. 1-10. People are important resources in maintaining a transportation system.

Fig. 1-9. Inputs are the ingredients we put into cookies or any other product or service we provide.

The engine, in turn, may run the system. Materials that are used in a transportation system consist of solids, liquids, and gases, Fig. 1-13.

Energy

Transportation systems operate from a source of energy. Some sources of energy include human power, animal power, wind, solar, natural gas, and petroleum. Using various types of energy, transportation systems are powered. Energy powers vehicles that are used in a transportation system. See Fig. 1-14.

Time

Time is the duration (how long it lasts) of any activity. Transporting people and cargo takes time. While time can be considered a renewable resource,

Fig. 1-11. Capital is those tangible items, such as equipment or vehicles, that are needed in various areas of a transportation system.   (UPS)

Fig. 1-12. A train engineer must have knowledge of how to operate the train.   (Santa Fe Railway)

Materials

Materials are major resources used to make the transportation system function. Some materials can be used as they are and some materials are changed by the system. They may come into the system in the solid state and be processed into a liquid state. For example, corn (solid) may be harvested and hauled to a plant. At the plant it may be processed into a fuel known as gasohol (liquid). This gasohol may then be used as an input to fuel an engine.

Fig. 1-13. Gasoline is needed so that vehicles will operate effectively.

Fig. 1-14. Boats need a form of energy to be able to provide transport. Sailboats require wind energy. Power boats require some type of fossil fuel.

time lost or spent can never be recovered. When the movement of people or cargo is delayed, the time cannot be made up without changing another condition of the transporting.

Arranging time for transporting is called scheduling. Usually, companies in the business of transporting make up schedules. A schedule will indicate when a transportation vehicle departs and when it will arrive at its destination. People plan their travels by consulting a printed schedule.

Finance

Finance is money. A system of exchange is needed to pay for all inputs. Money is used to buy the resources used to begin a system. In the transportation system, resources like materials, services of people (skills and time), capital, energy, and knowledge all need to be paid for.

SYSTEM PROCESSES

Once you have the inputs of a system, it is time for some action. *Process* is the action part of a system. Let us use the previous example of baking cookies. The process is the mixing of the ingredients, the cutting out of the dough, and the actual baking in the oven. See Fig. 1-15.

During a process, the desired goal is in sight. The inputs you started with are now being changed.

This change will produce an output or desired result. So it is in a transportation system. The inputs are combined to make the system run. For the system to run properly, it must be managed. People manage systems. For transportation to be efficient, management is a necessity. The job of a manager is to plan, organize, and control the system. For example, people who manage bus lines route the schedules of the buses so that people can plan out their trips in advance. Railroads, as well as truck lines, also need to be managed. The movement of people and cargo begins once the transportation process is started.

System Outputs

The *output* of a system is the end result. The first two elements of a system, inputs and processes, assist in reaching the output. Without all three elements, there would be no system. In the example of baking cookies, the output is golden brown cookies, Fig. 1-16. If you didn't gather your ingredients, or perform the process of mixing and baking, you would have no output. A transportation system also has an output. The relocation of people or cargo is the output.

A transportation system will have other outputs besides the relocation of people or cargo. These are called unintended outputs. One of these is pollution. The burning of fossil fuels puts hydrocarbons and other pollutants into the atmosphere. Aircraft

Fig. 1-15. When the action takes place in a system, we call it the process.

Fig. 1-16. Golden brown cookies are the output of the baking system described.

cause noise pollution especially for those living near airports. Can you think of other undesirable outputs of transportation?

GOALS OF A SYSTEM

The success of all systems involves desirable goals. Using the example of baking cookies, the desired goal would be to have golden cookies but, if the cookies would have come out burnt, the goal would not have been met. You would still have an output, burnt cookies, but your desired goal would have been missed. A transportation system also has desired goals. For instance, the desired goal in transporting an athletic team from their home school to the opponents school by way of bus would be to get the team to the right place at the right time. If the bus breaks down or the bus driver gets lost then the desired goal of the system is missed. However, there are also societal and personal goals put on a transportation system. To arrive at a destination comfortably and in style is a personal, as well as, a societal goal. Society puts restrictions on a transportation system. Society also sets high expectations for a transportation system.

FEEDBACK

Feedback is also an essential part of any system. Feedback gives back information on how well the system has performed or is performing. In a transportation system feedback is also needed. An aircraft pilot, for example, looks at the instrument panel for feedback. Several gauges provide information as to the altitude, air pressure, and speed of the aircraft. This lets the pilot know the performance of the aircraft. In a similar manner the driver of an automobile observes gauges on the dashboard. These gauges feed back information on speed, mileage, oil pressure, engine coolant temperature, fuel reserves, and other conditions that may affect the operation and progress of the vehicle.

SUMMARY

Transportation affects our everyday lives. It is used to transport people and cargo from one point to another. Without transportation, you would not be able to do the things you are able to do now. Transportation is a technological system that has definitely made our lives easier. In the transportation system, as well as any other technological system, there are some major elements. These elements are inputs, processes, outputs, goals, and feedback. In this chapter, you have had a brief introduction to what transportation is.

To understand transportation more fully, you must also understand energy and power. Energy and power are essential components in the transportation system. Without them, transportation would not exist as it does today. For instance, cars would not run, bicycles would not move, and planes would not fly. Energy and power are, indeed, the foundation of any transportation system. They will be discussed in the following chapters.

KEY WORDS

All of the following words have been used in this chapter. Do you know their meaning?

Feedback	System
Input	Technological system
Output	Technology
Process	Transportation

TEST YOUR KNOWLEDGE

Write your answers on a separate sheet of paper. Do not write in this book.

Fill in the blank:
1. To move people or cargo from one place to another is called _____.
2. A technological system consists of what five elements?

True or False:

3. A transportation system is a technological system. True or False?

4. An output is used to begin the system. True or False?

Short answer:

5. Define a system.

6. Define technology.

Multiple choice:

7. Indicate which of the following are inputs into a transportation system:

   A. Materials.

   B. People.

   C. Knowledge.

   D. All of the above.

ACTIVITIES

1. Prepare a report on the forms of transportation you used during one week. Set up two columns on a sheet of paper. In the first column, list the forms of transportation used. In the second column list the activity that would be affected if that form of transportation were not available. Suggest what changes would be made in your life to adjust to each situation.

2. Invite a representative from a school bus company to address your class on how the company sets up routes used to bring students to school.

3. On a map of your school district, prepared and supplied by your instructor, design a bus route to pick up students from a certain area or neighborhood.

Chapter 2
WHAT IS ENERGY?

After studying this chapter, you will be able to:
☐ Define energy.
☐ Identify the energy that surrounds us.
☐ Discuss potential and kinetic energy.
☐ Identify the sources of energy.
☐ Name and describe the six forms of energy.

Imagine what it would be like if you were the first person on planet earth. What would you think about the intensity of the big yellow spot in the sky? What would be one of the first characteristics of the sun you would discover? The heat it produced! You go through the day discovering all kinds of new things. You finally recognize that the warm, yellow, spot in the sky is beginning to turn orange. It's also getting farther away from you. You are starting to feel cooler. It's getting dark now. As you look up in the dark sky, you see very clearly another bright spot. You soon discover it is not producing heat. You then begin to feel something hitting you. It feels wet. It's coming at you very fast. What is it? Where is it coming from? All of a sudden you hear a big crack and bang resounding overhead. And a big flash of light rushes at you. What are you thinking at this time? It's all a new experience. You have just discovered the natural forces of your environment. Before long you will begin to gain more knowledge and understanding of such forces. And you will soon discover that they are going to help you survive!

HARNESSING ENERGY

Centuries ago, people stood in awe of nature more then we do today. Our ancestors had many questions about the natural forces around them.

They questioned the sun, the wind, and the rain, Fig. 2-1. They wondered what lightning was and the effects it was having on their planet. It was all new to them.

Over the years, and very slowly, they began to uncover the mysteries of these forces. People began to recognize that they could use the sun to help them survive. Primitive people began to use its heat to dry out fruit and animal hides.

Fig. 2-1. Primitive humans stood in awe of nature. They had many questions about rain, lightning, and the sun.

Next came the discovery of fire. Perhaps they saw lightning strike a tree and ignite it. Experiencing the heat from this fire, these primitives began to use fire for warmth, cooking, and developing tools.

The discovery of fire set the pace for advancements in technology. Tornadoes and floods were often frightening experiences until humans learned how to control small winds and waterfalls. They fashioned the first crude sails to power their boats. Water wheels were invented to capture the power of flowing or falling water for grinding corn, Fig. 2-2.

People also learned to make better use of their strength. They began making tools. Wooden clubs became a more effective way to kill animals than using the bare hands. Also, the plow was developed to make the tilling of fields more efficient. Still, the work was hard and time-consuming for humans. It was then that animal power was used to provide a greater amount of work and less toil for humans. We see energy at work all around us. Anything that causes movement has energy. It is time for a definition of energy.

ENERGY: THE ABILITY TO DO WORK

Most of the time we identify with the work produced from energy and often miss the energy being used. Work causes a change. Wind that causes a windmill to operate a pump and pump water is an example of seeing the effects of the work being done. However, we often forget that it is the energy produced by the wind that causes the work. Energy is at work all around us. The sun continues to heat and light the earth, Fig. 2-3. We, as humans, exert energy. Skipping, running, bicycling, and jumping are all examples of work being done due to the energy within us, Fig. 2-4. Energy affects our lives in many ways. It's easy to see some effects of energy. Still, we often fail to notice its influence on our world. For instance, you can see the sunlight and feel the sun's heat. You can feel the wind. You

Fig. 2-3. The sun wraps the earth with huge amounts of energy.

Fig. 2-2. A replica of a waterwheel like those humans first developed to run mills.

Fig. 2-4. Humans, too, convert energy sources into energies within us that are used in work or play. (Wisconsin Dept. of Tourism)

can even see the effects of big gusts of wind and tornadoes, Fig. 2-5. You can see an airplane as it soars through the air. It's harder, however, to see the effect of energy on plants and trees within our environment.

Granted, energy is used in many ways around us; but what is its source? Energy comes from many sources. These sources can be organized into the following groups:
- Renewable energy resources.
- Nonrenewable energy sources.
- Inexhaustible energy sources.

Renewable energy sources are those resources that can be replaced when needed. Food is one example; plants and livestock are other examples.

Nonrenewable energy sources are those that cannot be replaced once used. Coal is a good example of nonrenewable energy.

Inexhaustible energy sources are those that never will run out. At least they will last for the next several million years! The sun and wind are examples of inexhaustible energy sources. These different sources of energy will be discussed in detail with several examples in Chapter 4.

TYPES OF ENERGY

You have just been introduced to the different groups of energy sources. All energy formed from these sources can be classified as:
- Potential energy.
- Kinetic energy.

Potential Energy

Potential energy is energy that is waiting to happen. It is waiting to have motion. Potential energy is at rest. It's sitting still. An example of potential energy is a golf ball sitting on a golf tee, Fig. 2-6.

Kinetic Energy

Kinetic energy is described as energy in motion. This energy can be found in the movement of most objects. Any object in motion has kinetic energy. As the golf ball is hit off of the tee, it is now experiencing kinetic energy, Fig. 2-7.

FORMS OF ENERGY

As we just discussed, energy is of two types, potential and kinetic. Therefore, potential and kinetic energy are related to the form in which energy is found. All of the energy around us comes in different forms. These forms are:
- Light energy.
- Heat energy.
- Mechanical energy
- Chemical energy.
- Electrical energy.
- Nuclear energy.

All six of these forms of energy are used to aid us in our everyday lives. All are used to do work for us. These forms of energy will be discussed in more detail in Chapter 5.

Fig. 2-5. Tremendous amounts of energy are present in strong winds and tornadoes.

Fig. 2-6. A golf ball, resting on top of a tee, has potential energy. This energy would be changed to a small amount of kinetic energy if the ball fell off the tee.

Fig. 2-7. As the golf ball is struck by the club, its flight is an example of kinetic energy—the energy of motion.

Energy is important to understand because it affects our lives in so many ways. It affects our ability to function in a technological world. In learning about transportation, you must be familiar with forms of energy. Energy is what makes the entire system of transportation possible. The system begins with energy being converted to do work. Once the work is being done, you have power. Power is what runs all of the transportation systems.

SUMMARY

Energy is the ability to do work. Energy is all around us. We use energy without even recognizing it. Many sources of energy come from the natural forces within our world. The sun, wind, and water are examples of inexhaustible energy sources. Other energy sources are renewable and nonrenewable. Energy is classified as potential and kinetic energy. Potential energy is stationary (at rest) and kinetic is in motion.

There are six different forms of energy that can be converted and controlled from the main sources. They are heat, light, mechanical, chemical, electrical, and nuclear.

It is important to understand energy and where it comes from in order to understand transportation. Energy is the beginning of any transportation system.

KEY WORDS

All of the following words have been used in this chapter. Do you know their meaning?
Energy
Kinetic energy
Potential energy

TEST YOUR KNOWLEDGE

Write your answers on a separate sheet of paper. Do not write in this book.
Short answer:
 1. Define energy.
 2. List some ways in which energy affects your life.
 3. List the six forms of energy.
True or False:
 4. Energy that is waiting to happen is known as potential energy. True or False?

ACTIVITIES

 1. Build and demonstrate a device that changes a renewable source of energy into a form that will do work.
 2. Collect pictures from old magazines showing examples of potential energy in the world around you.
 3. Construct a device that demonstrates potential energy being converted into kinetic energy.

Chapter 3

WHAT IS POWER?

After studying this chapter, you will be able to:
☐ Define power.
☐ Understand how power is measured.
☐ Identify with the three basic power systems.
☐ Understand how electrical power is measured.
☐ Describe the basic elements of all power systems.

Power is something we so often take for granted. We seldom think about where we get power to perform specific tasks. As you ride your bicycle, think about what makes it move. First, you supply the energy to turn the pedals. Then the energy is changed into a form of power. As the pedals turn, the chain and gears power the bicycle, Fig. 3-1.

Power is energy that has been converted. When energy is converted, transmitted, and controlled to do useful work, we call this a power system. *Power* is the amount of work being done over a period of time. Power is a measurement of work. Power is the amount of work done in a given amount of time. Power can be measured by the following formula:

$$Power = \frac{work}{time} \text{ or } P = \frac{w}{t}$$

It can also be written as : $P = \frac{D \times F}{t}$

If a crane operator is going to move a 1000 lb. barrel of nails up 40 ft. to a second story window in 30 seconds, how much power is developed?

$$P = \frac{40 \text{ ft. x } 1000 \text{ lb.}}{30 \text{ seconds}} = \frac{40,000}{30}$$
$$= 1333 \text{ ft-lb per sec.}$$

Fig. 3-1. Once the energy is supplied by the human, the pedals, chain, and gears all work together to power the bicycle.

The standard unit of power is the *horsepower*. Horsepower is the rate of doing work. One horsepower is the energy needed to lift 33,000 lb. 1 ft. in 1 minute, Fig. 3-2. It can be computed by the following formula:

$$Hp = \frac{work}{time \text{ in minutes} \times 33,000}$$

If 200 lb. are lifted 165 ft. in 1 minute, how much horsepower is developed?
Here's how you can find the answer:

1. You must first find out how much work was done.

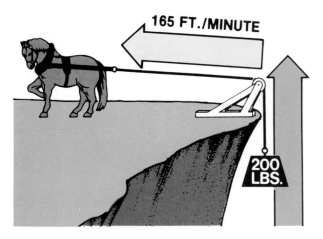

Fig. 3-2. The amount of horsepower is determined by dividing the amount of work done by elapsed time multiplied by 33,000.

$$W = D \times F$$
$$W = 165 \text{ ft.} \times 200 \text{ lb.} = 33,000 \text{ ft.-lb.}$$

2. Now you can find the horsepower by using the formula.

$$Hp = \frac{33,000}{1 \times 33,000} = 1$$

3. The answer is 1 hp.

Work is movement created by using a form of energy. In a technical sense, *work* is the application of force which moves an object (big or little) a certain distance, Fig. 3-3. Work is computed by the following formula:

WORK = DISTANCE × FORCE or $W = D \times F$

A force is anything that causes an object to move. Work is force times the distance through which the force acts. Work is measured in foot-pounds for conventional U.S. measure. A *foot-pound* (ft-lb) is the amount of force necessary to

Fig. 3-3. Work is the force applied times the distance moved.

move a 1 lb. load a distance of one ft. Mechanical power is measured in foot-pounds per second (ft-lb/sec).

Suppose that a rider in a canoe weighs 120 lb. How much work is being done if the canoe is paddled 600 ft.?

$$W = D \times F$$
$$W = 600 \times 120$$
$$W = 72,000 \text{ ft-lb}$$

POWER SYSTEMS

Power is needed in our technological society. Power lights our cities. Power in our homes cooks our food and washes our clothes. Power is also needed in our transportation systems. Without power in transportation, cars wouldn't function, airplanes wouldn't fly, and subways wouldn't run. Sources of energy such as wind, solar, and heat are harnessed to perform useful work. The harnessing of energy converts energy into a form of work.

In the harnessing of energy sources, machines are used to convert energy into movement. The machines that do the converting are referred to as *power systems*.

Basic Power Systems

Power systems come in many different shapes, sizes, and performance of jobs, Fig. 3-4. For instance, an automobile is a power system, fuel is converted into power. The tape drive of a video recorder is a power system. Energy has been converted into electrical power which is used to power the video recorder. An electric power plant is another good example of a large power system, Fig. 3-5. See the differences in power systems?

Three basic power systems will be discussed in greater detail in Section three. These power systems are electrical systems, mechanical systems, and fluid systems.

Electrical Systems

Electrical systems are those systems using electrical energy to do work. Think for a moment what your world would be like if there was no electricity available. You wouldn't have an alarm to wake you up for school. You wouldn't have any hot water for a shower unless you built a fire and heated the water, Fig. 3-6. You couldn't just go into the kitchen and pop a piece of bread into the toaster. See how an electrical system affects us personally!

We must also consider how electricity is important to our technological world. Manufacturing

Fig. 3-4. A jet plane and a dishwasher are vastly different machines but both use power.
(US Navy/Grumman; General Electric Co.)

Fig. 3-5. This electric power plant generates large amounts of electricity which is used to power many devices including electric appliances.
(General Electric Co.)

plants need electricity to run machines. Without electricity, products like stereos and bicycles could not be produced. The communication systems around us could not operate without electricity. For example, the television, the telephone, and the

Fig. 3-6. Chances are, an electric clock wakes you up every morning and keeps track of time.

radio would do us no good without electricity. Also, our transportation system would not be as efficient and safe as it is today without an electrical system. An electrical system is needed in an automobile to start the automobile and keep it running. Electricity is needed to propel and operate several different modes of transportation. Electricity is needed in most everything we use today.

Measuring Current

Electrical power is measured in *watts*. In order to measure wattage, you must know the amperage (rate of flow) and the voltage (pressure). You must know how to measure current. There are three basic units in measuring electric current. They are amperes, volts, and ohms. *Amperage* is the rate at which current flows through a conductor. It can be compared to the way in which water flows through a pipe. Amperes are measured with an *ammeter*. The formula sign for amperage is I.

Voltage is the pressure pushing the current through the conductor. Voltage can be compared to the pressure of water in a pipeline. Volts are measured with a *voltmeter*. The formula sign for voltage is E.

Resistance must also be mentioned in the study of measuring current. Resistance is the opposition to current flow through a conductor. Resistance produces heat and a drop in voltage. Resistance can be compared to friction. Resistance is measured in ohms with an *ohmmeter*. In the computing equation, the sign for resistance is R.

A law known as Ohm's Law can mathematically compute amperes, volts, and ohms. The formula is as follows:

Voltage = Amperage x Resistance, or

$$E = I \times R$$

The formula can also be written to find amperage and resistance. The Ohm's Law circle makes it easy to identify the correct equation to use, Fig. 3-7. Cover the one you want to find. For example, to find amperage, cover the I with your finger. Look at the circle and you see E/R. Voltage divided by resistance equals amperage. Thus, the following formulas:

$$I = \frac{E}{R} \text{ and } R = \frac{E}{I}$$

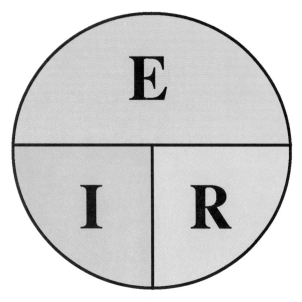

Fig. 3-7. Ohm's Law circle is used to calculate voltage (E), amperage (I), or resistance (R). By placing your thumb over the value you wish to determine, you will know whether to multiply or divide.

Measuring Electrical Power

As mentioned earlier, electrical power is measured in wattage. Wattage is the measurement of power produced by the flow of current under pressure. Both voltage and amperage are needed in order to measure wattage. One watt of power is produced by a flow of one ampere at a pressure of one volt. Thus, the equation:

Wattage = Amperage × Voltage
or
W = I × E

How electricity works will be discussed in greater detail in Chapter 8. The main concept to gather about electricity is that it is a system that is used to power many other systems in our society. Electricity is the most widely used and the most versatile type of energy.

MECHANICAL SYSTEMS

Mechanical systems are another basic type of power system that use mechanical energy to do work. *Mechanical energy* is the energy of motion. For example, the wind, waterfalls, and rotating gears on a bicycle are all forms of mechanical energy, Fig. 3-8.

Fig. 3-8. A windmill, a waterfall, and gears on a bike are all examples of energy in motion.

Mechanical energy also consists of machines which are used to produce work. A machine or a combination of machines can change the size, direction, and speed of force. Machines also change the type of motion produced.

We are often able to harness this energy. Such energy comes from the wind, from the force of water behind a dam, or from a machine. It can then be put to work and measured. When this conversion of mechanical energy takes place, it is referred to as *mechanical power*. Sometimes mechanical power is put directly to work without any changes. For instance, the blade on a lawn mower is connected directly to the power source which is the crankshaft. Most often, however, you need some change in the mechanical power before putting it to work. Mechanical power always has direction of motion. This may be linear (straight in one direction), reciprocating (back and forth), or rotational (spinning).

Machines are those devices used to manage mechanical power. Six simple machines are used to control and change mechanical power. These simple machines are the lever, pulley, wheel and axle, inclined plane, wedge, and screw, Fig. 3-9. These types of machines will be explained in more detail in Chapter 7.

Fluid Systems

Fluid power systems are those systems that do work using the energy found in liquids and gases. Fluid power can be referred to as the "muscles of industry." Fluid power can accomplish the movement of very heavy objects such as buildings. Yes, entire buildings and houses have been moved by the use of fluid power.

There are two types of fluid power systems: *pneumatic* and *hydraulic*. Pneumatic systems use a gas, such as air, to transmit power and to control the power. Hydraulic systems use a liquid, such

Fig. 3-9. These six simple machines all use mechanical energy in a way that benefits us. A—The lever allows one to lift heavy loads. B—The pulley changes the direction of the force applied. C—The wheel and axle is like a rotary lever. It multiplies distance or it multiplies force. D—The inclined plane allows us to lift loads using less force. E—The wedge is like two inclined planes placed back to back. Its principle is used in knives, axes, and chisels. F—The screw is an inclined plane wrapped in a spiral. A bolt and a wood screw use this simple machine.

as oil, to transmit and control power. Some examples of fluid power are air compressors and transmission lines. Landing gear on airplanes are controlled and operated by a hydraulic system. Likewise, in industry, forging of parts is done by the use of pneumatics.

Fluid power has been a great advantage in industries. It even has many advantages over the other forms of power. Mechanical power is often slow and awkward. On the other hand, electrical power is often expensive and very complex. Fluid power systems are easy to operate and control. They are also durable and accurate in their control. As you read on, Chapter 9 will explain in more detail the uses and principles of fluid power.

MEASUREMENT CONVERSION

It is important to know how to use measurements in power and other areas. The two measuring systems we use in the United States are U.S. customary and SI metric. It is important to know how to convert these measurements from one system to another. The chart in Fig. 3-10 will help you to do this.

Basic Elements of All Power Systems

The three basic power systems include electrical, mechanical, and fluid. All of these have just been introduced to you in the previous paragraphs. No matter how big or small these power systems are they all have basic elements or functions. Whether we are comparing a lawn mower or a power plant, they both include all the basic functions of a power system. These basic elements and their descriptions follow:

1. A *source of energy* is always needed before a power system can function. Often, fuel is used. It can also be another form of energy such as water or wind power.
2. A *converson method* is necessary in all power systems. There must be a way of changing the energy so that it can produce some kind of work. For example, falling water can spin a turbine that operates an electrical generator to produce electricity.
3. A *transmission path* is also needed in power systems. A transmission path is simply a way of moving the energy to the point at which it is to do the work for which it is designed. An example of a transmission line might be elec-

	U.S. CUSTOMARY TO SI METRIC				SI METRIC TO U.S. CUSTOMARY			
	Customary Units	×	Conversion Factor	= Metric Units	SI Metric Units	×	Conversion Factor	= Customary Units
Length	inches	×	2.54	= centimeters	centimeters	×	.4	= inches
	yards	×	.9144	= meters	meters	×	1.1	= yards
	miles	×	1.609	= kilometers	kilometers	×	.6	= miles
Weight	pounds	×	.4536	= kilograms	kilograms	×	2.2	= pounds
Force	pounds	×	4.448	= newtons	newtons	×	.2248	= pounds
Torque	pound-feet	×	1.356	= newton-meters	newton-meters	×	.7376	= pound-feet
Pressure	pounds per sq. inch	×	6895	= pascals	pascals	×	.000145	= pounds per sq. inch
Work	foot-pounds	×	.7376	= joules	joules	×	.7376	= foot-pounds
Meat	British thermal units	×	252	= calories	calories	×	.003968	= British thermal units
Mechanical Power	horsepower	×	.746	= watts	watts	×	.001341	= horsepower
Electrical Power	watts	×	1	= watts	watts	×	1	= watts

Fig. 3-10. A chart gives conversion factors between U.S. Customary and SI metric values.

trical power lines. You see them strung across the landscape.

4. *Control systems* are needed to control the work coming from the power system. It continues to check the energy to see that it does its work and no more. The throttle on a lawn mower is a control system, Fig. 3-11.

5. *Measuring devices* are an important part of the power system. A source of feedback is needed to see how well the system is functioning. This is done by using meters, indicators, and gauges, Fig. 3-12.

6. Finally, there must be an *output* or a *load*. This is the goal of the system. A load is the work done by the system. For example, a lawn mower's load is spinning the cutting blade. The goal of the mower is to cut the grass, Fig. 3-13.

SUMMARY

Power is energy that has been converted. When energy is converted, transmitted, and controlled to do useful work, it is referred to as a power system. Power is the amount of work done over a period of time. Power is measured in a standard unit known as the horsepower.

So often we take all power for granted. We don't realize how power affects our everyday lives. There are three basic power systems in our society. They are electrical systems, mechanical systems, and fluid systems.

Fig. 3-12. A meter is a measuring device used in a power system. Here a wattmeter measures the amount of electricity used.
(American Electric Power)

Fig. 3-11. The throttle of a lawnmover engine controls engine speed and power.

Fig. 3-13. The goal or output of a power system is to do the work for which the system is designed. This power system was designed to cut grass.

Electrical power systems range in size from a toaster to a big manufacturing power plant. Electrical power is measured in watts.

Mechanical power converts mechanical energy into work. Mechanical energy is the energy of motion. Machines are devices that are used to help change and control mechanical power.

Fluid power systems are referred to as the "muscles of industry." There are two types of fluid power systems. They are pneumatic and hydraulic.

All of the basic power systems contain the same basic elements. They all begin with a source of energy and use some sort of a conversion method. A transmission path, as well as a control system, is also evident in all forms of power systems. Finally, they all have a way in which to be measured.

KEY WORDS

All of the following words have been used in this chapter. Do you know their meaning?

Ammeter

Amperage

Electrical systems

Fluid systems

Hydraulic

Mechanical systems

Ohmmeter

Pneumatic

Power

Power systems

Resistance

Voltmeter

Watts

Work

TEST YOUR KNOWLEDGE

Write your answers on a separate sheet of paper. Do not write in this book.

Short answer:
1. Define power.
2. If a light bulb has the pressure of 120 volts and a rate of flow of 1.0 ampere, what is the wattage of the light bulb?
3. Name the two types of fluid power.
4. How do you compute work?

Fill in the blank:
5. The standard unit of power is _____.

Multiple choice:
6. Mechanical power is measured in:
    A. Watts.
    B. Ohms.
    C. Foot-pound.

True or False:
7. Electrical power is known as the "muscles of industry." True or False?

ACTIVITIES

1. Construct a machine that makes use of one type of energy to move the machine.
2. Set up a demonstration using as machine and an energy source and measure the output of the machine.
3. Research the subject of one of the three power systems and prepare as report. You may use a computer, a typewriter or longhand.

Transportation requires power to move vehicles from place to place. The power is developed through various propulsion units. Aircraft use reaction engines, as do space vehicles. Land-based vehicles usually get their power of motion through reciprocating heat engines. You will study more about these propulsion units and how they work in later chapters.
(NASA, General Motors Corp., U.S. Air Force)

Section II
ENERGY SYSTEMS

Chapter 4

SOURCES OF ENERGY

After studying this chapter, you will be able to:
☐ Define renewable energy sources.
☐ Identify the basic sources of renewable energy.
☐ Define nonrenewable energy sources.
☐ Identify the basic sources of nonrenewable energy.
☐ Define inexhaustible energy sources.
☐ Identify the basic sources of inexhaustible energy.

Evidence of the use of energy in our lives is all around us. What have you done today that took energy? Sometimes it just takes energy to get out of bed in the mornings. It takes energy to run the alarm clock. It takes energy to heat and pump the water for our shower. It takes energy to transport us to our destination, whether we are riding a bicycle or a bus.

From where does energy come? In order to make good use of our energy and to preserve the basic energy sources, we need to know. Most is energy nature has stored. For instance, the sun stores energy in plants and trees. This stored energy is released when plants or trees are burned. Plants and animals that have died millions of years ago also have stored energy. Today we use this stored energy in coal, oil, and natural gas. These are just a couple of examples. Energy comes from many sources. These sources, as you learned in an earlier chapter, have been divided into three categories:
• Renewable energy sources.
• Nonrenewable energy sources.
• Inexhaustible energy sources.

RENEWABLE ENERGY SOURCES

Renewable energy resources are those energy sources that can be replaced as needed. Renewable energy comes from plants and animals. Once you cut a tree down, it is important to replant one to maintain this form of energy, Fig. 4-1. The basic

Fig. 4-1. Once a mature tree is cut down a new tree must be planted. (Weyerhaeuser Co.)

renewable energy sources include animals, food, wood, and alcohol, Fig. 4-2.

Animals

Animals used to be a main source of energy for people of long ago. Animals were used to pull heavy loads on sleds or wheeled vehicles, Fig. 4-3. Animals were also used for food. They were the major source of energy until the development of mechanical machines. In some parts of the world, animals are still used as a source of energy. In the United States, the engine and other mechanical devices have taken the place of animals.

Food

Food is another source of energy. Energy from food allows you to do physical exercise, Fig. 4-4.

Fig. 4-4. Food provides energy for the human body.

Running, jumping, riding a bike, and skateboarding all require energy, Fig. 4-5.

Energy from food also keeps our bodies warm. Our bodies use the energy from the food to produce heat. This heat keeps our bodies at the correct temperature. People who are more active, in sports for instance, need to take in more energy.

Food is a renewable source of energy because it can be regrown. The supply continues to sustain us. For example, each fall farmers harvest their crops. The crops may be corn, soybeans, or wheat, or other plant life, Fig. 4-6. In the spring they plant again and care for the plants until it's time to harvest, Fig. 4-7. As this cycle continues, we are constantly supplied with a source of energy.

Some foods not only supply humans with energy but are used to supply vehicles with energy. For

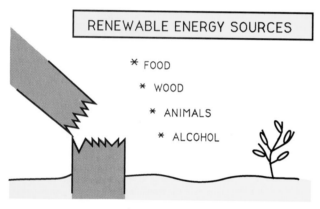

Fig. 4-2. These are the renewable energy sources. They can be replaced as needed.

Fig. 4-3. These farmers from the 1930s are getting their work done with the help of two horses. (John Deere & Co.)

Fig. 4-5. This boy is exerting energy as he performs intricate maneuvers on his skateboard.

Fig. 4-6. Matured crops are harvested and the fields will be replanted in the spring. (John Deere & Co.)

example, gasohol is made from grains to fuel automobiles. Food product waste is also burned or converted into fuel. Successful experiments in producing fuels from gardening and agricultural wastes have also been performed.

Fig. 4-7. Preparing for planting. New plants will grow from the reseeding to be harvested again in the fall.

Wood

Wood is a very old source of energy. Wood was used back in prehistoric times. Back then it was used to heat homes and for cooking, Fig. 4-8. By the early 1900s, the use of wood as fuel declined. Other sources of energy, such as oil and electricity, were beginning to be used. This caused the decline of wood use even more. However, today

Fig. 4-8. Wood was an important energy source for cooking in colonial America.

you can find wood burning stoves and fireplaces in modern homes, Fig. 4-9. Once again, wood has become a popular source of energy. One major disadvantage of burning wood is that it produces great amounts of air pollution. Wood does not burn clean.

Studies are continually being done on the various uses of wood. Wood can also be converted to another fuel. It can be changed into a liquid and used to fuel vehicles. One type of wood-based fuel that is being used is methanol.

As more studies are done, the more uses for wood will be discovered. The competition between using wood for an energy source and construction will increase. Large forests will need to be planted and maintained in order to have enough wood for all the uses. Since wood is a renewable source of energy, it offers a great advantage for future uses, Fig. 4-10.

Fig. 4-9. Many modern homes have woodburning fireplaces.

Fig. 4-10. Forests are essential for supplying us with the renewable energy source—wood. In this picture, large sections of the forest have been harvested. These sections will be replanted by the lumber company.

Alcohol

Alcohol is a liquid. It is made from different crops such as corn, sugar beets, and sugar cane. Alcohol is used for a fuel. It can be used to power automobiles. In some foreign countries, automobiles operate with 100 percent alcohol fuel. In the United States, we use a mixture of alcohol and gasoline to fuel some vehicles. These two types of alcohol fuel are gasohol and methanol. By using more alcohol and less oil, a huge amount of oil can be saved. Therefore, alcohol will have a positive effect on our total oil consumption.

Gasohol

Gasohol is a mixture of unleaded gasoline and ethyl alcohol. An ethanol plant is a plant where the crops are distilled and processed into alcohol. The alcohol is then mixed with gasoline. Gasohol is being used in many automobiles today. Approximately 10 percent of alcohol is mixed with the gasoline. This small percentage is a beginning of a big savings on oil.

Methanol

Methanol is a clean-burning liquid. It is also known as methyl alcohol. Methanol can be made from nonrenewable sources of energy. It can also be made from renewable sources of energy such as wood, plants, and waste products.

Methanol is also used as a fuel to power vehicles. It produces more energy than ethyl alcohol. Therefore, it does not need to be mixed with gasoline. Methanol also burns more slowly than gasoline. The redesign of engines has given methanol the ability to produce as much power as gasoline. Because it burns slower, it has smoother engine performance. Methanol is being substituted for gasoline in some transportation systems.

BIOCONVERSION

The process that produces energy from the waste products of our society is known as *bioconversion*. The waste is known as *biomass*. Biomass is organic material such as trees, plants, grains, and algae. Wastes such as manure, garbage, sewage, and paper are sources of biomass. All of these sources of biomass can go through a bioconversion. They can be burned or converted into alcohols like ethanol and methanol. Biomass conversion yields petroleum.

Several cities shred and burn waste. The heat energy is then used as a source of energy, Fig. 4-11.

Fig. 4-11. Garbage, part of the biomass source, can be used to produce fuel. (American Gas Assn.)

For instance, the heat from the waste may turn a turbine which will then generate electricity. This source of energy can be mixed with other forms of energy. Bioconversion also helps get rid of unwanted waste.

NONRENEWABLE ENERGY SOURCES

Nonrenewable energy sources are those sources you cannot replace once they have been used. Examples of nonrenewable energy sources are coal, oil, natural gas, and uranium. Over 90 percent of our energy needs are met by using these few sources of energy. Transportation uses up a big portion of the 90 percent. Nonrenewable energy sources can be divided up into two different groups: fossil fuels and uranium.

Fossil Fuels

What are fossil fuels? From where do they come? How often are they used in our society? All of these questions are going to be answered in this chapter.

Fossil fuels are coal, oil, and natural gases. These come from the ground. Fossil fuels are formed by the decays of plants and animals. These decays have been buried in the ground for millions of years. The remains of such plants and animals have gradually built up in layers over the years. As the years went by, soil continued to be piled on top of the deposits. Fossil fuels burn easily. One main use for them is to heat homes and other buildings.

Fossil fuels come in the form of coal, and in two other forms. They are liquids and semisolids which include petroleum and tar. Another form of fossil fuel is a gas. Gases are usually found with petroleum (oil). This type of gas is called *natural gas*. Since fossil fuels are nonrenewable, they are slowly decreasing in our environment. In a developing nation like the United States, it takes great quantities of fossil fuel in order for it to function. Because of the increases in industries, more fuel is needed. Due to the millions of years it takes for fossil fuel to form, we cannot replace them. Fossil fuels will one day run very low or run out completely. The need for finding other sources of energy is very important for this very reason.

Coal

The forming of coal in the earth began about 500 million years ago. For plant and animal decay to form into coal took approximately 85 million years. Coal is a soft rocklike material, Fig. 4-12. It is black or brown depending on its age. The older the coal is the more dense it is and the blacker it becomes. Coal is combustible (burnable). Coal is used to generate electricity by power companies, to power transportation vehicles, and to heat homes and buildings.

How do we get coal out of the ground? Removing the coal is called *mining*. Coal, once mined, can be burned immediately as a fuel. Mining can be done two different ways. These methods are

Fig. 4-12. Coal is changed to heat energy by burning. (Quaker State Oil Refining Corp.)

deep mining and surface mining. *Deep mining* is an operation that can become a very dangerous process. Deep mining uses shafts (passages) and special machinery to remove the coal from deep within the earth's surface, Fig. 4-13. Miners have been killed in mining accidents while in the shafts due to cave-ins and machinery accidents.

Surface mining is the mining or removing of coal that is close to the earth's surface. It is also known as strip mining. Surface mining is done mainly with the use of large pieces of machinery such as mechanical shovels and bulldozers, Fig. 4-14. Surface mining is much safer than deep mining.

Fig. 4-13. A mining machine removes coal from the wall of the mine. This is known as continuous mining. (Cyprus Mineral Co.)

Fig. 4-14. This bulldozer is clearing away burden (top soil) to expose a coal vein for strip mining.

There is one major disadvantage to surface mining and that is the condition it leaves the land in after the coal has been gathered. Several laws require that the land be restored to its original condition after strip mining has taken place.

Oil

Oil is also known as *petroleum*. Like coal, petroleum is a fossil fuel. In its natural state, petroleum is called *crude oil*. As crude oil comes from the ground, it is a mixture of semisolids, liquids, and gases. Oil has many uses. One of the biggest users of oil is the transportation systems. Almost all transportation vehicles are fueled by a form of oil. Like coal, oil is found underground. To get oil out of the ground an operation known as drilling is necessary.

Before drilling for oil, there are several tests that need to be done on the surface and underlying rock. Certain drill bits are selected depending on the method that is going to be used to drill. Large drill bits are used to cut through layers of the earth. Drilling has gone for 3-5 miles below the earth's surface. Once the bit has struck an oil pocket, natural pressures cause the oil to rise to the earth's surface. The oil is then controlled by valves. Pumps are also used to bring oil to the surface, Fig. 4-15.

Once the oil is brought to the surface, it is transported by pipeline to the refinery. A refinery is a place that turns oil into other useful products. For instance, a refinery will take crude oil and refine it into other products such as gasoline, diesel fuel, kerosene, and lubricating oil. In a large tower

Fig. 4-15. A pump like this is often set up over an oil well to bring crude oil to the surface. Some wells operate from natural underground pressure.

called a *fractionating tower*, crude oil is separated into various products. The crude oil travels through a pipe into a furnace. The furnace heats the crude oil and at different temperatures a variety of useful products are developed, Fig. 4-16. The different products are then transported by way of pipeline to storage tanks or another refinery.

There are two other places in which to find oil. This is sometimes referred to as alternate sources of oil. These two sources are oil shale and tar sands. *Oil shale* is a rock that was formed millions of years ago from fossils that were mixed with clay. The oil shale is a dark, flaky rock. Some shale have enough oil in them to catch fire. Oil is removed from the rock by using heat. The shale is mined similar to coal. It is then crushed and heated. The heat releases oil from the shale. *Tar sands* are fossils that have been formed millions of years ago and became mixed with sand. Heat is also used to extract the oil from the tar sands. Tar sands do not need to be crushed. The largest deposit of tar sands is in Alberta, Canada. The tar sands in this particular area could possibly contain a trillion barrels of oil.

Oil is measured in barrels. The barrel is the basic unit of measurement in the United States oil industry. In the early days of the oil industry, the crude oil was shipped from the well to the refinery in wooden barrels. Since those days, railroad tank cars, oil barges, and pipelines have replaced the bar-

rel. But it is still used as a standard unit of measurement. One barrel equals 42 gallons, Fig. 4-17.

Natural Gas

The gaseous portion of petroleum is called natural gas. Natural gas is always found wherever oil deposits are discovered, Fig. 4-18. Natural gas is made up of ethane, propane, methane, and butane. These are all combustible (burnable) gases. Natural gas is the cleanest burning and the least expensive of the fossil fuels. Natural gas has become one of the major sources of energy because of these characteristics.

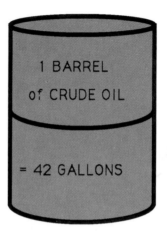

Fig. 4-17. The barrel is the standard unit of measure for oil in the U.S.

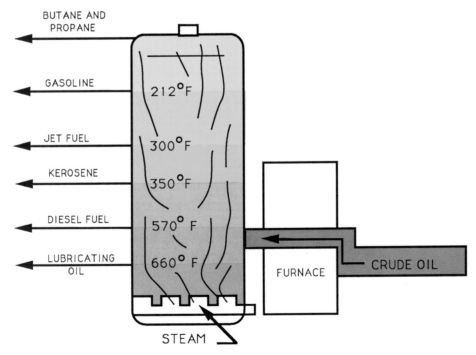

Fig. 4-16. Crude oil is boiled and turned into a vapor. Once the vapor rises, it cools and different products are formulated at different temperatures.

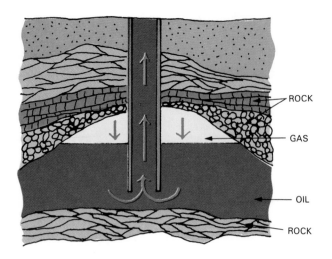

Fig. 4-18. Cross section of an oil well. Natural gas is always found wherever there is oil.

Removing gas from the ground is done in much the same way as the recovery of oil. Wells are drilled into the ground. The gas is then removed and transported by way of pipeline to a processing plant. At the plant, all of the impurities like dirt, moisture, and sulfur are removed. The gas is then transported to homes and industrial establishments for use.

Gas can be transported through pipelines in its natural state. It is usually stored underground. During the warm months, when not much gas is needed for heating purposes, the gas from the pipelines is stored in underground reservoirs. These reservoirs are called *aquifers*. An aquifer is a rock formation underground. The aquifers hold large quantities of water. When the gas is pumped in under pressure, it pushes the water down farther into the ground, Fig. 4-19

The transporting of gas in pipelines could get rather expensive. Building pipelines to transport gas

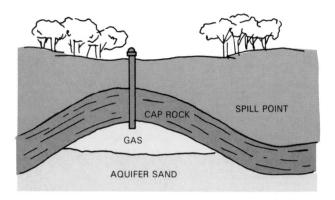

Fig. 4-19. Some natural gas is stored in natural underground aquifers where it forces the water deeper underground.

everywhere would be hard as well. Therefore, to solve this problem, gas has been placed under pressure at very low temperatures to create **liquefied natural gas** (LNG). With liquefied gas, transportation can be done by using railroad tankers, truck tankers, and ships. Also, more liquefied gas can be stored in a holding tank than gas in its natural state.

Uranium

Uranium is the other type of nonrenewable energy source. *Uranium* is thought to be a substance in volcanic ash. It probably spewed from a volcano onto the earth's surface millions of years ago. Rains dissolved the uranium out of the ash. It was then carried back into the ground where it has hardened into ore over the years. It is located near the surface of the earth. Therefore, it is mined in much the same way as coal. Like fossil fuels, uranium supplies will one day run out. Uranium is the most common type of nuclear fuel. It is used to fuel large nuclear power plants. Uranium can generate large amounts of energy in the form of heat. The heat that is produced is used to boil water thus creating steam. The steam is then used to drive turbine-powered generators which produce electricity, Fig. 4-20.

Uranium is an atom with a large and heavy nucleus (center). Therefore, a lot of energy is bound up inside that can be used as nuclear fuel. Uranium atoms are bombarded by neutrons. This causes the nuclei to split apart. This splitting is known as *nuclear fission*. Lots of energy is released at the time of the splitting. When one nuclei splits, it releases energy and other neutrons which, in turn, split other nuclei. A chain reaction thus occurs. This reaction produces huge amounts of energy in the form of heat. All of this reaction takes place inside of a strong, closed container called a *reactor*. A *nuclear reactor* is to a nuclear power plant what a furnace is to a home. It produces the heat that is used to produce power from the plant, Fig. 4-21.

The fission of uranium is the only developed source of nuclear power to the present day. The use of nuclear power produces about 13 percent of all the electricity produced in the United States per year. Nuclear power in the form of electricity is produced at a *nuclear power plant*. The amount of energy produced by uranium is incredible. One pound of uranium can produce as much electricity as three million pounds of coal.

There is one major concern about using uranium to produce electricity. Uranium is a very hazardous

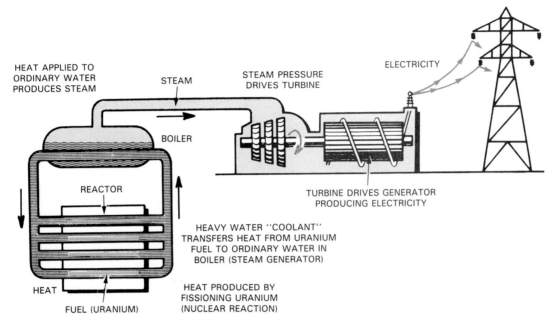

Fig. 4-20. Sketch shows how a nuclear reactor works.
(Nuclear Power in Canada/Canadian Nuclear Assn.)

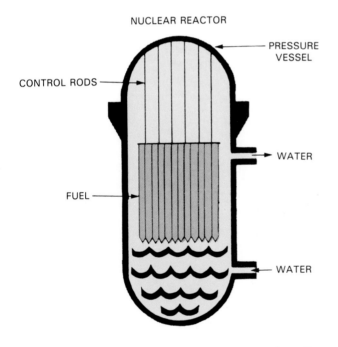

Fig. 4-21. A pressure vessel is where nuclear fission takes place in a nuclear reactor. Water also circulates through the vessel to cool the reactor and to carry steam to the steam turbines.
(Edison Electric Institute)

substance. When the atoms of uranium decay, they give off atomic particles. This reaction produces *radioactivity* which is harmful to humans and other living things. Research is being done, especially at the Argonne National Laboratories to make spent nuclear fuel less hazardous.

INEXHAUSTIBLE ENERGY SOURCES

Inexhaustible energy sources are those sources of energy that will never run out. We are fortunate to have such energy sources. It does not matter how much or how often we use them. Solar energy, hydroelectric energy, geothermal energy, the wind, and hydrogen are the most common sources of inexhaustible energy. These sources are renewed by forces beyond our control.

Solar Energy

The sun supplies the earth with an extremely large amount of energy. The sun's diameter is 110 times that of the earth. If the sun were 18 in. in diameter, the earth would be 1/16 in. across. The sun is so huge, it is twice the weight of the earth. The sun is 93 million miles away from the earth. Considering the distance, it is hard to imagine that we receive so much energy from the sun. Only one of every 2 billion portions of the sun's rays reach the earth, Fig. 4-22.

The sun provides us with two forms of energy: light and heat. Light and heat energy is often referred to as *solar energy*. If we knew a way to collect a bigger portion of the sun's energy, we would have all the energy we would need. Solar energy is not that easy to collect because it is spread out all over the surface of the earth. The methods used to collect the sun's energy are insufficient and rather

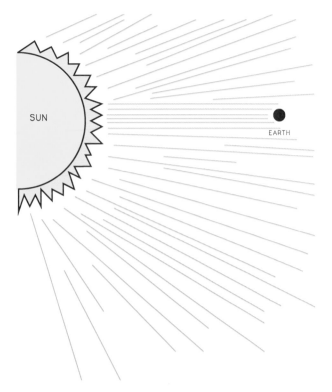

Fig. 4-22. For every two billion parts of energy sent out by the sun only one part reaches the earth.

Waterwheels were built to move water from a river into a trough. The water would then shoot out the end of the trough into the wheel. The force of the water on the wheel would cause the wheel to turn, Fig. 4-24. A machine of some sort was hooked to the wheel's shaft. The turning motion of the wheel would operate stone grinders for grain, spindles, and large hammers. Although flowing waters do not operate machines anymore, flowing water is still a valuable source of energy.

Hydroelectric energy is using flowing waters from waterfalls and dams to produce e'ectricity, Fig. 4-25. About 15 percent of the electricity used in the United States is generated from flowing water. Hydroelectric energy is produced by using hydroelectric dams or waterfalls. Dams are used to trap and store water, Fig. 4-26. The water is let in by a gate. When the gate is open, the water rushes through a tunnel known as a sluice. At the end of the sluice is a water turbine. The turbine turns as the water comes rushing in. As the turbine turns, this causes the generator to spin. The mechanical energy that spins the generator is converted into electricity. The electricity is then sent off to power companies through electric lines and distributed to customers.

expensive compared to the other energy sources. It is also hard to store solar energy.

Solar energy does provide a great amount of heat for homes and industries. *Solar panels* are used to trap solar energy, Fig. 4-23. The energy is then used to heat water or air. Hot water or air can then be used directly. Heated air can be stored in a tank for later use. Heated air can be stored in a bin full of rocks.

Hydroelectric Energy

Years ago, flowing water was used as a source of energy. Have you ever seen a waterwheel?

Fig. 4-23. Solar panels on the roof collect solar energy as heat and transfer the heat to water or air in the building.

Fig. 4-24. A waterwheel uses moving water as power to do work.

OUTSIDE DAM

INSIDE DAM

Fig. 4-25. Top. Force of water can be seen as it passes through this dam. Bottom. Interior shot shows generator room of a modern hydroelectric generating station.

The storage of electricity is difficult and expensive. Therefore, as the need for electricity increases or decreases, the amount of electricity produced is controlled at the hydroelectric plant. Once the electricity is produced it must be used. The amount of electricity being produced is controlled by adjusting the amount of water running through the sluice. The more water running through the sluice, the faster the turbine will turn thus causing the generator to spin faster. This will then produce more electricity. The largest dam in the United States used to generate electricity is the Grand Coulee Dam in the state of Washington.

Tidal power and wave power are also sources of water energy. Tidal power is the force that comes from the gravitational pull of the sun and moon. Thus, the power from a tide delivers much energy. Wave power is caused by the wind driving the water toward the shore. This, too, delivers much energy.

Nearly all power taken from water energy is from hydroelectric plants at waterfalls or dams.

Geothermal Energy

Geothermal energy is heat from the earth. Geo means earth and thermal relates to heat. This heat that is within the earth comes mainly from a molten rock called *magma*. Magma is located miles beneath the earth's surface. Heat from magma is trapped underground. Sometimes, magma erupts from the earth in a volcano.

Water that is underground turns to steam when it comes near this molten rock. Great amounts of steam are produced from the earth.

The high pressure from the steam is used to turn turbines which are connected to generators. The

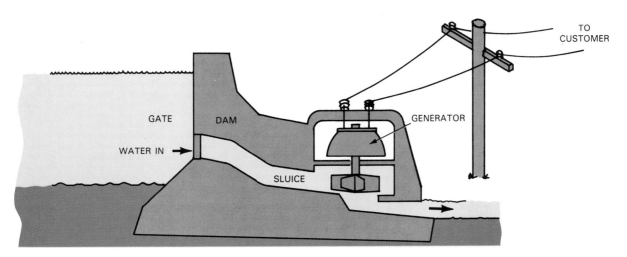

Fig. 4-26. How a dam for a hydroelectric power station is designed. Water flows through a pipe called a sluice to spin a turbine. The turbine drives an electric generator that converts mechanical power into electrical power.

generators then produce electricity. The production of electricity is the greatest use of geothermal energy.

In San Francisco, there is a location where magma is about five miles below the earth. This location is known as The Geysers. The first geothermal plant was built at The Geysers in 1960. Now there are several power plants in the area. So much steam boils out of the ground that all of these power plants together produce enough electricity to power a city of over a million people.

Wind

For years, people built windmills in places where the wind blew much of the time, Fig. 4-27. The windmills helped them to live. They would pump water, grind grain, or do other useful tasks.

Unfortunately, the wind has never been a predictable energy source. You never know when the wind will blow. One day it may blow all day another day it may blow very lightly or not at all. Windmill usage decreased when fossil fuels became available.

Today the windmill is back in use. Mainly, it is being used to generate electricity. A way to harness this free energy produced by the wind is by a wind turbine. Today most windmills are referred to as *wind turbines*. A wind turbine has two different designs. One type of turbine is the horizontal-axis design. The other type of turbine is the vertical-axis design, Fig. 4-28. On both designs, the wind drives a propeller or turbine that is connected to a generator. The wind makes the turbine turn the generator which produces electricity.

Wind is also used to power sailboats. Designers are experimenting with large sails for ocean going freighters. Wind is a great source of energy to harness and put to work.

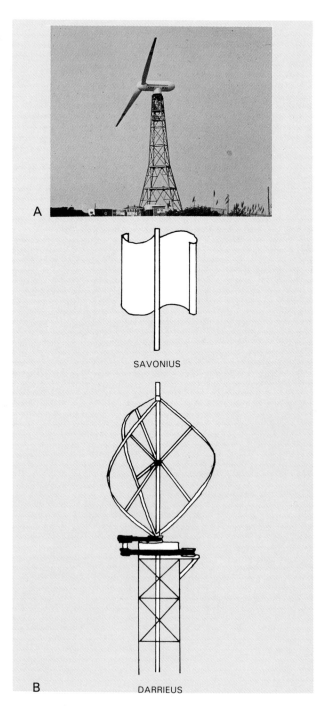
A

SAVONIUS

B   DARRIEUS

Fig. 4-28. Examples of wind turbine types. A—Horizontal axis type. B—Vertical axis types include the Savonius and the Darrieus.

Fig. 4-27. Years ago, windmills such as this helped people with their daily tasks.

Hydrogen

Hydrogen is found in water. Two atoms of hydrogen are found in one molecule of water. The two hydrogen atoms are bonded tightly with one atom of oxygen, Fig. 4-29. Water covers about two-thirds of the earth's surface. Therefore, hydrogen is considered inexhaustible since it is found in water. Not only is the supply of hydrogen plentiful but it is also a very powerful fuel. Hydrogen is combustible (will burn). There are a lot of ways in which hydrogen can be used. Some uses of hydrogen are to operate turbine generators, power rocket engines, and power automobiles.

There are very few problems with using hydrogen. However, it is hard to remove hydrogen from water. The bond that holds water molecules together is very strong. And the bonds need to be broken in order for the hydrogen to be released.

This process of releasing the hydrogen requires large amounts of electricity. The electricity passes through the water and breaks the strong bonds between the hydrogen and oxygen atoms. At the present time, it costs more to produce hydrogen than the hydrogen is worth. A solution to the high cost of electricity could be to use a free source of energy to produce electricity. For instance, if we could convert solar energy into electricity then the process of producing hydrogen would be more efficient.

Hydrogen may be used to replace gasoline one day. We may burn hydrogen in our automobiles instead of gasoline. It may also replace natural gas used for heating.

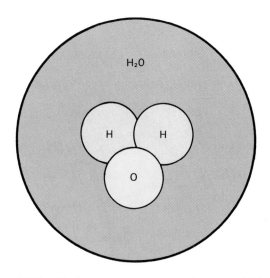

Fig. 4-29. Hydrogen as a source of power. If cheap electricity can be found, it might be used to separate the hydrogen found in water molecules. (Two hydrogen atoms are found combined with one oxygen atom in every molecule of water.)

SUMMARY

Energy begins mostly with nature. Energy comes from many sources. These sources have been broken down into three categories. They are renewable, nonrenewable, and inexhaustible. Renewable energy sources are those sources that can be replaced. They mainly come from plants and animals. Most of the basic renewable energy sources are animals, plants, food, wood, and alcohol. Nonrenewable energy sources are those sources that cannot be replaced once they have been used. For example, coal, oil, natural gas, and uranium are nonrenewable. Inexhaustible energy sources are those sources of energy that will not run out. Some examples of these are the sun, the wind, geothermal energy, falling waters, and hydrogen.

All of these sources of energy aid in the transportation system in some fashion. Whether it be a direct input into the system or a conversion of energy into the system, either way, we must have energy sources to operate our transportation systems.

KEY WORDS

All of the following words have been used in this chapter. Do you know their meaning?

Aquifers	Nuclear fission
Bioconversion	Nuclear power plant
Biomass	Nuclear reactor
Crude oil	Oil shale
Deep mining	Petroleum
Fractionating tower	Radioactivity
Gasohol	Reactor
Geothermal energy	Renewable energy
Inexhaustible	Solar energy
Liquefied natural gas	Solar panels
Magma	Surface mining
Methanol	Tar sands
Natural gas	Uranium
Nonrenewable energy	Wind turbine

TEST YOUR KNOWLEDGE

Write your answers on a separate sheet of paper. Do not write in this book.

Short answer:
1. List the three categories of energy sources.
2. What is an advantage of using more alcohol in a gasoline mixture?
3. How are fossil fuels formed?

Fig. 5-2. Even when we play, producing movement is defined as work.

Fig. 5-4. This train uses electricity from the power cable overhead to operate electric motors to turn the wheels. The electric motor in the train converts electrical energy into mechanical energy to move the train.

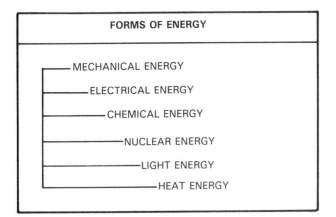

FORMS OF ENERGY

- MECHANICAL ENERGY
- ELECTRICAL ENERGY
- CHEMICAL ENERGY
- NUCLEAR ENERGY
- LIGHT ENERGY
- HEAT ENERGY

Fig. 5-3. The six different forms of energy. It is not always possible to observe the motion even when the form of energy is at work. For example, while we can see the motion of mechanical energy in wind we cannot see change or movement in electrical energy until it is converted to another form.

make 36 different conversion possibilities. Even so, humans have put only about half of all types of conversions to use. Two of the more obvious ones are the conversion of chemical energy to light and heat in the form of fire. The second is electrical energy used to light lamps or power trains, Fig. 5-4.

Potential and Kinetic Energy

The six forms of energy in our universe can be further divided into potential energy and kinetic energy. Energy that is stored is called potential energy. Coal is an example of a substance with potential energy. The chemicals stored in coal can be converted to other forms of energy through combustion (burning), but remain stored until the fire is started. Potential energy can also be found in wood, uranium, and fossil fuels.

"Kinetos" is a Greek word that means moving. From this we derive the term kinetic energy. Kinetic energy is energy in motion. It is this kinetic energy that enables us to do work and perform transportation activities. Kinetic energy is found in a moving body of water, a skydiver falling from an airplane, and even in sand flowing through an hourglass.

It is not always possible to see kinetic energy. In boiling water, the atoms that make up the water are moving very fast. We cannot actually see the atomic movement, nor do we want to look for fear of burning ourselves!

Let us consider the relationship of potential and kinetic energy. It is not possible for potential energy to move or work by itself. It must be converted to kinetic energy. For example, the water held behind the gates in a lock is recognized as having stored (potential) energy. Until that water is released through valves it cannot perform work. When it is released, the flowing water possesses kinetic energy. Can you see how stored energy is changed to the energy of motion?

By controlling this energy, we can lower or raise large ships to various water levels when the ships are moving from one body of water to another. How many other examples can you think of where potential energy is changed to kinetic energy to be used in transportation?

Heat Energy

Heat energy, also called thermal energy, is the energy produced by movement of molecules in our surroundings. Molecules are the "building blocks" of everything in our environment, and are always in motion in any substance. Thus, a trace of thermal energy can be found in all gases, liquids, and solids. As the speed of molecules in a substance increases, its thermal energy also increases. Therefore, the faster the molecules of these substances move, the greater the amount of heat energy possessed and released by the substance.

Heat energy is a very important type of energy for our world. If it were not for the thermal energy generated by the sun, life could not exist on earth, Fig. 5-5. As we look at all of our technological processes that help us survive and make life easier, we can realize just how much we rely on heat energy. Heat is used to cook our food, warm us when our environment is too cold, and melt metal and other materials so that we can form them to suit our needs, Fig. 5-6. Heat is also used to generate electricity.

There is a customary unit of measurement for heat energy. It is known as the **British thermal unit** (Btu). One Btu is the amount of heat energy needed to raise the temperature of one pound of water one degree Fahrenheit, Fig. 5-7. A Btu is used to measure the amount of heat coming from a furnace. It is also used to measure the cooling of air conditioners. Fuels can also be rated as to how many Btus they can produce.

In the field of transportation, our major source of propulsion at the present time is the heat engine. There are many types of heat engines which will be explored in later chapters. Have you ever seen a hot air balloon? Look at Fig. 5-8. This is a transportation vehicle that owes its existence to thermal energy.

Fig. 5-5. Thermal energy is generated by the sun. Without the sun, planet earth would be too cold to support any kind of life.

Fig. 5-6. Heat is essential in getting a pan of water to boil.

Fig. 5-8. A hot air balloon operates by blasting heated air into the opening at the bottom of the balloon. Why does heated air cause the balloon to rise?   (Conner Prairie)

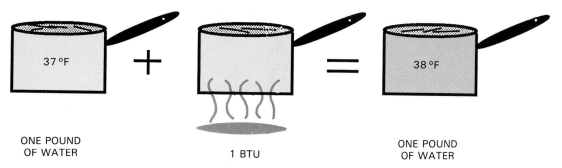

ONE POUND OF WATER   1 BTU   ONE POUND OF WATER

Fig. 5-7. How many British Thermal Units of heat would be needed to raise the temperature of the water from 50 °F to 212 °F?

Friction is a form of heat energy that often works against us when we are developing transportation systems. *Friction* is created by two surfaces rubbing against each other. It is the cause of a large amount of energy loss in a machine. However, it is also used to help control vehicles. Clutch and brake devices rely on friction to operate.

Light Energy

You have learned that *light energy*, like heat energy, is a type of radiant energy. It is given off by a source, the most important source of all, the sun. The light we see everyday has been radiated by the sun. Light travels at a speed of a little more than 186,000 miles per second. That means the light we see now left the sun about eight minutes ago. That is not a long time when you consider how far we are from the sun. The earth is 93 million miles away. Imagine the possibilities if we could travel safely at this speed.

Just as thermal energy is important, light energy is also important for life on earth. *Photosynthesis* is the process plants use to convert light energy into food for growth. Plants are natural "machines" that convert light energy to chemical energy, Fig. 5-9. Animals then utilize this chemical energy to feed their bodies. You and I also use the stored chemical energy in plants to survive.

We are also finding ways of using light energy from the sun to progress technologically. We have developed *photovoltaic cells*, or solar cells to produce electricity used to power lightweight vehicles, Fig. 5-10. Photovoltaic cells are also used to convert sunlight to the electrical energy that powers satellites in outer space, Fig. 5-11.

Mechanical Energy

Mechanical energy is the energy of motion. This is probably the easiest type of energy to see. Mechanical energy can also be described as kinetic energy. Any object that can be observed in motion possesses mechanical energy. Examples of mechanical energy include a person walking, a race

Fig. 5-10. Solar cells are located in the hood and roof of this converted Honda. It has a gasoline engine-powered generator to extend its driving range. It took first place in the 1990 American Tour de Sol Solar and Electric Car Championships in the open category. The contest is sponsored by the Northeast Sustainable Energy Association. (Mark Morelli photo)

Fig. 5-9. Plant life is nature's storehouse for light energy. The storage process is called photosynthesis.

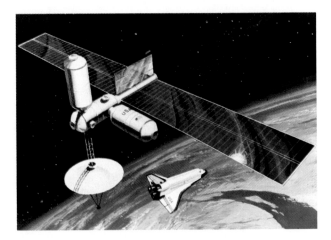

Fig. 5-11. Since satellites are far from any other source of electricity, solar cells convert the sun's energy to provide electrical power. Solar cells are located in the wing-shaped structure. (NASA)

car speeding around a track, a boat cruising into a marina, or even one of your friends riding a skateboard, Fig. 5-12. How many more examples can you name?

It should be recognized that all transportation systems are capable of, and rely on, mechanical energy. Refer again to the definition of transportation.

Electrical Energy

Electrical energy is produced by the movement of atomic particles called *electrons*. Electrons are the negatively charged particles in atoms. We cannot see this movement as easily as we can observe mechanical energy. The reason is because the atoms are very small in size. Even so, the use of electrical energy is widely seen by humans in their technological successes. This energy is converted to light energy by lamps, to mechanical energy by motors and solenoids, and to thermal energy by ovens and heaters.

Most of the technologies we use today rely heavily on electricity. Our emphasis on the use of computers, Fig. 5-13, as a tool in transportation, communication, manufacturing, biomedical, and other technologies proves this. Electrical energy is what computers use for "food." Telephones, televisions, and many other modern conveniences also owe their existence to the control of electrical energy.

An important advantage of electrical energy is that it is easily carried through wires over long distances, with little loss of energy. Those innocent

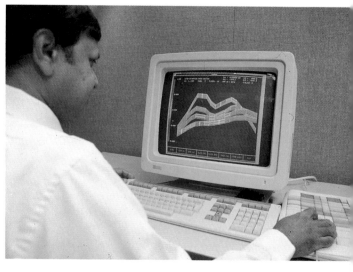

Fig. 5-13. Electrical energy is needed to operate this computer which is providing the operator with data needed by an oil company.   (Mobil Oil Co.)

looking wires hanging from towers and poles are hard at work transporting electrical energy. Should one of those wires fall or break, it can be very dangerous because electricity can kill if it is not respected. If you ever see an overhead electrical wire on the ground, DO NOT go near it. You should immediately get help from the local electric company, Fig. 5-14.

Fig. 5-12. Chemical energy stored in gasoline is converted to mechanical energy by the engine. This mechanical energy powers this car. Some of the mechanical energy is converted to electrical energy so lights, radio and electric motors in the car can operate properly.   (Ford Motor Co.)

Fig. 5-14. The wires strung along our highways conduct (carry) electricity to its point of use. Downed wires, also called cables or conductors, are dangerous and should be avoided. The electric company must be called to make repairs.

Chemical Energy

All changes in nature can be described in scientific terms as physical changes and chemical changes. Physical changes can be reversed. For example, ice can melt and become a puddle of water. It can then refreeze and be ice once again.

Chemical changes are those that cannot be reversed. For example, once a match has been lit, it can never be relit. The chemicals on the match head have been changed by the first fire. Look at Fig. 5-15.

Chemical energy is the energy produced by chemical changes. A typical chemical change is combustion. What types of energy are converted from chemical energy in combustion? How about the two types of radiant energy, heat and light? Many of the sources of energy discussed earlier are harvested for their chemical energy. Fossil fuels like coal, oil, and natural gas are all chemically changed through combustion so that they may produce work. Many transportation systems rely on these chemical changes for propulsion.

Cells are used when a portable energy source is needed, Fig. 5-16. They are designed so that when the two terminals (ends) of the cell are connected in a circuit, chemical changes occur inside and produce electrical energy. Cells have many uses in our technological world. Can you name any?

Nuclear Energy

One of the more recent developments in our utilization of energy sources is the exploitation of

Fig. 5-16 When we need a portable energy source to help us light our way, cells supply the energy in portable flashlights. (Eveready Battery)

nuclear energy. *Nuclear energy* is that energy which is stored in atoms. It is unlike electrical energy in one respect. The whole atom is used rather than just the electrons.

Nuclear energy is released in a chain reaction called *fission*. In this reaction, one atom is split by being hit with a neutron (another part of an atom). This atom releases heat energy as it splits. The parts of that atom then hit other atoms which release heat when they split.

Uranium-235 is the most common fuel for nuclear fission, Fig. 5-17. This reaction is allowed to continue only under carefully controlled conditions in nuclear reactors. The enormous amount of heat generated is used to create steam which drives turbines to produce electrical energy. Nuclear fission is also used to power the machines that propel some ships and submarines.

Fig. 5-15. A match stores chemicals that convert to heat energy when the match is rubbed along a rough surface.

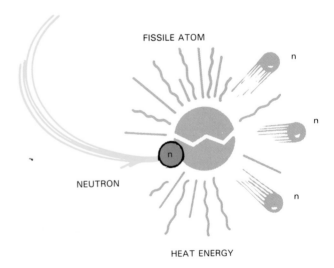

FISSILE ATOM

n

n

NEUTRON

n

HEAT ENERGY

Fig. 5-17. Fission is the ongoing process of splitting atoms. A free neutron resulting from the splitting of one atom strikes and splits another atom. This reaction continues and releases huge amounts of heat energy.

Another way we have learned to use the energy stored in atoms is through nuclear *fusion*. This process involves the joining of hydrogen atoms. When the atoms join, large amounts of thermal energy are released. This heat is then used to produce electrical energy. Nuclear fusion is not currently being used commercially because we cannot sustain a chain reaction like the one in the fission process.

You are probably aware that the use of nuclear energy is a debated issue. Some problems include the difficulty in containing the tremendous energy released and our current inability to safely store radioactive byproducts of nuclear reactions. However, some engineers do feel that we are almost able to produce safe ways to store these materials. Many people feel that we must continue to pursue nuclear energy as a safe and reliable energy source because we are quickly depleting our reserves of fossil fuels.

The Argonne National Laboratories near Chicago, Illinois has developed a new nuclear reactor design which promises to remedy part of the problem. Designers say that it will be able to reuse all but a few percentage points of its spent fuel. This would greatly reduce the amount of radioactive material that would need to be stored. Reports also indicate that the radioactive half-life of this material would be in the hundreds of years—not thousands. The design will be tested in a pilot reactor constructed for the purpose in Idaho.

EFFICIENCY IN ENERGY CONVERSION

We have just seen how energy is converted and used to feed our technological needs. Efficiency is a term used to describe how well we accomplish this conversion to meet our needs. When one form of energy is converted, it usually produces more than one other kind of energy. In order to be efficient, we must be sure to use as much of the energy converted as possible. Many times we lose energy through heat, or do not use all of the energy given off in a conversion. This leads to inefficiency.

Efficiency is stated in a percentage. The formula for determining efficiency follows:

$$\text{EFFICIENCY} = \frac{\text{ENERGY OUT}}{\text{ENERGY IN}} \times 100\%$$

For example, if 80 units of work were applied to a system of pulleys that lifted 20 units of weight, that system could be said to be 25 percent efficient.

Efficiency can be calculated for any machine known to us. Obviously, we should try to make this percentage as high as possible. Unfortunately, we do not always use very efficient systems of energy conversion for transportation. Only through further study of this technology can we improve our use of energy found in our universe.

SUMMARY

We use energy to produce the power needed to operate transportation systems. Energy can be categorized into six types. They are heat, light, chemical, mechanical, electrical, and nuclear energy. These energy types can be converted from one form to another. The law of conservation of energy states that energy can neither be created nor destroyed. Radiant energy includes heat and light energy. This is commonly seen in the life-sustaining energy given off by the sun.

Potential energy is the energy stored in substances. Kinetic energy is the energy possessed by all moving objects. Transportation systems use potential energy to create kinetic energy to move people and goods. Efficiency is the term used to describe how well we convert energy to meet our needs. The more energy in a system that is not used productively the smaller the efficiency percentage of that system.

KEY WORDS

All of the following words have been used in this chapter. Do you know their meaning?

British thermal unit	Friction
Efficiency	Fusion
Electrons	Photosynthesis
Fission	Photovoltaic cell

TEST YOUR KNOWLEDGE

Write your answers on a separate sheet of paper. Do not write in this book.

Matching:

1. ___ Heat energy.
2. ___ Mechanical energy.
3. ___ Light energy.
4. ___ Nuclear energy.
5. ___ Chemical energy.
6. ___ Electrical energy.

A. Produced by movements of molecules in our surroundings.
B. Energy used by photovoltaic cells.
C. Produced by movement of electrons.
D. Released through fission and fusion reaction.
E. Energy of motion.
F. Energy produced by chemical changes.

Fill in the blank:

7. _____ energy is stored in many substances.
8. The law of _____ states that energy can neither be created nor destroyed.
9. _____ energy is found in moving objects.
10. _____ is the process used by plants to convert light energy to food.

Short answer:

11. Name as many items as you can that use gasoline as an energy source for transportation.
12. What should you do if you ever see a fallen telephone pole or electrical wire on the ground?

13. What is the efficiency of a machine that uses 100 units of energy to do 35 units of work?

ACTIVITIES

1. Research books on physical principles concerning the Law of Conservation and write a class report. Explain what happens to energy after it has performed work.
2. Construct a device that changes one form of energy to another form.
3. Design, construct, and demonstrate a device to prove that there is energy in light.

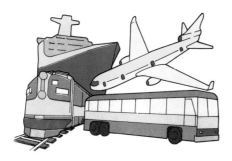

Chapter 6

USING ENERGY IN TRANSPORTATION

After studying this chapter, you will be able to:
☐ Understand the different uses of energy in transportation.
☐ Discuss the general uses of energy in society.
☐ Identify energy used in transportation vehicles.

You have been introduced to the different types of energy found in our environment. Energy sources, from wood to uranium, have been discussed. You have also been introduced to the conversion of energy. The changing of one form of energy to another has been alluded to. To conclude this section on energy, we will study how transportation consumes energy. You will look at some facts and figures about energy consumption in the transportation system. You will also be given some examples of how energy is used in specific transportation systems such as land, air, water, and space.

THE USE OF ENERGY

All the energy from various sources, whether renewable, nonrenewable, or inexhaustible, are distributed into four different sectors. These sectors demand energy to meet their needs. The four sectors are residential, commercial, industrial, and transportation, Fig. 6-1. The residential and commercial sectors consume energy for space heating, water heating, cooking, lighting, computer operations, air conditioning, and other similar uses. Industry uses energy for operating machines in the manufacture of products and foods. Finally, transportation demands energy to move cargo and people from place to place. Without fuel or some

other sort of energy the transportation systems could not function. Transportation uses about one-fourth of all of the energy consumed in the United States. Canada uses about the same percentage.

In the United States and Canada, about 90 percent of all the energy used comes from the three fossil fuels: coal, oil, and natural gas. The remaining 10 percent of the energy used comes from nuclear, hydroelectric, and alternative sources, Fig. 6-2. The alternate sources, including solar energy, account for less than one-half of one percent.

As you know, oil is a nonrenewable source of energy. One day the supply will run out. Notice on the pie chart in Fig. 6-2 the amount of oil be-

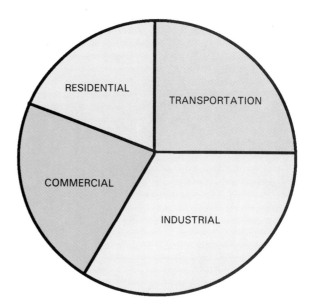

Fig. 6-1. These four sectors require the use of energy in our society.

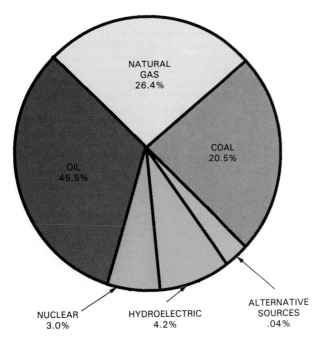

Fig. 6-2. Little more than 7 percent of our energy comes from inexaustible or renewable sources.

ing used at the present time. Most oil is used for the production of various types of fuels. Fig. 6-3 shows the different fuels produced from one barrel of crude oil. About 40 percent of the barrel of crude oil is used to produce gasoline. Approximately 18.2 percent is used to produce diesel fuel. About 4 percent is used for the production of petrochemical products such as plastics, fertilizers, paints, soaps, insect sprays, pharmaceuticals, and other products requiring petroleum. Look again at the barrel in Fig. 6-3. Compare the amount of fuels coming from one barrel to the amount of petrochemical products and other products coming from the barrel. Over half of the barrel of oil is used for

fuels burned in the transportation industries, Fig. 6-4. Transportation systems use more than half of all the oil that is produced or purchased in the United States.

Besides oil, another fossil fuel, coal, can be used to produce quality fuels for transportation vehicles. It can also be burned in stationary plants to produce electricity. This electricity can then be used in electric and hybrid vehicles. Natural gas is also used in the production of domestic and industrial fuels. Nuclear plants also produce electricity that can be used in transportation.

Alternative Energy for Transportation

The future holds a positive outlook for operating transportation systems with alternative sources of energy. Shale and tar sands when mined, filtered, and refined, can produce liquid fuels. Solar biomass when properly treated, can produce low hydrogen liquid fuels that can be used to power transportation vehicles. Hydrogen is an ideal fuel for transportation purposes. It is clean burning and produces water as its waste. Research is still being done on using hydrogen as an alternative fuel.

The problems with hydrogen have been its production, distribution, and storage. It is likely that in time technology will solve these problems.

You have just seen that most of the fuel for transportation vehicles comes from petroleum. The sun, the wind, and water are also sources of energy for transportation vehicles.

It may be that they propel a vehicle from their natural state. Take the wind for example. It may move a sailboat along at a rapid speed. As another example, it may turn a wind turbine which then generates electricity to operate an electric vehicle.

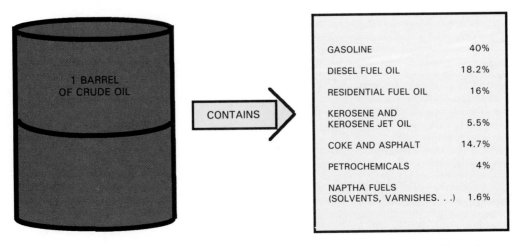

Fig. 6-3. A barrel of crude oil yields varying percentages of seven different products. Note that the largest percentage is converted into gasoline, one of several important transportation fuels.

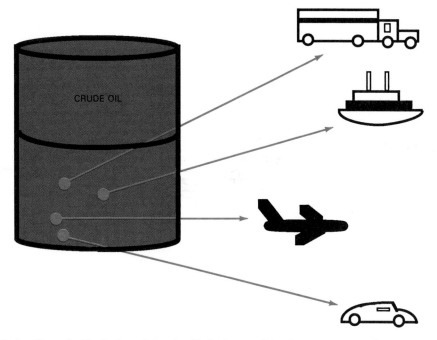

Fig. 6-4. Over half of the oil in the U.S. is used in the transportation systems.

One fact that you know for certain is that energy is definitely needed in our transportation systems! This will be discussed in more detail in Chapter 17. We will now look at some examples of energy used for land, air, water, and space transportation.

Energy Used in Transportation

For any transportation vehicle to function, it needs a source of energy to propel it. Whether it be a bicycle or a bulldozer, a ship, a jet plane, or a rocket, it must have an input of energy. Most of the energy used in transportation comes from fossil fuels. There are also other sources used to operate land vehicles.

Land Transportation

Human energy and animal energy are simple forms of energy but are still important to transportation on land. Riding a bike, a skateboard, or a buggy pulled by a horse are all examples of energy being used in transportation, Fig. 6-5. Human-powered vehicles (HPV) are similar to bicycles but they have a body like a car. They consist of two or three wheels and are pedal operated. They can travel up to 60 miles per hour. The designers of these HPVs are always looking for ways to make their vehicles go faster. In order to operate an HPV, you must be in good physical condition and have a great deal of energy stored up inside your body. Can you think of any other land transportation vehicles that operate from human energy?

Fig. 6-5. Where is the energy coming from to power this skateboard?

Solar energy can also be used in land transportation. The sun's rays can be transformed (changed) into electricity and stored in batteries. The transformation is done by using *photovoltaic cells.* The cells convert visible sunlight directly into electricity. The electricity that has been produced is then stored in batteries and used to power electric motors.

General Motors has built a solar-powered car, Fig. 6-6. The solar panels are placed on top of the vehicle so they can catch the sun's rays. The vehicle is battery powered. Called the Sunraycer, it weighs 390 lb. and travels at an average speed of 41.6 mph.

Fig. 6-6. The Sunraycer is a solar-powered, battery-operated vehicle designed by engineers at General Motors. (General Motors Corp., Hughes Electric)

Late in the nineteenth century and early into the twentieth century experiments were being done to use solar energy to power steam engines in ships and trains. The first design idea was to heat water and use the steam from the water to power the steam engine. John Ericsson, designer of the warship, Monitor, designed the largest solar engine ever known up to that time. Its collectors had an area of 200 sq. ft. These were linked to an engine that developed nearly 2 horsepower.

Later, A.G. Eneas designed a parabolic collector to heat water. It directed reflected sunlight onto a boiler that produced steam for a steam locomotive. His first solar "furnace" resembled an upside-down umbrella with the boiler where the umbrella handle would be. Steam generated in the boiler moved along a flexible pipe to the engine, Fig. 6-7.

It was soon discovered that a solar engine wasn't as cheap as a regular steam engine. This discouraged further design activity to develop solar power for heat engines.

What is the main source of energy in a vehicle? Most of us would say gasoline or diesel fuel. Both of these come from fossil fuel. See Fig 6-8. As the fuel goes through the fuel system, an igniting of air and fuel takes place. This igniting produces a power stroke which powers the vehicle.

Fig. 6-8. Fuel is the most important element in most transportation systems.

Fig. 6-7. This is an artist's conception of Eneas' design that used solar energy to drive a steam-powered locomotive.

Air Transportation

Some air transportation vehicles are powered, controlled, and guided by wind energy. A hang glider, for example, is a recreational vehicle that, like a kite, depends on the wind, Fig. 6-9.

Like land transportation, air transportation also uses human power in some air vehicles. A plane known as the *Daedalus* is a human-powered plane. It weighs a skimpy 70 lb. and has a 112 ft. wing span. With no energy except for the power of his or her, the pilot will take off on a flight that was inspired by a Greek myth. According to Homer, the legend suggests that Daedalus is one of history's first engineers. Daedalus was imprisoned in Crete. He needed to escape so he built wings made of feathers and wax or honey. His son Icarus, flew with him. Icarus ignored his father's warnings and flew too close to the sun and melted his wings. Icarus fell to his death while Daedalus flew on to safety. This myth has captured the imagination of many inventors. In 1988, Daedalus was constructed and flown 72 miles over the Agean Sea.

The direct use of the sun's rays has given transportation new designs and experimental vehicles. One such solar powered aircraft, known as the Gossamer Penguin, flew across the English Channel.

Petroleum is also the source of aircraft fuels. One of the byproducts of petroleum distillation is kerosene. Other hydrocarbons are used to operate an aircraft. *Hydrocarbons* make up natural gas. Natural gas has four major types of hydrocarbons. They are methane, ethane, propane, and butane. The fuel is mixed with air which forms a combustible mixture. This combustion operates a compressor which turns a turbine. A small portion of energy from the fuel-air mixture is used to operate the compressor in the jet engine. The rest of the energy is released through the exhaust with great force. This is where an aircraft gets its thrust to move in a foward direction.

Water Transportation

The energy supplied by the wind has also aided water transportation. Centuries ago, ships were built with big sails and were driven across the oceans by the wind. Today, more experiments are being done to put big sails on ocean-freighters and once again use the wind as a source of energy. For water recreation, the wind is a frequent energy source. Para-sailing, windsurfing, and sailboating are some examples of using the wind to transport, Fig. 6-10.

However, fuel remains the main energy source for water transportation whether it be a jet-ski or a cargo ship. Fuel is injected into the engine where combustion is produced. The force of the expanding gas creates power to move the vehicle.

Water transportation has introduced nuclear power into the transportation system. In 1955, the first nuclear-powered ship became operational. It was a submarine known as the *Nautilus.*

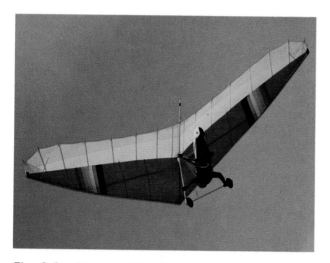

Fig. 6-9. A hang glider depends on air motion and the amount of air it can capture under its canopy.

Fig. 6-10. Wind surfing depends on the kinetic energy of moving air.

The major advantage of ships operated by nuclear power is that a small amount of fuel can power the vessel for years. Conventional ships need to be refueled every one or two months. The Nautilus traveled 62,562 miles in two years before it needed refueling. It was the first ship to ever reach the North Pole. In doing this, it proved that nuclear power could be safe and efficient.

Today, many ships are powered by nuclear reactors. The reactor core holds fuel rods which are filled with uranium. The fission reaction takes place within the fuel rods thus creating a great amount of heat. The heat is transferred to water which produces steam. The steam is then used to turn large turbines that drive large propellers. The pressure of the propellers against the water drives the ship forward.

Space Transportation

Launching a space vehicle into orbit requires some form of power. The power comes from a rocket engine. The rocket engine provides an extreme amount of force which sends a shuttle sailing out of this atmosphere. Rocket engines are of two types: solid fuel and liquid fuel. The main source of energy for the liquid- fueled rocket engine is hydrogen. Hydrogen is found in water. It is a gas that can be converted to a liquid. The largest use for hydrogen now is to propel liquid-fuel rocket engines.

Solar energy may one day be used in space transportation. Sounding much like science fiction, solar sailing is a proposed exploration system powered by the sun's rays. The design would be such that the rays would fall on a sail and provide a push. The force would build up and become greater than the thrust of a rocket engine.

We have briefly looked at some examples of sources of energy being used in transportation. These were mentioned to give you some practical ideas on the importance of all sources of energy as they relate to transportation vehicles. In the following chapters of this book you will gain a greater knowledge and understanding of how vehicles operate using a particular source of energy. Power that is generated from a source of energy puts a vehicle in motion. Power systems will be discussed in detail in the following section.

SUMMARY

Energy used in our society meets the needs of residential, commercial, industrial, and transportation sectors. Transportation uses approximately one-fourth of all the energy consumed in the United States and nearly half of the fossil fuel energy. Over 90 percent of all energy in the United States and Canada comes from the three fossil fuels: coal, oil, and natural gas. Most of the fuel for transportation vehicles comes from petroleum. The sun, wind, and water also provide for sources of energy for transportation vehicles.

Human power has powered a lightweight aircraft and a lightweight car, as well as bicycles, skateboards, and scooters. The sun and the use of solar energy has a great outlook for the future. Experimental solar vehicles have been developed for land and space transport.

KEY WORDS

All of the following words have been used in this chapter. Do you know their meaning?

Daedalus   Photovoltaic cell
Hydrocarbons   Nautilus

TEST YOUR KNOWLEDGE

Write your answers on a separate sheet of paper. Do not write in this book.

Short answer:
1. List the three fossil fuels.
2. What is an advantage of using hydrogen as a fuel?
3. Define a photovoltaic cell.

Fill the blank:
4. The _____ was the first nuclear-powered ship.

True or False:
5. Over three-fourths of all energy is consumed by transportation systems? True or False?
6. About 40 percent of a barrel of crude oil is used to produce gasoline. True or False?

ACTIVITIES

1. Using the school library or resource center, draw up a list of references on modern transportation.
2. Research the use of electricity to power automobiles. Prepare a talk or paper on its challenges and benefits.
3. Suppose that fuels were in short supply and that your community has been asked to conserve energy. Take part in a brainstorming session on ways to conserve.

4. Involve your family in a month-long effort to reduce electricity usage in the home. Compare that month's electric bill (kilowatts used) with the one from the previous month or from the same month in the previous year. Calculate the amount of money saved and the number of kilowatts saved. Find out the number of households in your community or a neighboring community and compute the amount of savings in electricity if each household conserved an amount equal to your household. Prepare a bar graph of your findings.

Transportation is an important technology. Most of us use land and air transport at some point for getting from place to place.

Section III
POWER SYSTEMS

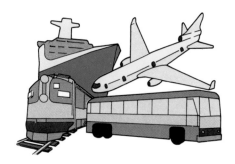

Chapter 7
MECHANICAL SYSTEMS

After studying this chapter, you will be able to:
☐ Explain and give examples of mechanical advantage.
☐ Describe the difference between ideal and actual mechanical advantage.
☐ List the six simple machines.
☐ Explain and give examples of the six simple machines.
☐ Describe various mechanical transmission devices.

Mechanical systems are power systems that use mechanical energy to produce work. They consist of one or more *machines*, which are devices that can change the size, direction, and speed of forces. Machines can also change the type of motion produced.

A block and tackle is a machine that enables a person to lift extremely heavy loads with little effort. Its effect is to multiply the force acting upon it.

A seesaw is a machine that changes direction of force. Pushing down on one end lifts the other end.

An eggbeater changes the speed of an applied force. The blades of the beater move fast even when you turn the crank slowly.

Other machines can change the type of motion. Transportation vehicles make use of three types of motion. The motions are reciprocating, rotary, and linear. Fig. 7-1 illustrates these.

Reciprocating is back and forth in the same line. Rotary means the motion is going around in circles. Linear is straight in one direction.

MECHANICAL ADVANTAGE

The machines we will explore are very important. They provide *mechanical advantage*. This is the increase in force provided by a machine. This means the force you apply to a machine is actually multiplied. The block and tackle discussed earlier is a machine that produces a great amount of mechanical advantage. Can you explain why? Did you ever try to lift a rock out of the ground with a long metal bar? If you did, you increased the effort you could produce by using the long bar. This is a simple machine, called a lever. It has found uses in all parts of our technological world.

Mechanical advantage can be found by dividing the input distance by the output distance. For example, suppose that you are using the metal bar wedged between two rocks as shown in Fig. 7-2. You exert a force 4 ft. away from the smaller rock. (The rock is the fulcrum.) The load is 2 ft. away from the fulcrum. This means that the machine provides twice the force that you put into it. Can you see that the more mechanical advantage a machine produces, the less energy is required to power that machine?

Actual Vs. Ideal Mechanical Advantage

The method that we just used to calculate mechanical advantage will tell us the *ideal mechanical advantage* (IMA). It is a ratio of the distances involved. In the real world, however, we must account for the amount of energy lost (not

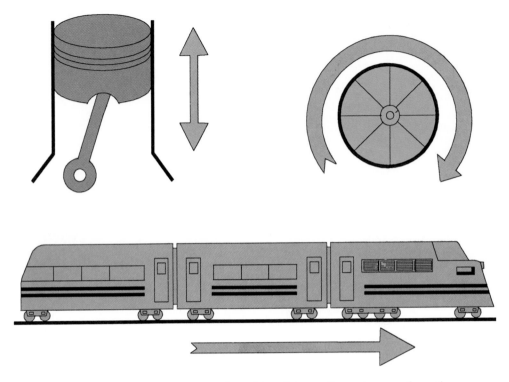

Fig. 7-1. Mechanical systems (machines) have three types of motion.

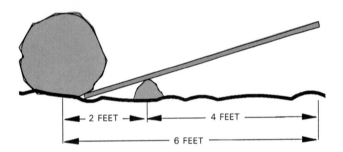

Fig. 7-2. Levers give their users a mechanical advantage. Less energy is required than if trying to move the load by lifting it.

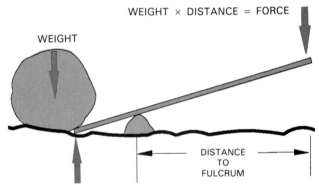

Fig. 7-3. Force of a first-class is determined by multiplying the weight of the load by the distance of the force from the fulcrum.

destroyed) through friction. Friction is the heat energy that is a common byproduct of mechanical energy. It is generated by two surfaces rubbing against each other. (You can experience this heat energy by rubbing the palms of your hands together rapidly for a few seconds.)

Actual mechanical advantage (AMA) is the ratio that we use to determine the increase of power by a machine, including the loss through friction. AMA is always less than IMA. Can you explain why? When we calculate AMA we must use a formula that involves the forces in the system. Force is weight (effort) times the distance from the fulcrum. Look at Fig. 7-3. Here we divide the output force by the input force to find AMA.

Very simply, the efficiency of machines is a comparison of the effort put in to the amount of ef-

fort put out. One way to calculate efficiency (in percentages) is to divide AMA by IMA, and multiply the answer by 100. See Fig. 7-4.

Simple Machines

You might think of washing machines, table saws, and drill presses when you think of machines. These are perfect examples of machines, but they are *complex machines*. They use more than one simple machine to accomplish their tasks. We can study these complex machines by picking out the smaller parts that actually do different types of work using mechanical energy. These smaller parts are the *simple machines*.

$$\%E = \frac{AMA}{IMA} \times 100$$

Fig. 7-4. To determine efficiency of a machine divide the Actual Mechanical advantage by the Ideal Mechanical advantage; then multiply by 100. The result is a percentage.

Six simple machines are used to control mechanical energy. They are the lever, the pulley, the wheel and axle, the inclined plane, the screw, and the wedge. Look at Fig. 7-5.

Although there are six types of machines, all rely on the principles of only two. These are the lever and the inclined plane. Keep reading to explore the different simple machines that you use every day.

Levers

A *lever* is a rigid bar that rotates (turns) around one fixed point. That fixed point is called the *fulcrum*. Remember the rock we moved earlier? The smaller rock the bar rested upon was the fulcrum.

We use levers to apply force on loads. There are three classes of levers; first, second, and third. The relationship of the position between fulcrum, load, and input force is used to determine which class lever we have. See Fig. 7-6.

First-class levers have the fulcrum between the input force and load. A seesaw is an example. We might use a screwdriver as a first-class lever to open a can of paint. Pliers are really an arrangement of two first-class levers that use one fulcrum. How many other examples can you name?

We can change the mechanical advantage produced in first-class levers by moving the fulcrum between the input force or the load. If the fulcrum

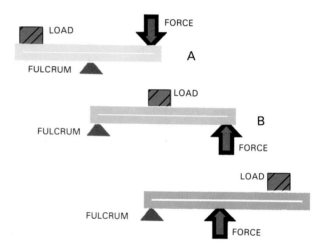

Fig. 7-6. Relationship between load, fulcrum, and force determines the type of lever.

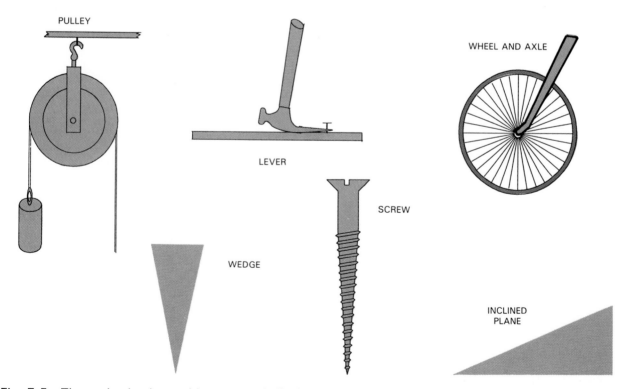

Fig. 7-5. These six simple machines control all of our mechanical energy. Complex machines are combinations of any of these six.

is close to the load, we will have a positive mechanical advantage, or an increase in force. When the fulcrum is exactly centered between the two, there is no mechanical advantage. As the fulcrum moves toward the input force, the machine loses strength but increases the distance we can move the load. Rowing teams use this positioning to increase the distance their oars move through the water, Fig. 7-7.

In *second-class levers*, the load is placed between the fulcrum and the input force. A wheelbarrow is a good example of a transportation system using a second-class lever, Fig. 7-8. Unlike first-class levers, second-class levers always provide a mechanical advantage in force. However, they can never increase the distance the force moves. Can you compare and see why this is so?

Third-class levers always move the load a greater distance than the movement of the input force. They never provide a mechanical advantage in the force applied.

Here the input force is between the fulcrum and the load. Many applications require increasing the distance rather than strength. Common shovels and rakes, as well as other gardening tools, utilize the principal of third-class levers. See Fig. 7-9. How many other machines can you think of that use third-class levers? How about baseball bats, golf clubs, and hammers?

Pulleys

Pulleys consist of solid discs that rotate around a center axis. The discs usually have a groove around the outside so that ropes or belts will ride

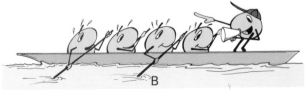

Fig. 7-7. A—Oars are based upon the principle of a first-class lever. They are designed to be distance multipliers. (Harvard University) B—Are these paddles examples of a first-class lever or a third-class lever?

Fig. 7-8. A wheelbarrow is a good example of a second-class lever. The fulcrum is the wheel and the load is between the wheel and the lifting force.

Fig. 7-9. A third-class lever like this rake is always a distance multiplier. Explain why.

around them easily. Pulleys are used to change forces in two ways. The direction of force is changed by a single fixed pulley, Fig. 7-10. We raise flags on poles with the help of fixed pulleys. Single movable pulleys are used to change the size of a

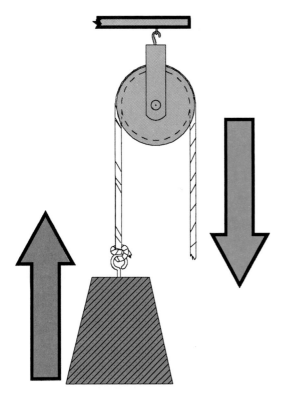

Fig. 7-10. A fixed pulley changes the direction of force to lift a load.

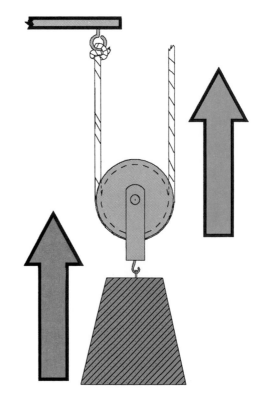

Fig. 7-11. A movable pulley does not change the direction of force.

force. Movable pulleys do not change the direction of the force. Look at Fig. 7-11.

Pulleys operate on the principle of levers. That means they have an input force, a fulcrum, and a load. In Fig. 7-12, these parts are labeled for fixed and movable pulleys. Notice that the distance between the fulcrum and input force is larger in the movable pulley. This is why it has greater mechanical advantage in force than the fixed pulley.

Several pulleys used together make up a block and tackle. With several pulleys in the same system, we can greatly multiply our input force. You may have seen piano movers or construction workers using these systems to lift heavy loads to great heights.

Wheels and Axles

The *wheel and axle* system is also based on the principle of levers. In this simple machine, the wheel has a large diameter while its axle has a small diameter. The two parts are attached to each other so that they move as one unit.

Wheels and axles can be used to change the size or distance of force. If the input force is applied to the larger diameter wheel, it multiplies the turning force as it turns the axle. What class lever does this resemble? It should look like a second-class

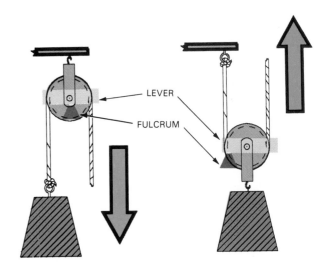

Fig. 7-12. Pulleys operate like levers.

lever. The steering wheel of an automobile is a good example. See Figs. 7-13 and 7-14. In contrast, when the input force is applied to the axle, the distance the applied force travels grows as it is transferred to the outside diameter of the wheel. See Fig. 7-15. What class lever does this resemble? How about a third-class lever? There are many common examples of wheel and axle systems. How many can you name? What about doorknobs, screwdrivers, winches, and drills?

Fig. 7-13. Did you know that the steering wheel of an automobile is a kind of lever? It multiplies the force used to turn the front wheels. (General Motors Corp.)

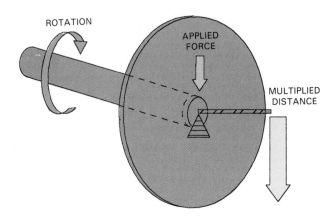

Fig. 7-15. A wheel and axle is a distance multiplier when the force is applied to the smaller-diameter axle.

Fig. 7-14. Without the leverage of the steering wheel it would be impossible to keep an automobile on a winding road.

Fig. 7-16. Greater force is needed to lift this barrel than to roll it up an incline.

Inclined Planes

Inclined planes are simple machines that make use of sloping surfaces. Loading ramps are a good example of this machine. It is hard for a person to lift a 100 lb. object up to the tailgate of a truck, Fig. 7-16. By rolling that object up a gently sloped ramp, the worker exerts much less energy to get the same result, Fig. 7-17. If there is one drawback with this system it is that the amount of energy used is spread over a greater distance. However, the increased mechanical advantage makes this machine worth using.

Inclined planes are often found in the roads that lead up steep hills or mountainsides. These roads switch back and forth to make the slope more gentle so that vehicles going up use less energy. See Fig. 7-18. Wheel chair ramps use the same princi-

ple. Wheel chair patients often have the energy to negotiate a ramp but would need assistance to mount steps.

Screws

A *screw* is another simple machine that operates on the principle of inclined planes. Actually, it is a very long inclined plane that is wrapped around a shaft. Fig. 7-19 illustrates this principle in a recognizable object. Can you see the similarity to an inclined plane?

The longer the slope in the inclined plane on a screw, the more turns it takes to advance up its

LESS EFFORT
GREATER DISTANCE

Fig. 7-17. Rolling a barrel up a ramp (inclined plane) requires moving it a longer distance. However, less force is used. The inclined plane is a force multiplier.

Fig. 7-18. Hilly, winding roads work like an inclined plane. (Fruehauf Corp.)

Fig. 7-19. Looking at the threads on this screw it is easy to see that it is an inclined plane wrapped around a shaft.

shaft one inch. Screws that have 16 threads per inch have a greater mechanical advantage than screws that have two threads per inch. This also creates more surface area to produce friction. Because of this, the screw is a very inefficient machine for some uses. Screws are commonly used as mechanical fasteners for wood, metal, and plastic. In such use, friction is desirable to grip and hold parts better. Screws are also used on vises and car jacks. In such usage they function as force multipliers. Can you name other things that make use of screws as force multipliers?

Wedges

Wedges are simple machines that are also based on the principle of the inclined plane. If you have ever driven a nail, or chopped wood with a hatchet, you have used a wedge. Wood-splitting wedges and door stops are also types of wedges. Look at Fig. 7-20 to see how a wedge operates. As the hatchet enters the wood, it forces the wood fibers apart until they separate or "split."

If you calculate the mechanical advantages of different-shaped wedges, you find that the longer the wedge (compared to thickness) the greater the advantage. Study this concept in Fig. 7-21. This is the reason you can split logs easier with thinner wedges.

Fig. 7-20. A hatchet uses the principle of a wedge. Its weight and fast movement combine to enable it to split the piece of wood.

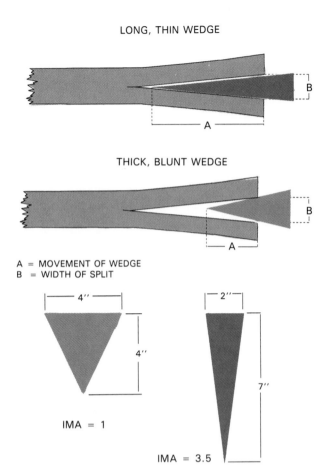

LONG, THIN WEDGE

THICK, BLUNT WEDGE

A = MOVEMENT OF WEDGE
B = WIDTH OF SPLIT

IMA = 1

IMA = 3.5

Fig. 7-21. A long, thin wedge has more mechanical advantage than a short, fat one. Look at the illustrations and explain why.

TRANSMISSION OF MECHANICAL ENERGY

We learned before that complex machines are made up of more than one simple machine. In order to transmit or pass power from one part of a vehicle to another, we may use variations on these simple machines. The following devices are specialized components in industrial machines and transportation vehicles whose operation relies on the principles of one or more simple machines.

Clutches

Clutches are mechanical devices used to connect the power source (motor or engine) to the rest of the machine. In many transportation vehicles, clutches connect the power system to the drive system. When the operator of the vehicle wants to disconnect these two systems, she or he simply activates the clutch. This device is needed so vehicles can remain at rest with the engine running, start slowly without stalling, and shift gears while moving.

Clutches operate on the principle of friction. Usually, two surfaces are made to rub, then lock against each other. This enables the two parts to move at the same speed, powered by one source.

The two types of clutches widely used in transportation vehicles are the friction clutch and the centrifugal clutch. These will be explained in more detail when you study control systems of vehicles.

Pulleys and Belts

Have you ever looked under the hood of an automobile? If so, you have probably seen many different belts that go around pulleys. See Fig. 7-22. Remember, pulleys are one of the simple machines we studied earlier. The belt and pulley systems you see under the hood are used to transmit power from the engine to drive engine components like water pumps and fans. Other belt/pulley systems are used to power accessories like air conditioning.

Belt and pulley systems are used on a wide range of other machines in our technological society. In fact, they have played an important part in the technological development of humankind. Many industrial applications have used these transmission systems. Old machine shops used complex systems of pulleys and belts to drive the machinery.

Belts and pulleys control mechanical energy through any of five different arrangements. Through their use, we can connect and disconnect power like a clutch, change direction, reverse rota-

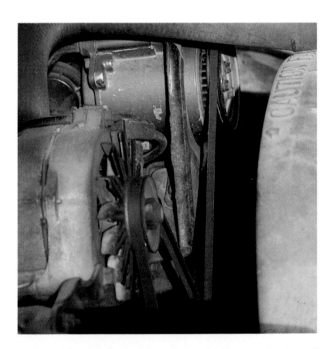

Fig. 7-22. Automobile engines make use of belt and pulley systems.

tion, change speed, and change torque. Fig. 7-23 illustrates the different arrangements to accomplish these tasks.

Chains and Sprockets

No doubt you recognize the chain and sprocket setup shown in Fig. 7-24. This mechanical transmission system is found on bicycles, mopeds, and motorcycles. They are usually used as the drive system to bring power to the driving wheel of the vehicle.

Like belts and pulleys, these systems can change speed and torque. By shifting the chain to different sprockets on a bicycle, you can control the input force that you give the system. You can make it

Fig. 7-24. A chain and sprocket transfer power from the bicycle pedals to the rear wheel.

easier to climb hills, or deliver power to the wheels even when you ride down hill. An advantage of chain and sprocket systems over belts and pulleys for drive systems, is their ability to provide positive power transfer. This means that the chain cannot slip like a belt on a pulley.

Gears

A *gear* is basically a metal wheel with small notches cut into its rim. Fig. 7-25 shows a typical gear.

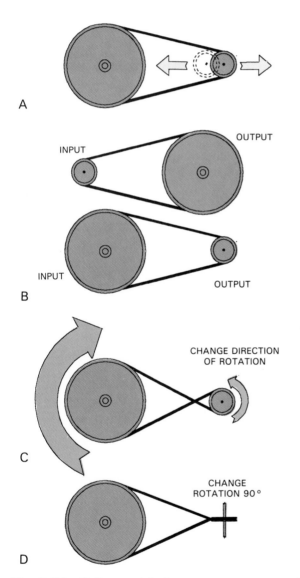

Fig. 7-23. Pulley and belt arrangements transfer power from one point to another. They also can change power and speed through pulley sizes. Sometimes belts are used to change direction of a force.

Fig. 7-25. This arrangement of gears is designed to change either force or speed. If the smaller gear is the driver, more force can be delivered at the axle of the larger gear. If the larger gear is the driver, more speed is delivered at the axle of the smaller gear. (Boston Gear)

Can you see the teeth around the outside of the gear? Teeth are on all gears, and *gear sets* are made so that the teeth on the gears interlock and drive each other. The gear powered by the engine or motor is the drive gear. The gear to which power is transferred is called the driven gear. Like chains and sprockets, gears will not slip, thus producing positive power transfer.

Although there are many different types of gears, the most common ones are the spur, helical, rack-and-pinion, worm, and bevel gears. Fig. 7-26 illustrates some common types. Can you see how they are able to control mechanical power in the same way as belts and pulleys? They can change direction of power, and speed and torque. Gears are widely used on transportation vehicles. We will discuss special transmission systems that use gears in later chapters. As you continue your study of transportation technology, you will see special transmission systems that use gears.

Shafts and Bearings

Shafts are long, cylindrical pieces of metal used to transfer mechanical energy in many machines. They look like pieces of solid pipe. Shafts are vital parts of automobile engines and drive systems, Fig. 7-27. Because of their solid construction, they permit positive power transfer.

Fig. 7-27. The drive shaft of a rear-wheel drive car shows the normal relationship of a shaft and bearing.

Bearings are specially shaped pieces of metal that are used to support shafts and reduce friction between metal parts as they move past or revolve around each other. They are made to be strong, yet allow the shaft to turn inside them. Although there are many types of bearings, the ones most common in vehicles are smooth circles of metal that are shaped to fit the outside of the shaft exactly.

The bearings are very important in the operation of any shaft-driven machine. They must be

Fig. 7-26. Gears are of several types. Some are shown here. Clockwise: A—Worm wheel. B—Spur gear. C—Helical gear. D—Pinion gear. E—Bevel gear. F—Small spur gear. G—Worm. (Boston Gear)

able to conduct heat away from the shaft as well as resist softening from heat. Bearings must also be soft enough to glide over uneven shaft surfaces and tough enough to resist corrosive properties of some engine liquids. Fig. 7-28 illustrates a typical shaft and bearing relationship.

Because the shaft is a solid piece of metal, it cannot bend easily and still accurately transfer mechanical energy. In cases where flexibility is needed, *universal joints* are placed on the ends of the shaft. Fig. 7-29 is an illustration of a common universal joint. These allow free spinning of connected shafts, while permitting a change in direction. For example, if you drive down the road next to a truck, you may be able to see the spinning drive shaft running from the engine to the rear axle. If you look closely, you will see that the drive shaft is at an angle with its connecting shafts. When the truck stops you will be able to see a universal joint at both ends of the drive shaft. In this way, you can observe how universal joints allow for free rotation of separate shafts pointing in different directions. Look at Fig. 7-29 again.

SUMMARY

Mechanical power systems are those that control mechanical energy to do work. They consist of machines which are devices that can change size,

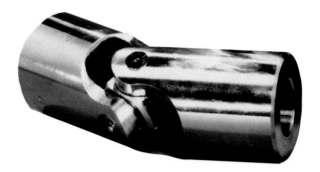

Fig. 7-29. A universal joint is often placed between two shafts that are not on the same plane. It allows the two shafts to turn together without binding or breaking.   (Boston Gear)

direction, and speed of forces. Machines can also change types of motion. The three types of motion studied in transportation technology are reciprocating, rotary, and linear.

Mechanical advantage is the increase in force provided by a machine. Ideal mechanical advantage is found by dividing distances, while actual mechanical advantage is found by dividing forces. Actual is always less than ideal mechanical advantage because of friction.

There are six simple machines that are used to control mechanical energy. They are the lever, pulley, wheel and axle, inclined plane, screw, and wedge. All six rely on the principle of either the

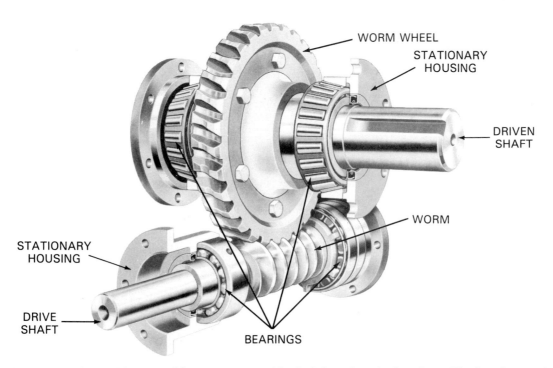

Fig. 7-28. The shafts in this assembly are supported in their housings by bearings. The bearings reduce friction between the rotating and stationary parts. The worm gear, comprised of worm and worm wheel, transmits power between drive and driven shafts.   (Cleveland Gear)

lever or the inclined plane. Mechanical power systems move mechanical energy through special transmission devices. These include clutches, pulleys and belts, chains and sprockets, gears, shafts and bearings, and universal joints.

KEY WORDS

All of the following words have been used in this chapter. Do you know their meanings?

Actual mechanical advantage	Mechanical advantage
	Pulleys
Bearings	Screw
Clutches	Second-class lever
First-class lever	Shafts
Gears	Third-class levers
Ideal mechanical advantage	Universal joints
	Wedges
Inclined planes	Wheel and axle.
Lever	

TEST YOUR KNOWLEDGE

Write your answers on a separate sheet of paper. Do not write in this book.

Matching:

On a separate sheet of paper, match the definition in the left-hand column with the correct term in the right-hand column.

1. __ Friction.
2. __ Actual mechanical advantage.
3. __ Fulcrum.
4. __ Mechanical advantage.
5. __ Complex machines.

A. Increase in force provided by a machine.
B. Calculation that involves forces in a system.
C. Reason AMA is always less than IMA.
D. Made up of many simple machines.
E. Point around which a lever rotates.

Fill in the blank:

6. Machines change _____, _____, and _____ of forces.

7. Six simple machines are the _____, _____, _____, _____, _____, and _____.
8. A wheelbarrow is an example of a _____ lever.
9. Shovels and baseball bats are examples of _____ levers.
10. Third-class levers always increase the _____ of the force.
11. Screws and wedges operate on the principle of the _____.
12. _____ are the devices that link power to drive systems.
13. _____ means that the power transmitting device will not slip when used.
14. _____ are used on the ends of shafts where flexibility is needed.

Short answer:

15. Explain the difference between first, second, and third class levers.
16. In what ways do single fixed and single movable pulleys differ?
17. List five different ways gears and pulley and belt systems control mechanical energy.

ACTIVITIES

1. Set up a demonstration to prove the mechanical advantage of a simple machine.
2. From the information gathered about the amount of force used and the amount of change (work) produced, determine the mechanical of a simple machine. (You may use the previous activity for this purpose.)
3. Survey your lab and list the various types of equipment on a blackboard or flip chart. As a class project, tell what simple machines are found in each.
4. Design and demonstrate the operation of a useful complex machine that combines two or more simple machines.

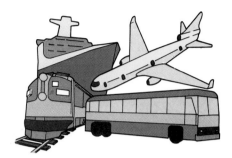

Chapter 8
ELECTRICAL SYSTEMS

After studying this chapter, you will be able to:

☐ Describe how atoms act to produce electrical current.

☐ Explain the types of current and how they are produced.

☐ Give examples and uses of different types of electrical circuits.

☐ Explain how electricity and magnetism are related.

☐ Describe the types of electrical circuits used in transportation vehicles.

Electrical systems are those that use electrical energy to perform work. Electricity is our most widely used, and versatile type of energy. Both simple and very complex electrical systems can be found in all aspects of modern technology. They are used to power home appliances that make our lives easier and safer. To save and maintain life, hospitals use electrical systems to run special machines. Manufacturing facilities rely on electrical systems to run the machines that produce needed products. See Fig. 8-1.

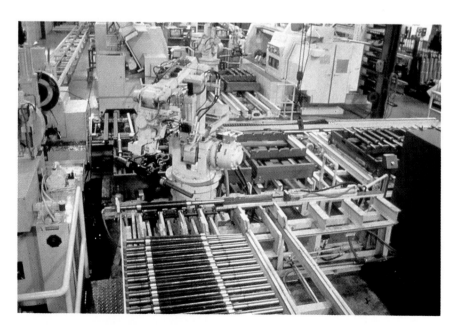

Fig. 8-1. Factories use electricity to operate various types of machines and equipment. Electric motors and other types of electricity-using tools are a common sight. This picture shows a robot that moves workpieces to and from a machine tool and conveyors. (SI Handling)

Electrical systems are also an essential part of most transportation systems and vehicles. An electrical system in an automobile lets us start the engine and keep it running. Separate electrical systems operate the lights, dashboard displays, radio, and other accessories. As shown in Fig. 8-2, electrical systems can provide the source of propulsion for transportation systems like elevators, moving sidewalks, and escalators. Often, vehicles are propelled by electric motors. Auto manufacturers are beginning to develop electric automobiles as an alternative to the gasoline or diesel engine.

Any electrical system relies on the use of *atoms.* Atoms are the "building blocks" of everything that we know of on earth. Rocks, trees, people, air, metal, and plastic objects are just a few examples of things made up of atoms. Since atoms are at the root of all electrical systems, that is where we'll start our study.

ATOMIC STRUCTURE

Atoms are extremely small, but even they are made up of several parts. Three particles make up an atom: protons, neutrons, and electrons. *Protons* have a positive (+) electric charge; *electrons* have a negative (-) electric charge; and *neutrons* have no charge at all. They are neutral. In an atom, unlike charges attract each other while like charges repel one another. The type of charge an atomic

particle has is called its *polarity*. Fig. 8-3 illustrates the parts of a simple atom.

At the center is the **nucleus** which contains the protons and neutrons. Electrons travel around the nucleus in elliptical (egg-shaped) paths. There are exactly as many electrons as there are protons in the nucleus. The number of separate paths followed by the electrons depends on their number. We call these paths rings. As the rings fill up with electrons, new rings are formed to allow room for more electrons. Compare the two atoms illustrated in Fig. 8-4. Notice how the number of protons equals the number of electrons in both. Note, too, that the atom with more electrons has more rings.

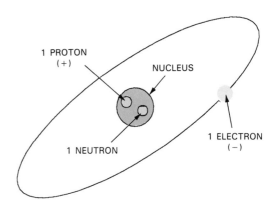

Fig. 8-3. Atoms are made up of a nucleus of protons and neutrons while electrons orbit around the nucleus.

Fig. 8-2. Electrical energy powers the people mover and the elevator system shown here. (United Airlines and Murphy/Jahn, Architects)

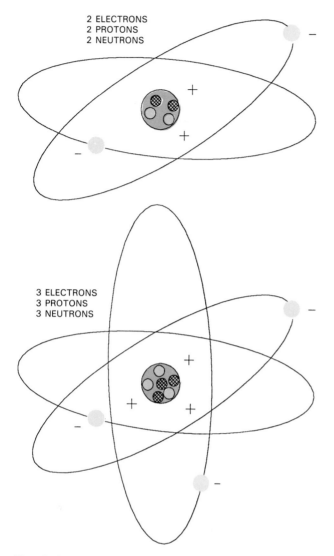

2 ELECTRONS
2 PROTONS
2 NEUTRONS

3 ELECTRONS
3 PROTONS
3 NEUTRONS

Fig. 8-4. Atoms always try to remain stable. This means that the number of electrons will balance the number of protons.

Atoms remain stable (neutral) by keeping the numbers of protons and electrons equal. Sometimes atoms need to lose electrons or gain electrons to keep their stability. Electrons in the outermost ring, called the *valence ring*, are the ones that are gained or lost. If an atom has more electrons than protons, it will lose some electrons from its valence ring. When the number of protons is greater than electrons, the valence ring will pick up electrons from nearby atoms so that it is stable. It is the electrons in the valence ring that lie behind the whole story of electricity.

Some atoms are able to lose and gain electrons easily, while others have a difficult time. Materials made of atoms that transfer electrons easily are called *conductors*. Wires that are used to carry electricity are good conductors. They are often made of copper. Materials that are made of atoms that

do not transfer electrons easily are called *insulators*. Insulators resist the flow of electricity. Some materials are both conductors and insulators. These materials are called *semiconductors*. Electrical systems depend on the action of electrons in relation to insulators and conductors. A semiconductor is a good example of how materials can be adapted to control movement of electrons from one atom to another. Fig. 8-5 shows one type of semiconductor (called a diode) and how it operates.

ELECTRON THEORY

Normally, an atom is neutral (has no charge). This tells us that the number of protons equals the number of electrons. When we are able to force electrons from their valence rings, electricity is produced. Fig. 8-6 diagrams the movement of electrons through a conductor. As a negatively charged electron is forced from its valence ring, the atom becomes positively charged (one more proton than electrons). The electron forced away is attracted to the positively charged atom to its right. Next, the atom that just lost an electron is positively charged and picks up an electron from an atom on its left. According to the *electron theory*, electrons flow from a negative point to a positive point. The

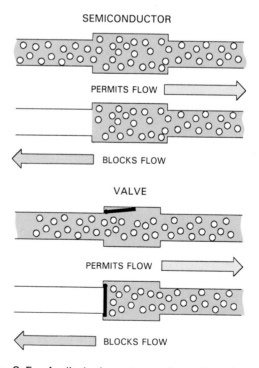

SEMICONDUCTOR

PERMITS FLOW

BLOCKS FLOW

VALVE

PERMITS FLOW

BLOCKS FLOW

Fig. 8-5. A diode is a type of semiconductor. It allows electrons to jump from one atom to another in one direction but not in the opposite direction. The diode controls electron flow the way a check valve flow of water in a plumbing system.

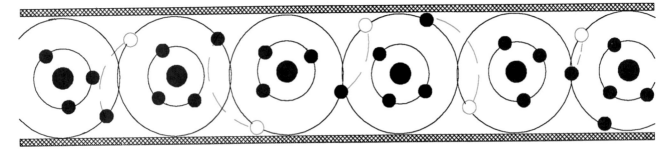

Fig. 8-6. When electrons migrate from one atom to another in a conductor, they produce an electric current.

negative point has an abundance of electrons, and the positive point has a shortage. Can you see this is in the conductor illustrated? The flow of electrons in a conductor is called *current*.

ELECTRICAL CURRENT

Current can move through a conductor (wire) in two different ways. In **direct current** (DC), electrons move only in one direction. Batteries are common devices that produce direct current. This type of current is used in modern automobiles as well as in many other transportation vehicles. See Fig. 8-7.

Alternating current (AC) involves the electrons flowing first in one direction, then reversing and flowing the other direction, Fig. 8-8. Alternating current is easier to send long distances through wires. This is the type of current used in houses and businesses to provide energy for lights, appliances, and machinery.

Fig. 8-7. Batteries chemically store electricity and release it as direct current. (Gould)

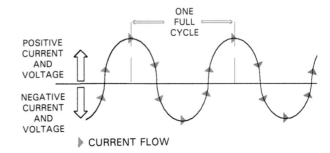

Fig. 8-8. The forward and reverse flow of alternating current is represented by a sine wave, like the one shown. Household current goes through 60 full cycles every second.

ELECTRICAL CIRCUITS

An *electrical circuit* is the heart of any electrical system. It is made of several components that are connected together to let electrical current flow in a complete path. An electrical circuit must have a power source that has both negative and positive terminals (connection points). Electricity flows from the negative terminal, through the circuit, to the positive terminal. Remember, according to electron theory, electricity flows from negative to positive.

We can manipulate the electricity in the circuit by adding components such as light bulbs, motors, and switches, to name a few. By placing these objects in the circuit, we allow electricity to flow through them so that they can operate. How many other objects or devices can you name that are parts of electrical circuits? How about car headlights, doorbells, and computers? Components that use electricity in a circuit are called *loads*.

Fuses are an essential part of any electrical circuit, no matter what the circuit's purpose. Fuses are made of filaments that melt and break the circuit if too much electrical current passes through them. A fuse prevents damage to the rest of the circuit should there be an overload. It is important to place the fuse between the energy source and the rest of the circuit. Fuses are made with different ratings. This means that some fuses allow more current to pass than others before they break the circuit. Fig. 8-9 shows various types of fuses used in transportation vehicles.

When planning and describing electrical circuits, it is easier to do it graphically (with drawings) than by describing them in words. *Schematic drawings* are used to draw an electrical circuit on paper, Fig. 8-10. They are like a road map. The road map shows the path taken by roads while schematics trace the path electron flow will take in an elec-

trical or electronic circuit. These drawings include symbols that show all the components that are in the circuit. Fig. 8-11 explains some symbols used for showing components in an electrical circuit.

There are three basic types of electrical circuits. They are *series, parallel,* and *series-parallel circuits.* These circuits have different characteristics and can be used for many applications. Circuits can be compared by the way they allow current to pass through them.

Fig. 8-9. Fuses like these are designed for transportation vehicles. They will open (break) a circuit so that neither the circuit nor the load is damaged by excess current.

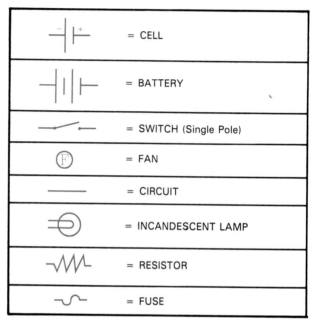

Fig. 8-11. Chart labels electrical and electronic symbols used in circuits.

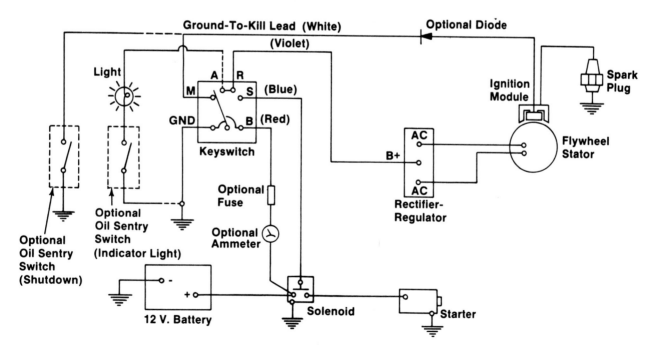

Fig. 8-10. Schematic drawings are the "road maps" of electrical/electronic circuits.

Series Circuits

Series circuits have one continuous path for electric current. If there is a break in the conductor or a bad connection, the whole circuit becomes useless. Fig. 8-12 illustrates a series circuit. Notice the single path for current between the components of the circuit. Electrical current flows from the negative terminal on the power source (in this case a battery), through a single switch and the light bulbs, then to the positive terminal. One switch operates all three light bulbs in the circuit at the same time. When it is opened, no current can pass through the circuit to power the lights. Refer to the series circuit in Fig. 8-13.

Parallel Circuits

Unlike series circuits, parallel circuits allow more than one path for electical current. (Current means the same as electron flow.) Because there is more than one path, a break in the conductor or a bad connection can only shut off part of the circuit. Notice in Fig. 8-14 how the components of this circuit are arranged in branches laid out next to each other. By adding a switch for every light, we can turn each one on or off individually, without affecting the other lights.

Parallel circuits allow paths for current even when one or more paths is broken or turned off. Look at this concept in Fig. 8-15. Parallel circuits are used in house wiring. Can you explain why these are better than series circuits for home use?

Series-Parallel Circuits

Look at Fig. 8-16 for an example of a series-parallel circuit. You should be able to recognize that it is a combination between the two circuits discussed earlier. In the circuit illustrated, the first light bulb after the negative terminal is in series with everything else in the circuit. The other two light

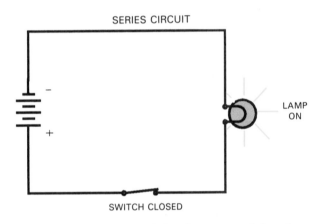

Fig. 8-12. A series circuit has but one path for electric current. When the switch is closed, the electrons flow through the circuit and the lamp is on.

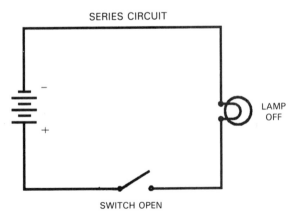

Fig. 8-13. This is the same circuit as in Fig. 8-12. The lamp will not light.

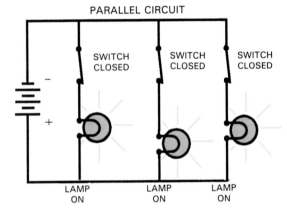

Fig. 8-14. An example of a parallel circuit. Even if one of the switches is opened, the other lamps would remain lit.

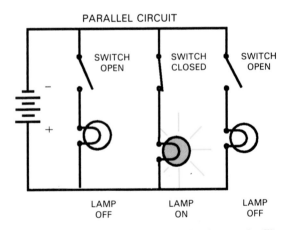

Fig. 8-15. This is the same circuit shown in Fig. 8-14 with two switches open. Can you trace the current in this illustration?

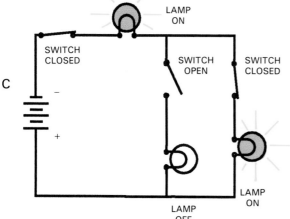

Fig. 8-16. In a series-parallel circuit, part of the circuit is in series and part is in parallel. A—All parts of the circuit are working. B—No current is found in the circuit. Do you know why? C—By looking at this circuit can you tell which parts of it are parallel?

bulbs in the circuit are arranged in parallel with each other. This means that a break at the first bulb would shut off the whole circuit. A break at any other bulb would still allow current to flow through

the circuit. Follow the path of current to see how this can work.

Magnets

Magnets are materials that are attracted to any metal that contains iron. They have an invisible force field that makes them stick to these metals. You might use magnets to hang things on your refrigerator at home. Magnetism is important in the study of electricity because the two can each affect the other. Electrical current produces magnetism, and magnets can induce, or cause electrical current in conductors.

Magnets usually contain two poles, one north and one south pole. These poles are on opposite ends of the magnet. There are *lines of force*, called *flux*, that run between the poles on the outside of the magnet. You cannot actually see the flux unless you place the magnet on a piece of paper, then sprinkle iron filings on the paper, Fig. 8-17. The filings form arcs between the north and south poles in the magnet, representing the lines of force.

When two magnets are brought together, their magnetic poles influence each other. Like poles repel each other, unlike poles attract each other. In other words, one north and one south pole are attracted to each other. Two north poles, or two south poles force themselves away from each other.

Electromagnets

About 150 years ago, Hans Oersted, a Dutch scientist, found that electricity produces a magnetic field. This discovery brought about the *elec-*

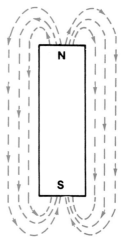

Fig. 8-17. The dotted lines are called lines of flux. They are always present in a magnet. Passing a conductor through a magnet's lines of flux induces an electrical current in the conductor.

tromagnet. An electromagnet consists of a conductor wrapped around an iron core. The two ends of the conductor are attached to a power source. When current passes through the conductor, the iron core becomes magnetized. When this happens, the iron core will be attracted to anything that has iron in it. Fig. 8-18 shows one application of an electromagnet.

Electromagnetic Induction

As mentioned earlier, we can produce electricity in conductors with the use of magnets. This process is called *electromagnetic induction*. Most of our electricity is produced this way. Remember that electricity is made when we are able to force electrons from their valence rings. When we pass a magnetic field through a coil of wire, the flux causes electrons to be forced from their atoms, producing electricity. See Fig. 8-19 for a description of electromagnetic induction.

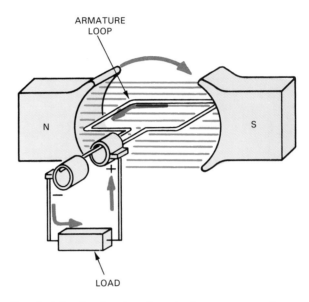

Fig. 8-19. A simple electrical generator demonstrates the principle of electromagnetic induction. The coil of the generator rotates through lines of force from a magnet to produce an electric current.

PRODUCTION OF ELECTRICAL POWER FOR TRANSPORTATION

We have seen that an important part of an electrical system is a power source. In fact, we could

not have a working system without one. The electrical power source provides a method for producing electrical current in a circuit. You have probably had to put *cells* inside a toy or flashlight at home. Cells, often mistakenly called batteries, are a common device for producing electrical power.

Have you ever seen or used a pocket calculator that would only work in a well-lighted area? That calculator used a special electricity-producing *photovoltaic cell*. These and other current-producing devices will now be studied in greater detail.

Cells and Batteries

There are many different types of cells and batteries. You may already recognize the cells used in flashlights. The same cell may be used in some clocks and smoke detectors. Batteries are used in transportation vehicles. These are tougher and more powerful than flashlight cells. All cells and batteries produce direct current.

A battery is made up of one or more *cells*. Cells and batteries are devices which change chemical energy to electrical energy. They consist of two different materials, called *electrodes*, and an *electrolyte*. The electrolyte is usually a liquid or paste that surrounds and touches both electrodes. The chemical reaction between the electrodes and electrolyte produces electrical current. Look at Fig. 8-20. The terminals that you learned about earlier are actually the electrodes. Remember that one has

Fig. 8-18. Scrap iron and steel can be picked up by an electromagnet.

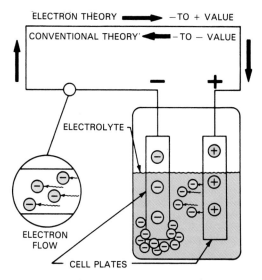

Fig. 8-20. A simple battery illustrates how a difference in electrical potential can cause electrons to flow in a circuit. In a chemical reaction between battery terminals and the electrolyte, electrons migrate from the positive to the negative terminal. If the other ends of the electrodes are connected, the electron flow causes a current through the circuit. (Kohler Co.)

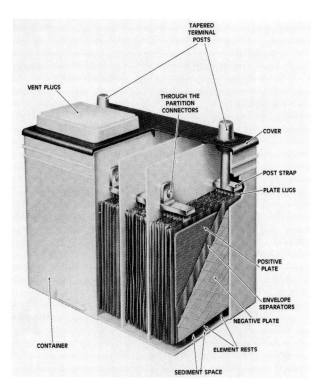

Fig. 8-21. A battery is made up of a number of cells. Three cells are visible in this cutaway. (Battery Council International)

a positive charge, and the other has a negative charge.

There are two kinds of cells, primary and secondary. **Primary cells** cannot be recharged. They can produce electrical current only while the chemicals in the electrolyte are reacting with each other. When the reaction stops, the cells are discharged and must be replaced.

It is this type of cell that powers toys and flashlights. A *carbon-zinc* battery is the most common primary cell used in these applications. In this type of cell, the carbon is the positive electrode and the zinc in the case is the negative. Other types of primary cells are alkaline, zinc chloride, mercury, and silver oxide cells. The very small batteries that are used in watches and cameras are mercury cells.

Secondary cells can be used up (discharged) and recharged many times. Recharging is done by sending electrical current through the secondary cell in a reverse direction from normal electron flow when it is producing electricity. The number of times a secondary cell can be recharged depends on its size, type, and the conditions under which it operates.

Refer to Fig. 8-21. It shows a common secondary cell used in automobiles. It is known as a *lead-acid battery*. This type of battery is a combination of several cells. It includes a series of positive and negative metal (lead) plates in a weak sulfuric acid

electrolyte. Other types of secondary cells are nickel-cadmium, nickel-iron, and rechargeable alkaline cells.

Alternators

Alternators are devices that can convert mechanical energy to electrical energy. They can do this by using electromagnetic induction. In a simple alternator, coils in a wire conductor pass through a magnetic field. See Fig. 8-22. As the conducting

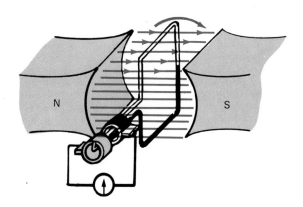

Fig. 8-22. This is a diagram of a simple alternator. As the conductor (wire loop) cuts through the magnetic field, magnetism causes electrons to flow in the wire loop and through the external circuit.

coil rotates through the magnetic field, current flows through the coil to the circuit. From an initial coil position, current flows through the external circuit in one direction for one half of a revolution. In the second half revolution, current flows through the circuit in the reverse direction. This action produces what is known as alternating current (AC). Alternators are sometimes referred to as AC *generators.*

Many of our large dams, Fig. 8-23, produce electricity with the aid of AC generators. (Alternating current is easier to conduct over power lines than direct current.) Mechanical energy is supplied to the generator through water channeled to a **turbine.** (A turbine is a wheel with blades on it that capture the energy in steam or water that is forced against the blades.) The turbine is connected by a shaft to the generator, located above it. As the turbine spins, it rotates the generator. See Fig. 8-24. The fast-moving water pushes on blades of the turbines, spinning the magnets inside the generator. The rotating magnetic field has the same effect as does a rotating coil in a *fixed* magnetic field.

With hydroelectric power, we can create as much electricity as we want by using an inexhaustible source of energy—moving water. Steam is also used to move turbines in many power plants. Unfortunately, we must use exhaustible energy sources to create the steam.

Photovoltaic Cells

Photovoltaic (solar) cells are used to convert light energy into electrical energy. They consist of thin

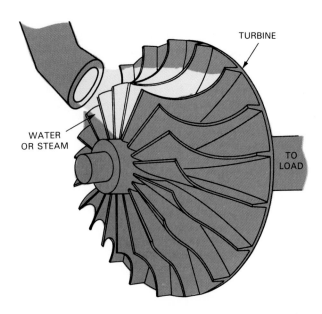

Fig. 8-24. Generators are powered by turbines which can convert steam or water pressure into mechanical energy to spin the generators.

pieces (wafers) of crystal, usually silicon, whose atoms are easily excited by light energy. Basically, *photons* given off by light, force electrons from their valence rings. This sets up an electric current on the treated surfaces of the silicon wafer. One cell generates only a very small amount of current but many may be hooked together to combine current or voltage. This way, we can produce as much electricity as we need.

We do not rely on photovoltaic cells to produce electricity except in hard-to-reach places and space because they are not efficient enough and they are very expensive. We do use solar cells to provide electric current to operate some satellites and space exploration vehicles. Fig. 8-25 shows one application of solar cells used on a spacecraft.

Fig. 8-23. View of the generators at the Hoover Dam hydroelectric plant. The huge generators (left background) are powered by turbines, which are situated beneath the generators and are driven by water. (Suzanne Silagi)

Fig. 8-25. Spacecraft rely on photovoltaic cells to provide power for their operation.

DC Generators

Like alternators, *DC Generators* rely on the principle of electromagnetic induction to create direct current. Look at Fig. 8-26 to see a simple DC generator. It consists of a wire loop mounted on a shaft that rotates. On two sides of the loop are magnets, one north and one south pole are toward the conductor loop. As the loop rotates between the magnetic fields, a current is produced inside it.

Remember that different magnetic poles produce different directions of current flow (AC generator). To solve this problem and produce direct current, DC generators make use of a *commutator* and *brushes*. Look again at Fig. 8-26.

As the loop rotates through the magnetic field, it turns the commutator. Brushes that touch on each side of the commutator carry the electric current away from the loop.

Notice that the commutator is split so that the conductor loop is not a complete circuit. The two parts of the commutator touch the brushes at different times. This way the current produced by the north magnetic polarity will always be carried away by one brush. The same is true for the opposite magnetic field, its induced current will always be carried away by the opposite brush. Can you see how this makes one brush negative, and the other positive, thus producing a DC output?

Transformers

Many times, the electrical power supplied to a circuit is either too much or too little. If there is a need to increase or decrease voltage, we use *transformers*. When we need to reduce the amount of voltage, we use a *step-down transformer*. When we have too little current and need more, we can use a *step-up transformer* which boosts the amount of electricity available. Transformers work on the principle of electromagnetic induction. Fig. 8-27 compares the two types of transformers with a simple illustration. They are both made of two separate coils wrapped around the opposite sides of an iron core. The coil that is attached to the input side is

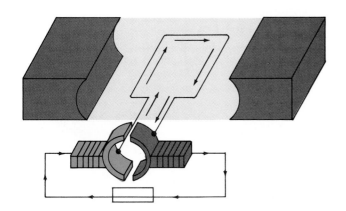

Fig. 8-26. Top. This is a simplified drawing of a DC generator. Note the names of its different parts. Bottom. This cutaway shows the inside of a DC electric motor. What parts can you recognize? (Baldor Electric)

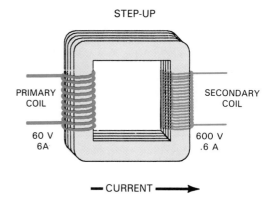

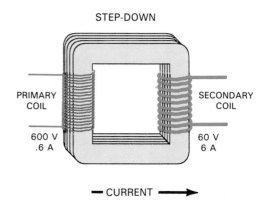

Fig. 8-27. A transformer is made-up of an iron core with wrappings of wire to increase the voltage. The two coils of wire are not electrically connected. Electromagnetic induction caused by a current in one of the coils causes a current in the other coil.

Electrical Systems   81

called the *primary coil*. The coil opposite this one, on the output side, is the *secondary coil*.

Notice that the primary coil is smaller than the secondary coil on the step-up transformer. As the current in the primary coil induces a magnetic field in the iron core, it is carried to the secondary coil. The extra wraps on the secondary coil allow more voltage to be induced in it by the magnetic field. This lets the transformer put out more electrical voltage than it was given.

Now, notice that the primary coil is larger than the secondary coil on the step-down transformer. Again, the induced magnetic field travels from the primary coil to the secondary coil through the iron core. This time the smaller secondary coil is not able to induce as much voltage as the larger primary coil supplied. Can you see how transformers are able to boost or reduce the amount of voltage in a circuit?

ELECTRICAL SYSTEMS IN TRANSPORTATION

Most modern vehicles rely on electrical power systems for one or more functions. Truck and automobile engines use a battery to supply the electric energy to start. Whenever the engine is run-

ning, alternators or generators are used to supply the electrical energy for the vehicle's computers, accessories (things like lights, heater, and radio), and other functions that require electrical power. These devices use the mechanical energy of the engine to produce electricity.

Some mass transportation systems receive electrical energy from overhead lines or tracks. The electricity is used to run electric **motors** which move the vehicles. Intercity subway trains and buses often use electrical systems this way. Fig. 8-28 shows examples of vehicles that use electrical systems. Can you identify the electrical systems that they use?

Lights

One of the more obvious uses of electricity on a car is to energize the headlights. Usually all the parts of a headlight are sealed in a closed, airtight container. The front of the container is a clear glass lens. The back is coated with a shiny material that makes it reflect light out the front. Prongs are used to connect the headlight to the car's electrical system so that they may be replaced easily. Fig. 8-29 shows a headlight assembly used on an automobile.

Other light bulbs in the vehicle may have either one or two filaments. Bulbs with two filaments may be used for two separate lighting functions. For ex-

Fig. 8-28. All of these transportation vehicles have electrical systems. Without electrical power, the vehicles could not operate. (Mark Van Manen, BC Transit; Airbus Industrie; Bayliner; Freightliner Corp.)

Fig. 8-29. LEDs (light-emitting diodes) use very little electricity and are used widely in computers and digital dashes of automobiles. (Ford Motor Co.)

ample, taillights on the rear of automobiles are used as both taillights and brake lights. Some may also be used as turn signals. Bulbs are also used in dome lights and dashboard lights inside the vehicle.

With more use of advanced electronic systems in modern vehicles, you will see more dashboard instruments using *light-emitting diodes* (LEDs). You might have already seen the orange, red, or green lights similar to the ones illustrated in Fig. 8-29. Their color is produced by the materials used in making them. These materials include phosphorus, gallium, and arsenic. LEDs operate on a very small amount of direct electrical current.

Electric Motors

Electric motors are devices that convert electrical energy to mechanical energy. They use the same principles of electromagnetism as alternators and generators, but they perform a totally opposite function. Electric motors have many applications in transportation technology. They are used in subway trains, golf carts, escalators, and elevators, to name a few transportation vehicles. There are two types of electric motors. The *universal motor*, which can operate on either AC or DC electricity, and the *induction motor*, which can use only AC.

The universal motor, Fig. 8-30, basically uses two separate electromagnets which produce magnetic

Fig. 8-30. A universal electric motor.

fields that repel each other. This repulsion causes part of the motor (armature) to spin. By switching the direction of current in one electromagnet, we can switch the poles on the device. This means that there will always be like poles repelling as the armature is spinning. A commutator and brushes make it possible to switch the direction of current flowing through the armature.

Induction motors use similar electromagnetic principles to operate. However, the alternating current they use creates a magnetic field that builds up, then collapses. This off-and-on magnetic field induces another one in the armature, the part of the motor that rotates. The alternating current affects the buildup and collapse of the magnetic fields so that there are always like poles repelling each other. Thus, the armature will spin as long as there is current going to the motor.

SUMMARY

Electricity is produced when atoms trade electrons between their valence rings. Conductors are materials that carry electrical current easily. Devices like bells, lights, motors, switches and fuses are connected together with a conductor, then attached to a power source to form a circuit. These circuits are the heart of an electrical power system when they do work, create light, or heat.

Magnetism is important in the study of electricity. Magnets are used to create electrical current by a process called electromagnetic induction. Iron can be magnetized by passing an electric current around it. This is called an electromagnet. Electricity-producing generators and alternators, as well as electric motors, use principles of electricity and magnetism to operate.

Photovoltaic cells convert light energy to electrical energy. Batteries convert chemical energy to electrical energy. Both may by used for transportation vehicles. Some batteries are also able to store electricity for later use. Transformers are used to increase or decrease the amount of electrical current supplied to a circuit.

Most transportation systems rely heavily on one or more electrical systems for proper operation. Electricity provides lights for night time operation. Electricity power electric motors that operate various components in a vehicle. Electricity is necessary for the operation of most heat engines. On-board computers need a reliable source of electricity to perform their many functions. Likewise, radios and other accessories depend on a reliable source of electricity.

KEY WORDS

All of the following words have been used in this chapter. Do you know their meaning?

Alternating current
Alternators
Atoms
Conductors
DC generator
Direct current
Electrical circuit
Electrical systems
Electrodes
Electrolyte
Electromagnet
Electromagnetic induction
Electron theory
Electrons
Fuses
Insulators
Light-emitting diode
Lines of force
Magnets
Motors
Neutrons
Nucleus
Parallel circuit
Photons
Photovoltaic cell
Polarity
Primary cells
Protons
Schematic drawings
Secondary cells
Semiconductors
Series circuit
Series-parallel circuit
Step-down transformer
Step-up transformer
Transformer
Turbine
Valence ring

TEST YOUR KNOWLEDGE

Write your answers on a separate sheet of paper. Do not write in this book.

Short answer:

1. What are the three parts of an atom?
2. What type of drawing is used to represent electrical circuits on paper?
3. What is the difference between series and parallel circuits?

Fill in the blank:

4. _____ are materials that transfer electrons easily, and are used to connect the parts of an electrical circuit.
5. According to electron theory, electricity moves from _____ to _____.
6. AC stands for _____ _____.
7. DC stands for _____ _____.
8. The process of using magnetic fields to create electrical current in a wire is called _____ _____.
9. _____ use an electrical current to produce a magnetic field in a piece of iron.

Matching:

10. __ Electrolyte.
11. __ Batteries.
12. __ Transformers.
13. __ Alternators.
14. __ DC generators.
15. __ Photovoltaic cells.

A. Devices which reduce or increase electrical current in a circuit.
B. Surrounds electrodes in a battery to help produce current.
C. Device that produces direct current.
D. Converts light energy to electrical energy.
E. Converts chemical energy to electrical energy.
F. Produce alternating current using mechanical energy.

Description:

16. Sketch a simple universal motor and describe how it works.
17. Make a sketch showing how moving water causes a turbine to create electricity.

ACTIVITIES

1. Connect two flashlight cells (batteries) in series (positive poles to negative poles). Ask your instructor to help you use a voltmeter or VOM to measure voltage. Be sure the function switch is turned to the DC voltage position. Use rubber bands to hold meter leads to the cell's terminals. Report the voltage reading to the class and also tell the voltage of each cell. Research circuit theory in an electricity reference and explain why the measured voltage is different from the individual voltage of either battery.

2. Study Fig. 8-14 and set up a similar parallel circuit using suitable power source (battery or cell), switches, conductors, and lights.

SAFETY NOTE: Wear eye protection for Activity 3. Automobile batteries contain acid that could cause blindness. Even a film of battery acid on the case could cause serious injury if it comes in contact with the skin or an eye.

3. Check an automotive battery for leakage across its top. Set a voltmeter at its lowest setting. Attach the probe with the black conductor to the negative terminal of the battery. Then, touch the positive probe to the battery case on the opposite side near the positive battery terminal. If the voltmeter registers voltage, there is an electrical leak because of a dirty top. Using a brush, clean the top of the battery case with a solution of warm water and baking soda. Retest as before. Is there any leakage now?

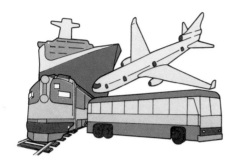

Chapter 9

FLUID POWER SYSTEMS

After studying this chapter, you will be able to:
- ☐ Describe components needed to operate fluid power systems.
- ☐ Explain how hydraulic cylinders can increase mechanical advantage.
- ☐ Describe physical characteristics of fluids used in fluid power systems.
- ☐ List the advantages of using fluid power systems.
- ☐ Expain the differences between hydraulic and pneumatic power systems.

Ancient societies found many uses for the movement of water. Some uses were simple plumbing systems to move fresh water and crude transportation vehicles like rafts and hollowed-out logs. These early societies found that by using the fluid properties of water, their work could be made easier. Look at Figs. 9-1 and 9-2. Fluid power systems are those that use the energy found in liquids and gases to do work.

WHAT ARE FLUID POWER SYSTEMS?

Hydraulic systems are those that control and transmit energy through liquids. Oil-like liquids are usually used in hydraulic systems. Various components have been developed to control liquids under pressure so that they may do work for us. These include cylinders, pumps, and transmission lines.

Fig. 9-1. Primitive people learned very early that it was easier to move a vehicle along on water than to move any type of vehicle on land.

The study of fluid power systems also includes *pneumatics.* In pneumatic systems gases are used in place of liquids. Air from our atmosphere is usually the gas chosen. Gases and liquids behave the same in many aspects, they both can be described as fluid. Devices for the control and transmission of gases under pressure have been developed, similar to those used in hydraulics.

This chapter will focus on the technology involved in using fluid power systems to do work. The principles behind hydraulic and pneumatic systems will be explained. You will discover the devices that are used to control the fluids. First, you should be aware of the benefits of using fluid power systems.

Fig. 9-2. The waterwheel is usually not thought of as a fluid power system, yet it is since the water (fluid) is used to operate machines.

WHY USE FLUID POWER?

Basically, fluid power systems involve the transfer of mechanical energy. Because fluids do not break like solid machine parts, fluid power systems have a long life expectancy. This means that they will last longer with less wear and tear than other mechanical power systems. Other advantages of these systems include:

- An almost unlimited amount of power can be produced and maintained in a fluid power system.

- Easy and complete control over a wide range of power in a fluid system. This allows for smooth, quick control of energy transfer.
- A characteristic of the fluids used is that they have a natural springiness, which produces a cushioning effect that reduces shock in the system.
- The components in fluid power systems can be located far apart and power can be transferred quickly, with little power loss in the system.

Fluid power systems offer a wide range of mechanical functions. They are used to produce linear and rotary motion, while remaining mechanically efficient. Many industries using modern technology employ fluid power systems. They can be found in manufacturing plants, on construction sites and farms, and as important parts of vehicles that transport people and cargo world-wide. See Fig. 9-3.

THE PHYSICS OF FLUID POWER SYSTEMS

The liquids and gases that are used in fluid systems have some similar characteristics. They exert pressure, take the shape of their container, and they can flow freely from one container to another. These characteristics have been studied and used for centuries. It is important that you learn them so that you can better understand fluid power systems.

Fig. 9-3. Hydraulics are used on farms to lift heavy loads with a front end loader on a tractor. One of the uses of pneumatics is to power tools such as this jackhammer.

Fluids Exert Pressure

Long ago, scientists found that liquids exert pressure in all directions, not only on the bottoms of their containers. *Pressure* is a force acting upon an area. Because pressure is caused by the amount (weight) of liquid in a container, more pressure is exerted on its lower sides. The more liquid a container holds, the more weight will be pushing down and out. Large tanks that hold water and oil are made so that the bottoms are stronger than the tops for this reason. Look at Fig. 9-4.

How Fluids Act

Have you ever heard the phrase, "Water seeks its own level"? This is true; water will flow from a higher level to a lower level until both levels are the same.

It is also true that water and other fluids will flow from high pressure to low pressure. It will continue flowing until both pressures are equal. Notice that the containers are connected at their bottoms by a pipe, Fig. 9-5. Even though the water levels are different at first, water flows between them until they both have the same level of water. If one container had more water at the start, it would be able to exert more pressure than one with less water.

Fig 9-4. Water tanks of the type used by communities for water storage and to provide good flow into water taps have to be built to withstand tremendous pressure because of the weight of the water stored in them.

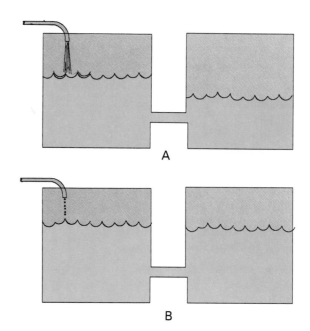

Fig. 9-5. Imagine two containers connected by a tube. A—If you were to start filling one of the containers it would also start filling the other one. B—Once the flow of water stops, the water flow will continue into the other container until the water levels are equal.

The water would flow from the high-pressure container to a low-pressure container until the pressures balanced. The system is balanced when all containers show the same height of water regardless of shape or size.

Blaise Pascal and Mechanical Advantage

Over 340 years ago, a French scientist, Blaise Pascal, was studying the properties of confined liquids. He wanted to know how liquids acted in closed containers. He found that when there was nothing but liquid in the container, compression applied on any part of it was distributed in all directions equally inside the container. He also noted that this initial pressure multiplied as it was distributed in the container. These properties are what make hydraulic devices capable of increasing mechanical advantage.

Fig. 9-6 shows two closed containers that represent hydraulic cylinders. Assume that one is 100 times smaller than the other one. If we exert a force of 1 lb. on the smaller container, it will transfer that pressure to the larger cylinder. Because the other cylinder is 100 times larger, and pressure is exerted in all directions, there is 100 times more pressure in the larger cylinder. In other words, the force on each square inch of both cylinders is the

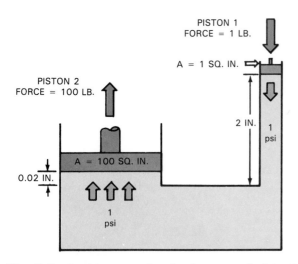

Fig. 9-6. In this example, the force applied to the smaller cylinder is increased 100 times at the larger cylinder. That is why the larger cylinder can lift extremely heavy loads with less force from the smaller cylinder.

same. Because the large cylinder contains more square inches, it will exert a larger total force. Can you see how this system of cylinders increases mechanical advantage? Fig. 9-7 shows a common vehicle that uses one or more hydraulic cylinders.

Comparing Liquids and Gases

Liquids and gases act differently because the molecules in liquid are closer together than the molecules in gases. Remember that a molecule is the smallest unit of any substance. These states can be observed in boiling water. The high temperature causes the water molecules to speed up and get far-ther apart, turning water (a liquid) into steam (a gas). See Fig. 9-8.

Because pressure is involved in doing work with fluid systems, we are concerned with the *compressibility* of the fluids involved. Compressibility means how much of any matter can be squashed into a smaller size (volume). Liquids cannot be compressed much at all. In fact, they compress so little under enormous pressure that, for all practical purposes, they are not compressible. Gases, on the other hand, may be compressed because of the amount of space between their molecules.

Temperature is an important factor in the amount of compressibility of a gas. Remember that

Fig. 9-8. Boiling water creates steam. Perhaps you have seen steam raise the lids from cooking pots. This is due to the expansion of the fluid as steam is created.

Fig. 9-7. A—Hydraulics are employed on dump trucks to raise the truck box allowing the load to slide out the back end. Back hoes also use hydraulics to control the digging claw and bucket.

the hotter a gas becomes, the more active its molecules become. Therefore, they have more space between them, making them more compressible. This relationship between pressure, volume, and temperature was studied by Robert Boyle, an English scientist. He concluded that if temperature remained constant, increasing the pressure on a gas will reduce its volume. In fact, if the pressure is doubled, the gas is compressed to half its original volume. When people design pneumatic systems, this concept must be considered. Can you think of any reasons why?

Another important difference between hydraulic and pneumatic power systems is that one can use an open system and the other has to be closed. The hydraulic system must be closed because the liquids used need to be returned to a reservoir (container) so that the system can be used again. Also, if the fluids were allowed to leak they would pollute our environment. Pneumatic systems, like the pneumatic cylinder on a door closer, Fig. 9-9, can be open because the air used can be returned to the atmosphere. Air that is input into the system is drawn from the atmosphere. There is no need for a reservoir to contain the air.

COMPONENTS OF FLUID POWER SYSTEMS

Like other power systems, fluid power systems require that different components be used together so that they may do work. When planning and designing these circuits, engineers or drafters make schematic drawings to describe fluid circuits on paper. Fig. 9-10 displays some symbols used in drawing schematics for fluid power systems. Some

TYPICAL FLUID POWER SYMBOLS			
CONNECTOR	•	FLOW METER	
LINE, FLEXIBLE		PRESSURE GAGE	
MOTOR, OSCILLATING		TEMPERATURE GAGE	
LINE, JOINING		PUMP, SINGLE FIXED DISPLACEMENT	
LINE, PASSING		MOTOR, ROTARY FIXED DISPLACEMENT	
FLOW DIRECTION HYDRAULIC PNEUMATIC		MOTOR, ROTARY VARIABLE DISPLACEMENT	
MANUAL SHUT-OFF VALVE		ELECTRIC MOTOR	
CYLINDER, SINGLE-ACTING		LEVER	
CYLINDER, DOUBLE-ACTING		SPRING	

Fig. 9-10. Drafters and engineers use symbols to mean different parts of a pneumatic or hydraulic system when they are drawing or designing systems.

of the components are used to produce the pressure, some are used to control the pressure, and others are used to make the pressure do the work. These devices will now be explored. Be sure you understand whether they have been developed for hydraulic or pneumatic power systems. Some you will find are used in both systems.

Hydraulic Pumps

Hydraulic pumps are used to supply and transmit the pressure needed to operate a hydraulic power system. They convert mechanical energy into fluid

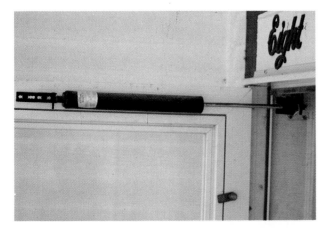

Fig. 9-9. Pneumatic systems such as those found in door closers and air tools can be open since they use atmospheric air in their systems.

power causing the necessary flow in the system. Pumps have many applications in modern industry and technology. They move water and coolant around boilers and nuclear reactors, move water out of ship bilges, and move bulk liquids from the holds of ships. Pumps are also used to move clean water in the plumbing systems of skyscrapers. These are only a few examples of applications for hydraulic pumps. Can you think of any other uses?

Gear Pumps

Gear pumps are used to create the pressure needed to operate many hydraulic systems. In this pump, two gears are placed so that they mesh with each other inside a housing. See Fig. 9-11. One gear is turned by a power source. It then turns the other gear in the opposite direction. On one side of the housing is the low-pressure port where oil enters the pump. Oil is drawn through the housing by the two spinning gears. This action forces the oil around the gears, to the other side of the housing where it goes out the high-pressure port. The oil under pressure is then used to do work.

Centrifugal Pumps

Centrifugal pumps are also used to produce pressure in a hydraulic system. This type of pump uses *centrifugal force* to move fluids in the system. Centrifugal force is what makes things want to fly outward when they are spinning around. It is this force that keeps water in a bucket when you swing it over your head very fast. See Fig. 9-12.

Fig. 9-12. A bucket of water whirled around rapidly has an outward pull known as centrifugal force.

Centrifugal pumps use a device commonly found in many pumps and propulsion systems. It is called an impeller. An impeller consists of many small blades mounted on a shaft. As the impeller spins inside its housing, it draws oil through the inlet port from a reservoir. Because the impeller is driven from an outside power source, it can be made to spin very fast. This movement of the impeller forces oil outward against the housing, then through the outlet port to the rest of the system. Fig. 9-13 is a simplified drawing of such a pump. Can you see how the impeller produces the centrifugal force similar to your arm swinging a bucket of water?

Reciprocating Pumps

Reciprocating (moving back and forth) pumps can also be called positive displacement pumps. They use a piston that moves back and forth in a cylinder to move hydraulic fluid. Each stroke of the piston moves a certain volume of liquid through the system. Fig. 9-14 illustrates the inside of a reciprocating pump. Each time the piston moves

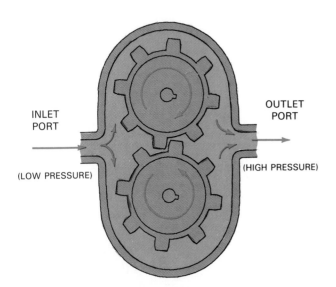

Fig. 9-11. A look at the inside of a gear pump. Two gears, one driven by a power source, pull the fluid into the pump housing and place it under pressure at the outlet port.

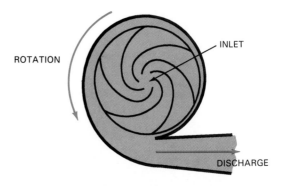

Fig. 9-13. This simplified drawing shows the inside of a centrifugal pump. As the impeller spins, fluid is forced off the vanes and becomes pressurized as it moves out of the pump housing.

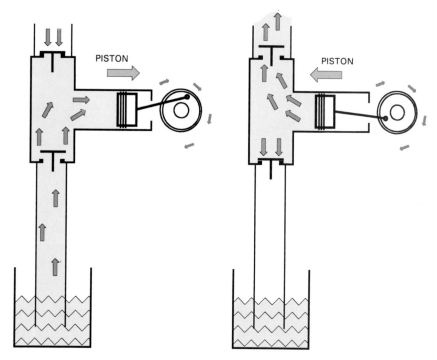

Fig. 9-14. A reciprocating pump has a piston driven by an shaft located off center on a revolving wheel or crankshaft. Note action of the intake and delivery valves as the direction of the piston changes.

in the cylinder, it forces oil out of the cylinder. Notice the check valves needed to keep fluid from moving backwards in the system. A simple type of reciprocating pump that you may have used to move water is a hand water pump, Fig. 9-15.

Air Compressors

Air compressors are to pneumatic systems what hydraulic pumps are to hydraulic systems. They convert the mechanical energy which is input into pneumatic power systems. This action causes the necessary flow to make the system work. Compressors are able to hold air under pressure in tanks so that it is available to the power system whenever it is needed.

The most common air compressor is also the reciprocating type, Fig. 9-16. It is sometimes called a positive-displacement compressor because its operation is similar to the reciprocating hydraulic

Fig. 9-15. Simple hand-operated water pump. You may have used one like it.

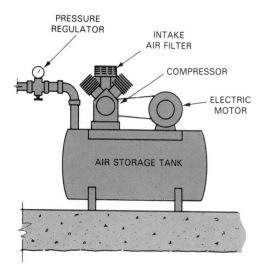

Fig. 9-16. Air compressors using a reciprocating type pump are a common sight in automotive shops. (John Walker)

pump. A piston moves up and down (reciprocates) inside a cylinder. The piston is powered by an external power source, like an electric motor. At the top of the cylinder there are two valves that let air pass only one direction. As the piston moves down, it creates a suction in the cylinder. This makes the intake valve open, letting air into the cylinder. As the piston moves up, the intake valve shuts and air is compressed in the cylinder until it forces the outlet valve open. The air is then allowed to enter the receiver where it is kept at a constant pressure.

Some compressors are a multi-stage type. This means that air passes through more than one piston/cylinder arrangement before it enters the receiver. As air passes between the stages its pressure is gradually increased. In multi-stage compressors, air reaches the desired pressure in the last compression stage.

It is important that pneumatic power systems do not allow water to enter the system. This could cause rust and corrosion of the systems' components. Filters and separators are placed in the system to remove any moisture from the air as it is compressed. These components are located in the compressor between the outlet valve and the receiver.

Control of Fluid Power

In a fluid power system, pressurized fluid is transported by way of transmission lines. Piping or tubing capable of withstanding high pressure is used for this purpose. Transmission lines carry the high-pressure fluids to where they will be used to do work. Components are placed in the system to control pressure, flow, and direction.

All fluid power systems must use control devices so that they will be functional (work right). *Valves* are the devices that control fluid power. Valves are used for:
- Flow control.
- Pressure control.
- Directional control.

Fluids used in fluid systems have many characteristics in common. Therefore, valves for hydraulic and pneumatic systems are almost the same in design. The important difference is that hydraulic systems need different seals to prevent loss of liquid.

Flow Control Valves

When we want to start or stop the flow of fluid in a system, we use a flow control valve. When you turn on the water at a kitchen sink, you are using a flow control valve. Many times there are two flow control valves at a sink, one for hot water and one for cold. Some valves are made so that they can control both hot and cold water. Which kind do you have at your house?

Flow control valves are also used to control how much fluid is allowed to go through a system. If the valve is only partially open or closed, it will not allow full flow.

Pressure Control Valves

Pressure control valves are also called relief valves. They are placed in a system to make sure that the pressure does not get too high. These valves can be compared to fuses in an electrical system, because they protect system components from overload. If pressure increases to dangerous levels, relief valves open automatically to reduce it.

In hydraulic systems, the relief valve directs extra liquid to the holding tank, or reservoir. In pneumatic systems where air is the fluid used, extra air can be released into the atmosphere. Fig. 9-18 shows a common type of pressure control valve used in fluid power systems.

Directional Control Valves

Many times, fluid power systems need to be designed so that there is more than one path for fluid to travel. When we need to control which path fluid is to take in a circuit, we use a directional control valve. These valves can be operated manually (by hand), mechanically, or electrically.

Check valves are another type of directional control valve. They only allow fluid to flow in one direction. If fluid starts to move backwards in a system, check valves close and stop the backward movement of fluid. Fig. 9-17 shows the operation of a common check valve. You should be able to see how they can easily allow fluid to flow in only one direction.

Making Fluid Power Work

Remember that the purpose of any power system is to do work. We have been studying the parts of fluid power systems that control fluid flow and pressure. Now we will look at components in a system that convert the fluid energy to mechanical energy of solid parts. The types of components we will look at are actuators and fluid motors.

Actuators

Actuators are devices that convert fluid power to mechanical power in hydraulic and pneumatic

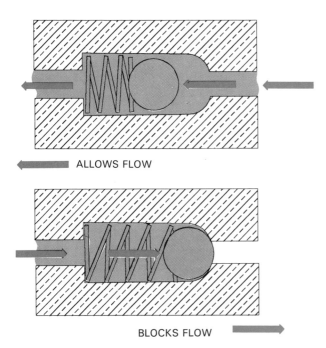

ALLOWS FLOW

BLOCKS FLOW

Fig. 9-17. A simple diagram shows the basic construction and action of a check valve in a fluid power system.

systems. Such a conversion is simple. It helps to make fluid power systems very easy to design and use. Fluid power can create just about any type of mechanical motion. Actuators are the devices used to make the reciprocating and rotary motion which allows fluid power systems to do work.

Cylinders, like the ones we studied earlier, are one type of actuator. They may be classified as either single-acting or double-acting. Both types of cylinders contain pistons which move back and forth (reciprocate) inside them. Single-acting cylinders use the force of fluid to move the piston in one direction, the weight of the load then forces the piston to its original position. Double-acting cylinders are able to use the force of the fluid to move the piston in both directions. Fluid pressure can be exerted on either side of the piston. These cylinders are used where there is a need for complete control, such as where we might need to reverse the movement of the piston. Fig. 9-18 shows some common applications of actuators, and the systems in which they work.

As was stated before, hydraulic and pneumatic components are very similar in design. The characteristics of the available fluids, liquid or gas, are used to determine which type of system is used. Remember that liquid is not compressible and gas is. Because of this, hydraulic cylinders (systems) are used where there is a need for quick and precise control of power. The liquids used in these systems

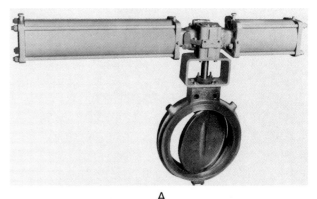

A

B

Fig. 9-18. Actuators convert fluid power to mechanical power. A—A butterfly valve with a hydraulic piston actuator. The piston moves to close or open the valve. B—This valve has a diaphragm actuator, which is pneumatically operated.
(Fisher Controls International, Inc.)

act as a solid link between the fluid and the solid parts. Pneumatic cylinders (systems) are used where a certain amount of cushioning is needed.

Fluid Motors

Fluid motors are devices that convert fluid power into rotary mechanical motion. Two basic types of fluid motors are the gear motor and the vane motor. Basically, gear motors operate like a gear pump, only the process is reversed. Fluid is forced into a housing that contains gears. As the fluid flows around the outside of the gears, against the housing, it forces the gears to spin. One gear is connected to an output shaft. The speed of the output shaft depends on the pressure of the fluid in the system.

Another common type of fluid motor is the vane motor. It is illustrated in Fig. 9-19. Basically, a rotor is offset inside a round housing. The rotor has vanes, which are spring-loaded so that they always touch the inside of the housing as the rotor spins. Fluid is forced through the housing. As it flows past the rotor it pushes against the vanes, causing the rotor to spin. An output shaft is attached to the rotor, and its speed depends on the pressure of the fluid in the system.

Torque Converters

Many transportation vehicles use a fluid coupling to connect one power system to another. For example, it may connect the engine to the transmission. *Torque converters* are devices that use fluid pressure to connect and disconnect moving parts. In a torque converter, a pump (impeller) is driven by the fluid that is put into the system. The pump forces the fluid forward through a housing which contains rotors. Fluid forced from the impeller causes the rotors to spin. The *impeller* and rotors are not mechanically attached. It is the force of the fluid in the system which connects the two. The speed of the impeller is controlled by the fluid pressure in the system. This directly affects the speed of the rotors. Can you see how the fluid coupling gets its name? It is a useful part of many transportation systems. Because there is no mechanical attachment, torque converters operate with very little wear.

SUMMARY

Fluid power systems are those that use the energy found in liquids and gases to do work. Systems that use liquids are called hydraulic. Those that use gas are called pneumatic. Both types of fluids in these systems have similar characteristics which lets the systems work with very little wear on mechanical parts. The basic difference, which must be considered when designing the systems, is the compressibility of the fluids. Liquids cannot be compressed while gases may be compressed into as much as half their original volume.

Like any system, fluid power systems require several components to do work. Pumps and compressors are devices that convert mechanical energy to fluid power. They supply the pressure and flow needed to operate the system. Fluid pressure is sent through transmission lines to other parts of the system. There are devices in the circuit that control flow, pressure, and direction of fluid power. These devices are valves. Other components convert fluid power back to mechanical power. These are the parts of the system that usually do the actual work. Generally, an actuator or fluid motor is the device that does this conversion. Like other power systems, schematic drawings are used to represent fluid power circuits on paper.

KEY WORDS

All of the following words have been used in this chapter. Do you know their meaning?

Actuators	Impeller
Air compressors	Pneumatics
Centrifugal force	Pressure
Compressibility	Reciprocating
Fluid motors	Torque converters
Hydraulic pumps	Valves
Hydraulic systems	

TEST YOUR KNOWLEDGE

Write your answers on a separate sheet of paper. Do not write in this book.

Fill in the blank:

1. Fluid power systems are those that use the energy found in _____ and _____.
2. Fluids exert pressure in all _____.
3. Fluids try to reach balanced pressure by flowing from _____ pressure to _____ pressure.
4. Of the two types of fluids used in power systems, _____ can be compressed and _____ cannot be compressed.
5. Two types of hydraulic pumps are _____ and _____.
6. Two types of air compressors are _____ and _____.

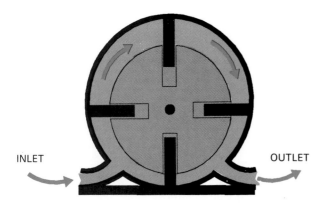

Fig. 9-19. A vane motor powered by air pressure from a pneumatic power source.

7. _____ are devices that act as a fluid coupling between mechanical systems.

Matching:

8. __ Air.	A. Fluid used in hydraulic power systems.
9. __ Robert Boyle.	
10. __ Oil.	B. Studied relationship between temperature volume, and pressure.
11. __ Blaise Pascal.	
	C. Gas used in pneumatic power systems.
	D. Described how hydraulic cylinders are able to increase mechanical advantage.

Short answer:

12. What are the advantages of fluid power systems?
13. Describe the parts of a hydraulic cylinder.

14. How do hydraulic cylinders increase mechanical advantage?
15. Name three applications of hydraulic cylinders.
16. What is an impeller? How is it used in pumps? How is it used in compressors?

ACTIVITIES

1. Using a length of clear plastic hose, set up a demonstration to prove that fluids will seek their level. Suggest to the class how this experiment could be used to check levels of structures like foundation walls, fences, patios, decks, and sidewalks.
2. Set up a lab demonstration using fluid power to do work.
3. Set up a lab demonstration of the operation of a fluid clutch. Explain its principle to the class.

Section IV
TRANSPORTATION SYSTEMS

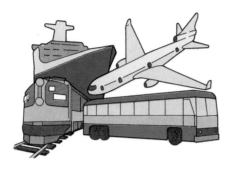

Chapter 10

WHAT IS A TRANSPORTATION SYSTEM?

After studying this chapter, you will be able to:
- ☐ Define a transportation system.
- ☐ Identify the components of a transportation system.
- ☐ Define inputs of a transportation system.
- ☐ Define the process of a transportation system.
- ☐ Define the output of a transportation system.
- ☐ Discuss the various goals of a transportation system.
- ☐ Describe feedback within a transportation system.
- ☐ List the four types of transportation systems.

We often limit transportation to riding around in a car. We may forget that there is a "moving" world around us. Forms of transportation we often overlook are:
- Escalators that move people from one level of a building to another.
- Satellites that circle the earth.
- Underground pipelines that transport several different types of materials.

In Chapter 1, you were briefly introduced to a technological system. It was said that transportation was one of our technological systems, Fig. 10-1. You are now going to broaden your knowledge of transportation. You will see how transportation functions as its own system. If you recall, a system is a combination of parts that work together to accomplish a desired result. A transpor-

tation system is a systematic way of relocating people and/or cargo by the use of the various modes of transportation. The whole process accomplishes a desired result.

Transportation systems, as we pointed out in Chapter 6, can be categorized as:
- Land transportation.
- Water transportation.
- Air transportation.
- Space transportation.

See Fig. 10-2. All four of these function as separate systems.

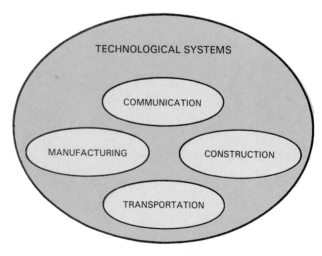

Fig. 10-1. Our technological systems include these four areas. This is one way of clustering them.

Fig. 10-2. There are four different ways or modes of transportation. Each has its own vehicles that can travel in that environment.

THE TRANSPORTATION SYSTEM

Transportation systems consist of inputs, processes, and outputs. Also, feedback from the system and several goals of the system are present, Fig. 10-3. First we'll take a look at how a transportation system functions. Then we will briefly discuss the four types of transportation systems.

Inputs in the Transportation System

Inputs into a transportation system are those resources needed in order to begin the system. The following are inputs into the transportation system: people, capital, knowledge, materials, energy, and finance.

People are an important factor in a transportation system. Persons like you and I are what make a transportation system function. People are needed to repair the system if something breaks down. We call them mechanics (because they repair machines). People are also needed to drive vehicles, read instruments, and monitor the progress of the system.

Regardless of the mode (kind) of transportation, the need for people is inevitable. A bus driver is needed to drive children to school. A truck driver is needed to haul cargo from place to place. A pilot is needed to fly people and cargo across the skies. As you observe our society, take a look at all of the people working in the different types of transportation systems, Fig. 10-4.

Capital within a transportation system includes those assets that are used to help operate the system. Using the example of an airport, the hangars, the airplanes, the runway, and the radio

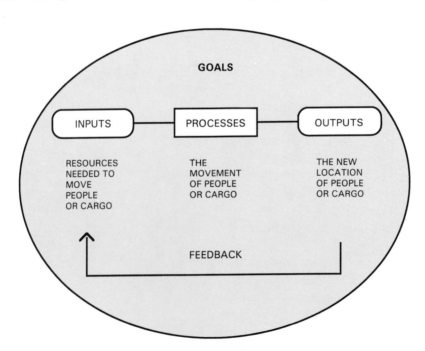

Fig. 10-3. Every technological system has these four distinct elements: inputs, processes, feedback, and outputs.

Fig. 10-4. What would our transportation systems be like without people? People repair broken equipment, drive land vehicles, fly airplanes, and assist travelers.
(United Parcel Service, United Airlines, and U.S. Postal Service)

tower are all forms of capital for this particular mode of air transportation, Fig. 10-5. Capital relates to the possessions of a transportation system. Vehicles, roads, and buildings are other forms of capital.

Knowledge within a transportation system is essential. Information is attained through application and experience of the various tasks performed by people. Once the information is understood, it becomes knowledge. This knowledge is then incorporated into different jobs within a transportation system.

Fig. 10-5. Without forms of capital, it would be difficult, if not impossible, for a transportation system to function. What would air transportation do without an airport control tower? (United Airlines)

Before you participate in a game of soccer, you need to have some knowledge of the sport in order to have a successful game. The same concept is true if you are involved in some part of a transportation system. If you are a ticket agent at a local bus station, then you need to know how to schedule people on the most efficient route. If you are the operator of a hot-air balloon, then you need to have knowledge of weather conditions, map reading, and the legalities of flying a balloon. Machines also aid us in knowledge. Technological advancements such as computers and robots have made many jobs within the transportation systems much more efficient and accurate, Fig. 10-6.

Materials within a transportation system are a very important input. Without materials such as raw materials, we wouldn't have too many functioning systems at all. Iron can be used to build railroad tracks, Fig. 10-7. Wood can be used to construct vehicles or support systems. Fuel is another important material needed as a material input into a transportation system. Fuel of various kinds is used to power different forms of transportation vehicles. Oil, coal, ore, and wood can make a system function in a different way. They can be burned and produce a type of energy needed to power a mode of transportation. They may even be used to help construct the system. Other types

Fig. 10-6. These people work together with computers to schedule people on correct flights. The computers make scheduling flight reservations very efficient. (United Airlines)

Fig. 10-7. Many materials are essential in a transportation system. Transportation means not only powering systems. Pathways, such as roadbeds, must be constructed. This railroad bed requires wood, gravel, and steel.

of materials within a transportation system may be synthetic (made by humans) materials such as plastic, rubber, and nylon.

Energy within a transportation system is one of the main inputs. Without a source of energy, you have no operating system. It takes energy to ride a scooter, peddle a bicycle, drive a truck, fly an airplane, and sail a sailboat. Without energy you have no power. Therefore, you are unable to be transported from one place to another, Fig. 10-8. Some different sources of energy include wind, solar, heat, nuclear, animal, human, and natural gas. If you wanted to go sailing in a sailboat on Lake Michigan and there isn't any wind, it may be a long trip! Without wind power, a sailboat cannot transport efficiently. All modes of transportation are powered by some source of energy. Therefore, energy is needed to begin a system of relocating people or cargo.

Finance within a transportation system, as with any system in our society, is needed in order for the system to function as efficiently and effectively as possible. Finance is simply money that is need-

Fig. 10-8. A scooter moves only under human power. Take away the power source and the scooter sits still.

ed to pay for equipment, materials, personnel (people employed by the system), and energy sources. Putting gas in a car or truck takes money. Paying a pilot for flying an airplane takes money. To repair a flat tire on your bicycle takes money. Customers of a transportation company pay a fee for services, Fig. 10-9.

Whenever a transportation system begins, it must have some form of input. The input may be immediate, such as the need for an energy source before the system can run. The input may be long-term such as the financing of equipment or services. Either way, you can see the importance of inputs into a transportation system. The system cannot function without some form of input.

Think of what our transportation systems would be like without any inputs. If you wanted to fly in an airplane across the country, but there was no pilot to fly the plane, you wouldn't get anywhere. Therefore, that particular air transportation system would not function without the input of a person. Can you think of other problems that might occur in a transportation system without adequate inputs?

Processes in a Transportation System

The processes within a transportation system are divided into two groups: production and management, Fig. 10-10. Working together they reach desired outputs.

Production

Production within the process of a transportation system is the "action" part of the system. In

Fig. 10-9. This delivery man is collecting payment from a customer for providing a delivery service. (UPS® and UPS® in the shield design are registered trademarks of United Parcel Service of America, Inc. Photo used with permission.)

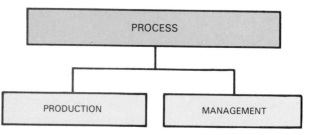
Fig. 10-10. Process has two areas of activity. Production involves those people and machines that move the cargo or people, that deal with customers, and that service the equipment. Management involves people and machines that organize the company and its affairs.

this "action" stage, the inputs are changed to accomplish an output. The production process is the most recognizable segment of a transportation system. It's the part you see or observe the most. For instance, when you see a train rolling down a track, trucks and cars on a highway, and a speed boat racing through the water, you have just observed the production (action) process of a transportation system, Fig. 10-11. Some preparations may be needed before beginning the production process. If you are going on a family vacation in the summertime, you will first need to pack the car with your luggage. You may also need to service your car. You can fill it with gasoline, oil, and also check the tires to make sure it is maintained for safety. Before take-off, your luggage is loaded into the aircraft and the aircraft is also serviced. Then you are ready for the operation to take place. You are ready for action! The car can now be put in gear and the plane can now take off.

Management

The *management* process within a transportation system includes activities that are necessary to keep

Fig. 10-11. An example of the transportation process. This bus is in the act of moving people around a city. The process is completed when passengers reach their destination and leave the bus.

people and cargo organized and on schedule. Without the managed portion of the process, our transportation systems could get very chaotic. If you got on a subway at one station and there was no direct schedule for the route you were on, you may never reach your destination. The subway would move down the track which represents the production process but would be lacking in the managed area, Fig. 10-12. Therefore, management is a necessity. Management processes are needed to plan, organize, and control the system.

In planning the transportation system, people are needed to decide what must be done. People plan the best route. People decide on what must take place to make the system more efficient. Also, how the system will run in the most efficient manner is determined. During the planning stage of management, goals are set and a course of action is determined.

Organizing a transportation system involves the preparation for transporting. It may be assigning jobs. If a newspaper route is getting too big for one person to handle, a need to assign new delivery persons is recognized. Any type of maintenance, such as putting air in tires and filling up the tank of an aircraft with fuel, are also examples of organization within a transportation system, Fig. 10-13.

The controlling of a transportation system is another function of management. In controlling a system, records are kept, computers are used, and systems are monitored. Computers may be used to control the flow of oil through a pipeline. The computer may control the on-off pumps, valves, and

Fig. 10-13. Another example of company management. Regular refueling of vehicles is required if the vehicles are to keep their schedule.
(United Airlines)

flow rate within the system. A guard with a stop sign at a school crossing is another example of controlling a system. The crossing guard controls the flow of vehicles when children are present. The control of traffic is evident by the use of various signals and signs, Fig. 10-14.

OUTPUTS

The output of a transportation system is the relocation of people or cargo. As a result of the inputs and processes a change is achieved. For in-

Fig. 10-12.   Management is a necessary part of transportation. No matter how well the transportation vehicle runs its route someone must schedule stops. Otherwise, some people or cargo will not be transported to their intended destination. Of the two illustrations which indicates the best management?

stance, a log truck is selected to transport logs from California to a sawmill in Iowa. Inputs are brought together to begin the system of transporting the logs by a land transportation system. You need fuel to power the truck. A person is also needed to operate the truck, read the map, and follow directions. Of course, money to operate the truck must not be overlooked. Once the inputs are there, the truck then goes into process or action. It begins its journey of transporting the logs. As the truck reaches the sawmill with the logs, the output has been achieved. The logs have been relocated, Fig. 10-15. That is the main purpose of a transportation system — relocating people and/or cargo.

Upon achieving an output in a transportation system, many events may occur that bring about change. For instance, upon delivering the logs, change will occur with the logs themselves, as well as, with the driver of the truck. The driver drops his load of cargo and will then move on to a new destination.

Consider other examples. As you travel to a vacation spot, change occurs upon reaching your new environment. You may do things you normally wouldn't do while at home. Maybe you have just transported grain from a farm to the grain elevator and you're receiving a payment. In these two examples, the relocating of people and grain brought about changes of some sort.

FEEDBACK

In a transportation system, feedback is essential. Feedback gives back information on how well the system is running. With feedback, you are able to evaluate the system. When driving down the

Fig. 10-14. Traffic is controlled by various signs and signals. This helps keep the transportation systems safe and functioning.

Fig. 10-15. These logs are being transported to their final destination, the saw mill. This will complete the truck's transport service.

highway, the speedometer is giving you feedback as you accelerate or decelerate the vehicle. The speedometer communicates if you are driving too fast or too slow. As you enter the 55 mph zone, you need feedback so you know whether to speed up or slow down. The speedometer enables you to make decisions. Instrument panels and gauges of various kinds also give you feedback which is needed in the control of a transportation system, Fig. 10-16.

GOALS

Within the transportation system, there are goals that need to be met. The first goal is the goal of the system itself. Then there are other goals such as personal goals and societal goals, Fig. 10-17. The goal of an entire transportation system is to relocate at the proper destination on time. If you had tickets for a concert in a nearby city, how would you get there? You may take a car, a cab, or maybe a subway. The main goal of the transportation system

Fig. 10-16. The instrument panel on this aircraft gives feedback to the pilot on how well the aircraft is functioning.   (United Airlines)

you choose would be to relocate you from your home to the concert on time.

Societal goals are those expectations we put on a transportation system. Such expectations may be traveling in a fast, comfortable, and safe fashion. These expectations can also be looked at as restrictions put on a transportation system by society. In the design of airplane seats, the company may be restricted from using a certain fabric for the seats because it may not be comfortable to the passengers. In the shipment of cargo, consumers (society) want the products to arrive safely and fast. Therefore, planners must consider the means by which the cargo will be transported. For instance, delivering a package by hand instead of by bicycle will help insure the safety of the product inside. Shipping cargo by plane instead of train may insure the speed at which the cargo is to arrive at its destination.

Personal goals also affect transportation. A Ferrari and a Chevrolet both transport people. Both produce the same output. One, however, has a better image. Driving a Ferrari suggests a higher step up the socio-economic ladder. People want to look good so they use this specific means of transportation to meet their own personal goals.

TRANSPORTATION SYSTEMS

You have been introduced into transportation. You have seen how transportation fits into our technological society as one of the many technological systems. You have had a foundation as to the structure of a transportation system. You've also seen how power and energy are needed before any form of transportation can begin. Thus far, you have been given information to introduce you to transportation. Now we are going to explore some more specific types of transportation. As you

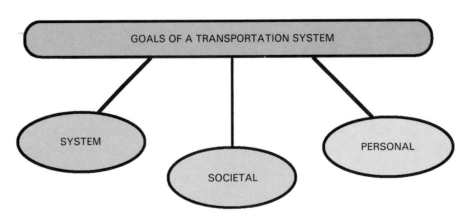

Fig. 10-17. A transportation system will have several different goals.

know, there are many ways in which to transport people and cargo. You know there are four different transportation systems: land, air, water, and space. All forms of transportation fall into a specific category under one of the four transportation systems, Fig. 10-18. We will now begin to look more closely into each of these systems.

Land Transportation

Think for a moment of all the forms of *transportation* you might find on the *land*. There are many: subways, buses, trains, trucks, bicycles, and motorcycles. These and other forms of land transportation can be categorized as mass transit (carrying many people), rail, roadway, pipeline, or recreational.

Air Transportation

What comes to your mind when you think about *air transportation*? One of the first things might be an airplane. What else? How about hot-air balloons, airships, hang gliders, military fighter planes, and helicopters? All of these examples can be categorized as either lighter-than-air or heavier-than-air transportation modes.

Water Transportation

How do people and cargo travel on the water? *Water transportation* systems are categorized as in-

land and transocean (across the ocean). Ways in which people and cargo are moved on water may be by a ship, a sailboat, a raft, a barge, a tugboat, and a submarine. These are just a few examples of water transportation systems.

Space Transportation

Can you think of different forms of *space transportation*? Missiles, rockets, satellites, space shuttles, and spacecrafts are a few modes of space transportation. All of these, and more, can be categorized as manned or unmanned systems.

SUMMARY

A transportation system is a systematic way of relocating people and cargo.

A transportation system includes inputs, processes, outputs, feedback, and goals. Various types of inputs are needed to begin the process of a system. Once a transportation system is in process, the action begins. The process of a system also needs to be managed. When the system is underway, an output is in view. The output of a transportation system is the relocation of people or cargo. Feedback within the system is needed in order to control the system. Goals within a transportation system are societal, personal, and systematic. There are four divisions of transportation systems. They are land, air, water, and space.

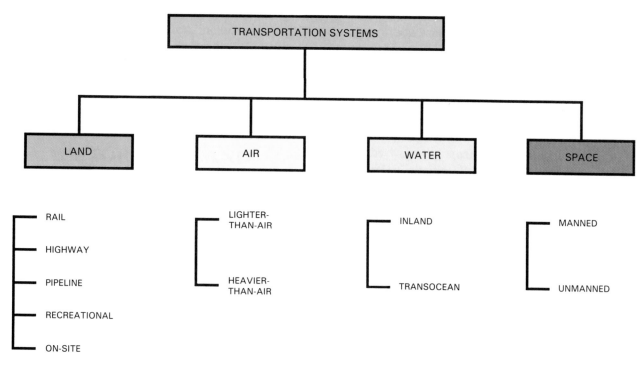

Fig. 10-18. All types of transport can be organized under one of the four transportation systems.

Fig. 11-1. The development of the wheel brought many advancements in land transportation. Horse-drawn vehicles, arising out of the wheel's invention, were in common usage until the early 1900s.   (John Deere & Co.)

ROUTES

Each type of land transportation vehicle travels on a route (pathway). These routes restrict the freedom of movement of the vehicle. Routes go by different names.

Random Routes

Automobiles are free to move to the left and right. They are also free to move forward and backward. Automobiles have a lot of freedom. They must stay on a road but they usually have a choice of which road to take. When a vehicle has such freedom, it is identified as a *random-route* mode. Random-route modes respond best to human needs and wants. For instance, if you were to drive from Pennsylvania to Oregon in a car, you would have the freedom to go through Indiana or down through Kansas and back up north. You could stop anytime you liked.

A disadvantage of random routes is that they use up excessive amounts of land. The building of roads often destroys a portion of our environment. Also, modes of transportation that use random routes consume a lot of energy and cause air and noise pollution.   On the other hand, there are vehicles that travel on *fixed routes*.

Fixed Routes

A fixed route is a pathway that stays the same. A railway or a subway line are examples of fixed routes. The train doesn't have the freedom to go wherever the operator wants. The driver must stay on the track and follow the designated route. Fixed routes are not so destructive of our environment. They are more efficient in energy consumption. However, a disadvantage of fixed routes is that they are less responsive to meeting human desires because they have to stay on a set guide way.

Stationary Routes

There is another transporting path that is a *stationary route*. This means that it does not move. Stationary systems usually move goods. The system may have moving internal elements such as belts or chains, but the basic supporting structure is stationary.

An example of a stationary system is a pipeline. Pipelines have no moving parts. The pipe extends from one point where material enters the system to a point where material is discharged. The materials are moved through the system by the use of pressure, gravity, or vacuum.

Conveyors are another example of the stationary system of transporting. Conveyors can be designed to move either people or goods.

Routes support vehicles

Routes are developed to support the vehicle. For instance, roadways and railways are used to support land transportation systems, Fig. 11-2. Through the use of routes, vehicles are able to reach their destination in a safe and efficient manner. Natural barriers seldom hinder a vehicle's travel. Mountains are tunneled. Rivers are bridged, Fig. 11-3. Routes allow vehicles to move about on the land without hurting people or bringing damage to property. Our cities, towns, and rural areas would be very dangerous if we did not set aside space to be used as pathways for vehicles. We would not be safe walking or driving!

Transporters

As we begin to look more closely at the development of land transportation, we will look at different modes of moving people and cargo. We will discuss the following:

- Passenger transporters. These systems move people over a long distance. Some examples are buses, railroads, and automobiles.
- Cargo transporters. These transporters are concerned with the movement of cargo over a long distance. Examples of this type of system are railroads, pipelines, and trucks.
- People transporters. These systems move people over short distances. Examples of this type of system include escalators, elevators, and moving sidewalks.

You will be reading about certain modes of land transportation, Fig. 11-4. Highways will be discussed, as will the types of vehicles that run on them. Also, railroads will be identified as a mode of land transportation. Pipelines will be included,

Fig. 11-3. The problems of natural barriers are solved with the construction of tunnels and bridges.

too. Recreational types of land transportation will be described.

HIGHWAYS

You need only look at a road map to get an idea of the miles of highways that criss-cross the landscape. Much of our travel would be impossible without them. Let us consider the history of roads.

History of Roadways

Highways or roadways are a mode of land transportation. Transportation on land encompasses many types of vehicles and carriers. Some run on roads and others on rails. As we review the history of transportation, we find that the development of roads is where American history really starts. It's amazing how large a role transportation has played in the settling of North America. Without roadways, we wouldn't be as developed as we are today. It was the roads that caused our founding fathers to continue on their journeys

Fig. 11-2. A highway is a route that a vehicle travels to reach its destination safely and efficiently.

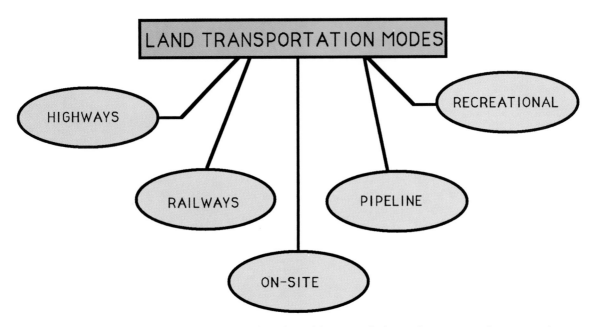

Fig. 11-4. All land transportation can be placed in one of these five categories or modes.

westward. Good roadways encouraged migration which led to people settling throughout the country.

However, let us go back even farther. Some of the first roads were built in Asia and Europe. They date back to the sixth century. Roads began as paths for wild animals, migrating people, and nomads. As time passed, horse-drawn chariots traveled the roads. With improvement of roads, more people and cargo began being transported.

What would your life be like today if there were no roads? Can you think of a way you could get to school without using a road? Taking trips would be a very limiting experience without roads.

See how important highways and roadways are? Let's look at some examples of highway or roadway transportation vehicles.

Automobiles

In the 1800s technology was advancing beyond the development of the wheel. In Europe the carriage was revolutionizing whole countries. It was an expensive mode of transportation mainly used by upper-class people. As railroads began to develop, the carriage gradually lost its popularity. During the same century, the bicycle was invented in Europe. It soon made its way to the United States. The United States fell in love with it. In 1900, one million bicycles were produced. The carriage and then the bicycle set the stage for another personal transport vehicle, the automobile.

The development of the automobile was driven by inventor genius and mass production. In the ear-

ly twentieth century it was in development stages in the United States, Great Britain, Germany, and France. Each country had added another dimension to the vehicle. Inventors in the United States first began by putting steam and gasoline engines on bicycles and buggies. The motor car was developed next and soon became appealing to most Americans. At the same time there was a distrust of the motor car. People were afraid that it would endanger people's lives and frighten horses that pulled the buggies and carriages.

A way to break this distrust was to make the automobile common to all—so common that the farmer and the working person, alike, would see it as a convenience and not just a toy for the wealthy. Any person who could achieve this was destined to put the world into machine-powered vehicles. Fig. 11-5 shows Henry Ford in his very first car. The year was 1896. Ford made the automobile a common sight on early twentieth century American roads. He mass produced 1700 automobiles in 1914. Ford made the automobile cheap, easy to operate, and easy to maintain, Fig. 11-6.

Since the early 1900s, the number of automobiles has continued to increase. Several automotive companies, begun in the early 1900s, still exist. The automobile has become one of the most significant vehicles in our society, Fig. 11-7. A two-car family is a familiar sight to anyone living in the United States but to people living in other countries it is unique. Most countries having automobiles operate them less often. Most of their travel is by bus, bicycle, and public transportation.

Fig. 11-5. Henry Ford's first car was powered by a two-cylinder, four cycle engine. It also had an electric bell attached to the front to warn pedestrians.

Fig. 11-7. The automobile has continued to advance in design and technological features. It has become a necessity in our society.
(Ford Motor Co.)

Out of all the energy used in the transportation system, over half of it is consumed by the automobile.

The design of the automobile has changed immensely over the past 100 years. From a carriage-like, steam-powered buggy that did a maximum of 10 mph, it has evolved into an aerodynamic turbo engine sports car that can reach speeds up to 200 mph. Indeed, the automobile has changed!

While we have shaped the automobile it has shaped our communities. What would our

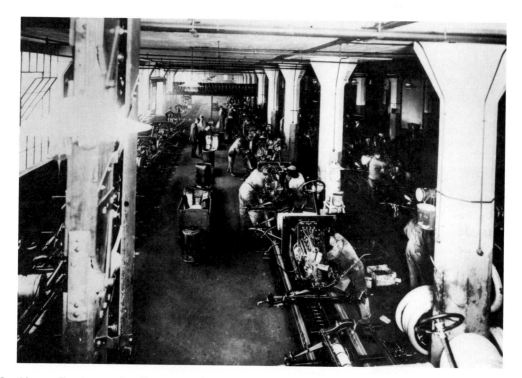

Fig. 11-6. Henry Ford was the first manufacturer to mass-produce automobiles using an assembly line. This was what his assembly line looked like in 1914 at Highland Park, Michigan.   (Ford Motor Co.)

neighborhoods be like if there were no automobiles? Certainly they would be much different than you see them today. Can you think what would be different? Look at Fig. 11-8 and try to imagine which of the structures shown would *not* be needed if there were no automobiles. Also, which structures would be changed?

Trucks

Trucks transport large amounts of cargo. Those that carry freight from city to city are major users of the highways. The truck does with freight what the automobile does for the passenger. In both cases, people and cargo are being relocated.

There are all kinds of trucks. Among them are dump trucks, cement trucks, grain trucks, garbage trucks, and delivery trucks, Fig. 11-9. Those usually seen on the highways are called "18 wheelers" or "semis." These trucks consist of a tractor and trailer.

The tractor is the front part of the truck that houses the engine, Fig. 11-10. The tractor is powered by a diesel rather than a gasoline engine. The reason for this is that more power is available for the hauling of heavy freight.

The trailer is the back end of the truck. The trailer can be of several different types, Fig. 11-11. Some trailers are tanks that haul liquid or gas. Some trailers are boxlike. They are good for hauling grain, livestock, or packaged goods from a manufacturing company. There are also refriger-

ator trucks that are used to transport food products. The standard length of semi-trailers is 39 to 45 ft. (12 to 14 m). The trailers are also made of lighter metals to reduce the overall weight of the truck. This allows them to carry more cargo.

Trucking has become a growing industry. Since the early 1970s, the development of new highways has increased the number of trucks hauling freight. This has also led to roadways replacing thousands of miles of railroad tracks.

The trucking industry includes three kinds:
- Private carriers.
- Contract carriers.
- Common carriers.

Private carriers own their own trucks and haul their own goods. Contract carriers haul goods only for the company with whom they have a contract. Common carriers haul goods for any shipper. Almost anything you wear or use has been transported by a truck somewhere in its journey to your community.

An advantage of moving cargo by truck is a reduction in damage to the cargo. Cargo also travels more safely in a truck. Packaging is not considered a necessity. Therefore, this saves on the cost of containers. It also saves on the packing material.

A great advantage of trucking, as opposed to any other form of carrier, is its flexibility. It is convenient for a truck to ship products door to door quickly. If you needed gravel for your driveway, how would you get it? The easiest way would be

Fig. 11-8. These pictures show how much the automobile has changed our society.

Fig. 11-9. Trucks benefit our lives in many ways. Can you name a few ways? (Ford Motor Co.)

Fig. 11-10. This tractor can pull great loads of freight. (Freightliner Corp.)

Fig. 11-11. Semi tractors haul different types of freight. This one is hauling a tanker loaded with gaseous fuel. (Freightliner Corp.)

for a gravel truck to deliver it to your house. It would be easier then having the next train stop at the nearest railroad yard and drop off a load of gravel. This method of delivery could take several days. This is just one example why the truck industry adds more convenience to our lives.

Trucks are loaded with freight at trucking terminals or warehouses. A supervisor checks the loaded freight. Once all information about the load is gathered, the truck is ready to roll on to its destination, Fig. 11-12.

Buses

The 1920s brought a distinct type of passenger vehicle, the bus. The first buses were no more than elongated passenger cars. Soon specialized buses were in demand. The first use of the bus was to extend railroad lines. When the tracks ended a bus would continue transporting people on into the city. Bus lines were soon established for cross-town transportation where there were no tracks.

Buses also were needed for the transportation of school children, Fig. 11-13. They are a necessity today in school systems. The bus brings the rural

Fig. 11-12. A truck can pick up in any community and deliver to any other community. (Freightliner Corp.)

Fig. 11-13. Many children travel to school on buses.

and suburban children into the city. Buses within school systems have aided the development of consolidating schools. The use of buses also led to the decline of small, one-teacher schoolhouses.

Buses have long been used to transport people on long runs. In 1929, the first nation-wide bus service was established. Several small bus companies consolidated into the Greyhound system.

One of the major advantages of a bus is that it can haul many passengers at once. Another advantage is that it has frequent pick-up and delivery points for the passengers.

In spite of the advantages of buses and other mass transportation systems, the sales of automobiles has increased almost yearly. This has contributed to more air pollution, more energy consumption, more traffic congestion, and more wear on roadways.

Despite all of these problems, ridership on buses has declined because of the convenience, comfort, and flexibility of the automobile. The bus lines have not been able to successfully compete with the automobile.

Some important factors bus companies need to consider are the scheduling, routing, comfort, and frequency of the bus service, Fig. 11-14. Buses must meet the needs of the people or people will not ride them. Can you think of any important advantages buses could offer people to attract more riders?

Motorcycles

Motorcycles are another kind of transporting vehicle. Motorcycles are often seen on the highways and streets. They are used by police departments, delivery services, and pleasure riders. Motorcycles can also be seen being ridden off the highway on dirt trails by sports riders. Motorcycles are of two types: a two-wheeled or three-wheeled vehicle. Both are powered by a gasoline engine, Fig. 11-15.

Today, motorcycles are built with heavier frames. A motorcycle engine is either a two-cycle or four-cycle design. The four-cycle engine pollutes less but the two-cycle develops more power for its weight.

Many people today travel on motorcycles across the country. The design of the motorcycle has changed to meet the personal needs and preferences of the operator and passenger. For instance, motor-

Fig. 11-14. The bus industry competes with the automobile in the transporting of people.

Fig. 11-15. Motorcycles are used for recreational purposes or for daily transport of people. (Harley Davidson)

cycles come equipped with radios and comfortable seats to make long trips easier. More control and a better suspension have made them easier to handle. Motorcycles play a limited but important part in land transportation systems.

Tractors

Tractors are mainly on-site farm vehicles. They do not require licensing and they are not often seen on the highways. Years ago, the tractor replaced the horse and made farming easier. On the farm a tractor has made it possible to prepare the ground for seed, plant the seed, and cultivate and harvest the matured crops. See Fig. 11-16.

Fig. 11-16. The modern tractor makes the process of planting crops much more efficient. The implement in the background can plant 12 rows of corn at a time while dropping fertilizer in each hill. The horse-drawn planter in the foreground plants but two rows at a time with no provision for fertilization.

Because of its design, versatility, maneuverability, and power, the tractor is also used in factories and in the construction industry. Tractors can be used to power other transporting devices when they have a Power Take-Off unit (PTO). For example, with a PTO, the tractor is a stationary power source and it can power an auger type elevator or conveyor which is used to transport such materials as grain and gravel. Also, due to its power and traction, a tractor is a prime mover of earth. With a grader, earth mover, or shovel on the tractor, trees and dirt can be moved to help in the clearing of land for construction purposes, Fig. 11-17.

RAILROADS

Railway lines form a network of tracks across the country. Railroads have been a factor in moving people and cargo for 320 years.

A railroad system consists of:
- Miles of roadbed and rails strong enough to carry the heavy weight of the trains and their payloads.
- A system of signal devices so that movement of trains on the same track can be safely coordinated.
- A variety of engines to pull the trains.
- Cars designed for carrying passengers or a variety of different products and materials.
- Stations for loading and unloading of passengers and handling cargo (freight).

History of Railroads

The first railway was developed in England in 1671. A railway is a road or way on which rails are placed for wheels to roll on. These first railways

Fig. 11-17. Tractors are also used for building roads and clearing a construction site. (John Deere & Co.)

were used to carry heavy loads of cargo on small cars. They were operated by hand and went back and forth on short runs in mines.

The first rails were no more than narrow wooden strips. Later, rails of wrought iron were placed on the wooden base of the track. In 1767, the first cast iron rails began to be used, Fig. 11-18.

In 1825, Colonel John Stevens of New Jersey built the first small locomotive. It was the first to run on American rails. The steam locomotive enjoyed considerable success. It provided the power to pull the train. At this time, the locomotive proved itself as a means of motive power. It was then that railways became railroads. *Railroads* are permanent roads made of a line of tracks that are fixed to wooden or concrete ties. A modern railroad provides a track for heavy equipment such as locomotives and rolling stock. *Rolling stock* are railroad cars that are pulled by the locomotive. Today, railroads are used for transporting large shipments of cargo over a long distance.

As the development of locomotives continued to increase, so did the construction of railroads. By 1860 there were more than 30,000 miles of tracks in the United States. As the railroads moved westward so did the people. The railroads played an important role in the settlement of the west.

Construction of the first transcontinental rail line, supported by President Lincoln, was delayed by the Civil War. In 1869, a railroad track stretching from Omaha, Nebraska to Sacramento, California was constructed, Fig. 11-19. It wasn't

Fig. 11-19. This photograph commemorates the laying of the last section of track that linked the east and the west.   (Santa Fe Railway)

long until other railroad companies linked on. This rapid growth soon connected the eastern states with the west coast. Business began to spread and towns were established along the railroads. A country still in its early development stages began to grow into a great nation with the help of the railroads and the people who worked for the roads.

Types of Rail Services

A rail transportation system offers service for the transporting of freight and passengers. Some trains transport only freight and others transport only passengers. In the following paragraphs you will look at some rail vehicles and the special transport services they offer.

Freight trains

A *freight train* is several freight cars coupled together and pulled by an engine or locomotive. Steam locomotives powered the first trains. Today, most locomotives are diesel-electric engines. The diesel-electric locomotive produces more power to pull heavier loads. In the United States, railroads are the largest freight-carrying business. Several different types of freight cars are used to transport different types of cargo. There are over 1.7 million freight cars in use in the United States.

It is more economical to haul large amounts of cargo by railroad. A single freight car can haul about the same load as four semi-trucks. It would also take four truck drivers to operate the trucks and more money to maintain four trucks.

Carrying freight by railroad also has fewer restrictions on weight and size of the cargo. Highway regulations place limits on the weight and length of the load trucks may carry.

Fig. 11-18. The laying of the first cast iron rails across a prairie was the occasion for this old-time photograph.   (Santa Fe Railway Photo)

The most common types of freight cars are box-cars, flat cars, gondolas, hopper cars, tank cars, and transport cars, Fig. 11-20.

Boxcars are boxlike cars with doors on both sides. They are used to carry a wide variety of products. Boxcars may also be refrigerated to carry frozen foods or any other product that must be kept cool.

Flatcars are sturdy platforms on wheels. They have no sides. Flatcars carry such material as steel, lumber, truck trailers, containers, and even very heavy equipment.

Gondolas have high or low sides with no tops and transport loose material such as stone, scrap metal, and iron. Basically, they can haul anything that can be loaded and unloaded from the top by a crane, auger, or magnet.

Hopper cars have hoppers (chutes) underneath. The hoppers make the cars easy to unload. Hopper cars carry bulk materials like coal and ore. Some have no tops while others are closed. Closed hoppers are used to haul materials that need to be protected from the weather. Such materials include corn, wheat, sand, salt, and fertilizer.

Tank cars are large tanks on wheels. Tank cars transport liquids such as oils and several kinds of chemicals.

Transport cars are flatcars with side rails. Usually, there is an upper and lower platform. Transport cars are mainly used for transporting new automobiles and trucks from manufacturing plants to car dealers.

A caboose is the last car on the freight train. It is used to house the train crew. With computers to automate and operate rail transportation, cabooses may no longer be necessary.

Most freight trains are made up of a combination of cars carrying different cargo. A unit train, however, carries only one type of cargo and all of its cars are alike. An example of a unit train is the coal train pictured in Fig. 11-21. A unit train goes to the same destination trip after trip.

A great advantage of freight train transportation is that it moves heavy loads and large quantities. The average size train powered by a diesel-electric locomotive can haul 70-100 cars at one time.

Passenger trains

Passenger trains are trains that transport people. This form of transportation causes little traffic con-

Fig. 11-21. Unit trains transport only one product such as coal. (Norfolk Southern Corp.)

| A | B | C |

Fig. 11-20. Photos show different types of railway cars. A—A tank car is designed to transport fluids, such as liquid or gaseous chemicals. B—A hopper can is designed to haul loose bulk such as coal and grain. C—A flatcar is designed to carry large machines or to "piggyback" semi trailers. (Sante Fe Railway)

gestion and is safe to travel on. Although, passenger trains aren't as convenient as automobiles. Riding a train causes personal set-backs. For instance, you have to be at a certain loading area to catch the right train. You also have certain times in which to catch the train.

The American Travel Track or Amtrak, is a passenger train system that transports people from one major city to another. Amtrak provides long distance travel for people. There are other types of rail transportation for passengers. This type runs within the city. Subways, monorails, and elevated trains are examples of rail transport systems within a city. These are forms of mass transit rail systems. Mass transit rail systems are forms of rail transportation that can carry many people at one time.

A *subway* is a train running on a rail below the earth's surface. It is found in many large cities. A great advantage of a subway is that it avoids the surface traffic in the city. These systems are very expensive to construct.

An *elevated train*, also known as the "EL," is a rail system that runs above the city streets. This, too, avoids the congestion that is common on the streets.

A *monorail* is a train that runs on a single rail. There are two ways in which a monorail can function. In one system it rides on top of the rail. In the other system the car or cars hang from the rail.

Some rail systems are fully automated. The train requires no driver. These systems are often referred to as automated transit systems (ATS). Such systems are used in large parking lots, airports, and shopping centers. One of the most highly automated rail systems is the San Francisco Bay Area Rapid Transit System (BART). The BART system travels in subway tunnels, on elevated railways, and in tunnels under the bay area. Other forms of rapid transit rail systems are the Washington Metro which operates in downtown Washington, D.C. and in suburban areas. The Shinkansen in Japan is another rapid transit system. Shinkansen means bullet train. It travels at speeds over 125 miles per hour (200 km/h).

Many of these high speed rail systems function by the application of electromagnetism. Magnetic levitation (*maglev*) trains in West Germany and Japan are capable of reaching speeds up to 300 mph (480 km/h).

Underwater Rail Systems

The Channel Tunnel project, also called the "Chunnel," is an underwater rail system linking Britain and France, Fig. 11-22. For nearly 180 years, the idea of tunneling under the English Channel has been contemplated and even attempted. This rail system consists of three tubes. Two tubes, 25 ft. in diameter, are linked at several points to a third tube about 16 ft. (4.8 m) in diameter. The smaller tube serves as a service tunnel. The rail line occupies the two larger tubes. The tubes or tunnels are 100 meters below sea-level. Tunnel workers have had to bore through chalk marl, which is the lowest layer of chalk under the channel. The tunnels are excavated using a boring machine, Fig. 11-23.

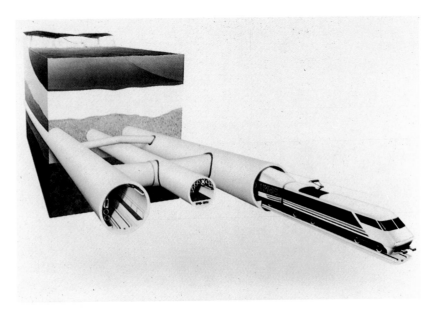

Fig. 11-22. Artist's rendering of the "Chunnel." Completed in 1994, it creates a rail link between England and France.   (Eurotunnel)

Fig. 11-23. A—Working 328 ft. (100 m) below sea level, a boring machine is excavating a tunnel 25 ft. (7.6 m) in diameter. B—The rail has been installed for one of the tunnels.   (Eurotunnel)

The trains carry passengers, cargo, and cars across the English Channel in one-half hour at 100 mph (161 km/h). The trains are driven by electric locomotives, Fig. 11-24.

PIPELINES

Pipelines are a mode of land transportation. Pipeline transportation is simply moving cargo from one place to another by the use of a pipe. Of course, the material being transported must be able to be moved through a pipe. Most are constructed

Fig. 11-24. The Channel Tunnel train pulls cars loaded with cargo and passengers. (Eurotunnel)

underground where they are seldom seen or heard. However, a few are constructed above the ground. Pipelines are a unique form of transportation. In a pipeline the cargo moves but the vehicle (the pipe) remains stationary. Pipelines cause little damage to the environment. They cause no traffic congestion, pollution, or direct damage to the land.

Centuries ago, pipelines were developed from bamboo. Water was transported through the hollow bamboo. Water-carrying pipelines were also made out of logs. The logs were hollowed out and fitted together. Being somewhat porous, the bamboo and the wood could not withstand the pressure of the water. Thus, by the late 1800s, iron pipelines were being constructed. Today, pipelines are made from steel or plastic and vary in diameter.

Pipelines are used to transport such products as oil, natural gas, water, coal, and gravel. Some of these substances are fluid and flow easily through a pipe.

If you wanted to transport water from your house to a garden that was 100 feet away, how would you do it? The most efficient solution would be to use a hose. Using this method demonstrates the efficient operation of a pipeline. See how fast the water can move from the house to the garden? It is much quicker than carrying water by bucket. This same efficiency would apply when transporting any product by pipeline. It's easy, fast, and efficient, Fig. 11-25.

Fig. 11-25. Pipelines stretch across many miles and carry several different kinds of materials. (The Coastal Corp.)

Construction of Pipelines

Most companies that transport by pipeline own their own pipelines. Construction of pipelines requires careful planning. Once a company decides to construct a pipeline, the route is first planned. The company will then contact the owners of the land where the pipeline will be constructed. The company expects to pay for this use of the land.

Once an agreement is reached with the land owners, the digging or trenching of the earth begins, Fig. 11-26. Pipe is laid in the trench and welded together. The trench is then refilled with earth. At this point, the pipeline is out of sight and the earth is returned to it's original condition.

One of the major pipeline constructions was undertaken in 1977. This installation is known as the Trans-Alaska Pipeline. It transports oil 775 miles across Alaska.

Fig. 11-26. It takes many workers and machines to lay a pipeline. (The Coastal Corp.)

Operation of Pipelines

To begin operating a pipeline, you need the actual product. In the operation of an oil pipeline, the crude oil is first pumped from underground. At the surface, it is transported through a line known as a *flow line*. The flow line carries the oil to storage tanks near the wells. From the storage tank, *gathering lines* transport the oil into *trunk lines*. Trunk lines then transport the oil to the refinery. There the oil is processed into such products as gasoline, heating oils, diesel fuel, and other petroleum products. From the refinery, the new products are shipped across the country by other pipelines. In an oil field, the gathering lines and trunk lines are constructed above the ground so they can be easily shifted when new oil wells are developed, Fig. 11-27.

Most pipelines are controlled by computers. In an automated pipeline system, oil can be transported 24 hours a day, seven days a week. Oil movement in the pipelines is controlled from a central dispatching station. The dispatching station consists of a control room, a pump room, and several offices. In this station, a scheduler is responsible for keeping the oil flowing from the refinery to the storage tank at the receiving station. The pipes need to be full at all times and the system must be controlled. Monitoring the system is done from an instrument panel. This panel monitors pressure, volume, and tank levels. Gauges give the controller a constant overview of the pipeline's activity.

To prevent pipeline clogging, a barrel-shaped brush, known as a *pig*, routinely cleans the line. The pig can be blown through the line or pushed through with moving cargo. In case of leaks or clogging, the controller has the ability to start or stop the oil flow. Also, a controller can speedup or slowdown the system.

Several different products can be transported through the same pipeline. Products are simply pumped into the pipeline in separate batches. For example, a batch of gasoline may be followed by diesel fuel or kerosene. This is called a *batch sequence*. Once the batches reach the terminals, they are separated by weight with a computerized device called a *gravitometer*. Each product is then pumped into its respective holding tanks and ready for distribution.

Solid products are moved through a pipeline in a *slurry*. A slurry is a mixture of a ground solid, such as coal, along with a liquid such as water. Nearly any solid material that can be ground into small pieces can be transported through a pipeline.

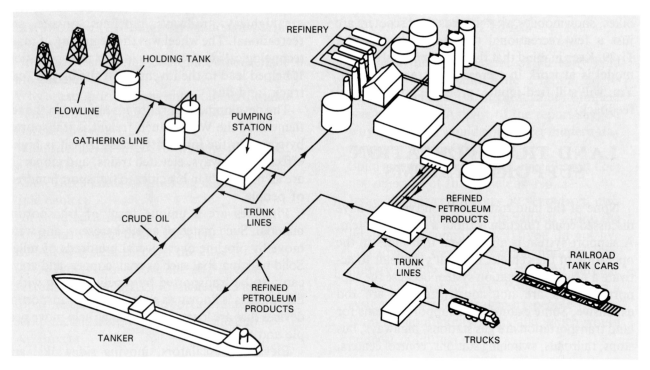

Fig. 11-27. An oil pipeline system moves crude oil to the refinery and then moves petroleum products to storage or to transport systems that will move them wherever they are to be used.

Other materials transported by the slurry pipeline system are limestone, minerals, clay, gravel, and copper.

There are millions of miles of pipelines crossing the United States. About half of the pipelines are used to transport natural gas which is mainly used for heating and cooking. The remaining pipelines carry oil, petroleum products, and slurry.

ON-SITE TRANSPORTATION

There is another mode of transportation that deals with moving people and products inside of buildings. Such transport is usually over a short distance. For instance, if you are in a department store and you want to get from the first floor to the third you may use an escalator or an elevator. Escalators, elevators, and moving sidewalks are all examples of people-moving transportation, Fig. 11-28. Moving sidewalks are often found in very large airports.

Products also are transported on-site. This is done by using conveyors which are material-handling devices. In industry, belt conveyors and roller conveyors are used to transport products down an assembly line. Trolley conveyors are still another method used to transport. A trolley conveyor moves overhead on a cable as it lifts and transports products.

Fig. 11-28. An escalator is a people transporter designed to move people between floors in buildings. It is a type of "on-site" transportation.

RECREATIONAL LAND TRANSPORTATION

There are a few forms of land transportation that are used for fun. Bicycles, mopeds, unicycles, dirt

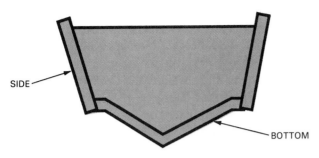

CROSS-SECTIONAL VIEW OF A HULL

SIDE

BOTTOM

Fig. 12-6. Boat hulls are designed for great buoyancy.

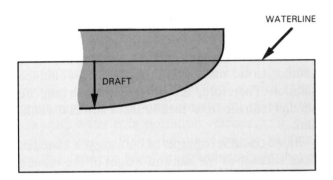

WATERLINE

DRAFT

Fig. 12-7. Draft is the depth a vessel sits in the water.

MODES OF WATER TRANSPORTATION

Modes of water transportation are of two types: inland and transocean, Fig. 12-9. As you learned earlier, inland waterways include rivers, canals, and

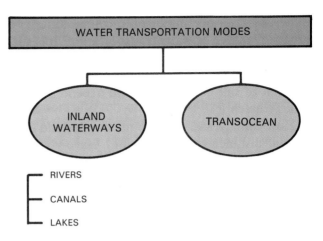

WATER TRANSPORTATION MODES

INLAND WATERWAYS

TRANSOCEAN

RIVERS

CANALS

LAKES

Fig. 12-9. Chances are, you have used at least one mode of inland water transportation.

lakes. In the following paragraphs, you will read more about the different modes of water transportation and watercraft. The vehicles can carry cargo or passengers or both, Fig. 12-10.

Inland Waterway Systems

Two important waterways are the St. Lawrence Seaway and Lake Superior. Both are located between the United States and Canada. The St. Lawrence connects the Great Lakes with the Atlantic Ocean. This waterway serves a large portion of North America. Many commodities are shipped in on the St. Lawrence and distributed throughout the U.S. and Canada.

The Mississippi River is another major inland waterway. Most vessels on the Mississippi are

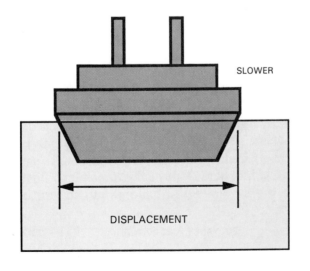

SLOWER

DISPLACEMENT

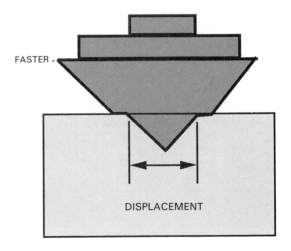

FASTER

DISPLACEMENT

Fig. 12-8. Draft has a direct relationship to speed and force needed to move a boat.

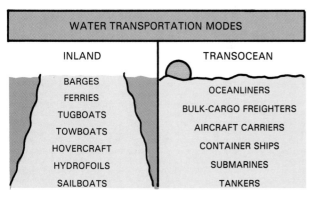

WATER TRANSPORTATION MODES

INLAND	TRANSOCEAN
BARGES	OCEANLINERS
FERRIES	BULK-CARGO FREIGHTERS
TUGBOATS	AIRCRAFT CARRIERS
TOWBOATS	CONTAINER SHIPS
HOVERCRAFT	SUBMARINES
HYDROFOILS	TANKERS
SAILBOATS	

Fig. 12-10. These are the vehicles used in the two modes of water transportation.

Fig. 12-11. Barges require tugboats or towboats to pull or push them.

barges carrying freight. This inland waterway can carry freight all the way from Minneapolis, Minnesota to the Gulf of Mexico.

Often, inland waterways are connected by canals. A *canal* is a channel that is constructed to connect two bodies of water. One of the most familiar is the Panama Canal in Central America. This canal was constructed to reduce the traveling time of vessels. Before it was opened, ships sailing from the East Coast to the West Coast of North America had to take a very long route. One route took them all the way north around Canada and Alaska and then back down the West Coast. The other route took them all the way around South America and back north. The construction of the Panama Canal saved over 10,000 miles on the trip from New York to California.

Various kinds of vehicles are designed for use on inland waterways. We will investigate the types in the following paragraphs.

Barges

Barges are flat with blunt ends and carry very heavy loads of cargo, Fig.12-11. A barge can carry up to five times its own weight. About three-fourths of all the cargo carried by water is transported by barge. A barge is not a very attractive vessel. It's not very fast either. However, barges are very safe. The smoothness of their ride and the amount of weight they can carry has no equal. Barges carry liquids, solids, and gases. The most common types of barges are the open hopper, covered dry cargo, liquid cargo, and deck. Such barges can carry coal, ore, oil, and grain.

Most barges have no engines. They must, therefore, be pushed or pulled by some other vessel or a series of vessels. A "tow" is a series of barges and smaller vessels linked together to form a single unit. They are moved by tugboats and towboats.

Towboats and tugboats

Towboats and tugboats are not often thought of as different from each other. They are very different. A *towboat* is designed to push barges, Fig. 12-12. A towboat has a wide flat front end to allow more surface area for pushing barges. *Tugboats*, on the other hand, are designed to pull a barge. Tugboats are very powerful. Tugboats are also used to pull

Fig. 12-12. These barges are being pushed by a towboat. (National Park Service, Natchez Trace Parkway)

ocean liners in and out of ports and help dock and undock other ocean-going vessels.

Hydrofoils

Hydrofoils operate on inland and coastal waters, Fig. 12-13. A hydrofoil is a passenger-transporting vessel. Depending on the size of the hydrofoil, up to several hundred passengers can be transported at one time. Most hydrofoils have seen service in New York, Long Island, Miami, and Pittsburgh. They have been used to transport people across big lakes, and up and down rivers, channels, and canals.

A hydrofoil is similar to a plane and ship put together. The term *hydrofoil* means "water wing." A hydrofoil has wings called foils. The foils lift the vessel out of the water due to the forward motion, like wings on an airplane. The hydrofoil develops its lift from the buoyancy of the water just as an airplane receives lifts from the air, Fig. 12-14. As

the watercraft reaches high speeds, the foils lift it out of the water. The boat is then sailing along at high speeds just skimming the surface of the water. The foils are the only part of the vessel making contact with the water. Due to the reduction of friction, hydrofoils can travel at high speed.

Hovercraft

A hovercraft is a vessel that rides on a cushion of air, Fig. 12-15. Hovercraft are also referred to as *air-cushion vehicles*. Air pressure allows the vessel to hover (remain suspended) in the air a few feet above the water. The vessel makes no contact with the water. It just rides along on a cushion of air, Fig. 12-16.

Fig. 12-15. The U.S. Navy is experimenting with hovercraft which can operate on water or land. (Standard Oil Co.—Ohio)

Fig. 12-13. Hydrofoils lift watercraft out of the water much like wings lift a plane into the air. In either case, power is needed to move the craft forward at high speed.
(Turbo Power, United Technologies Corp.)

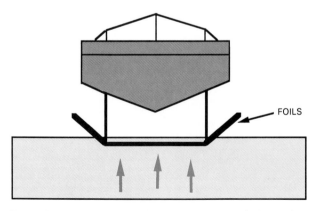

Fig. 12-14. The hydrofoil develops its lift from the buoyancy of the water.

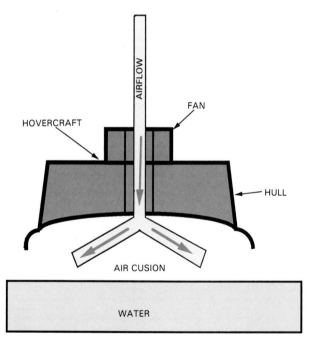

Fig. 12-16. The basic design of hovercraft. A cushion of air keeps the hull suspended above the surface.

Air is brought in by large, high-speed fans that are driven by gas turbine engines. The fans may be located on the top or sides of the vessel. The air is then forced down around the hull on all sides. This then forms the cushion of air.

Ferries

Ferries are vessels that move people and vehicles across narrower or smaller bodies of water, Fig. 12-17. Ferries are usually used along coastal waters and on inland waterways. Ferries transport passengers to and from islands and across rivers. One of the most popular is the Staten Island Ferry in New York Harbor. Another important ferry travels between the mainland and Vancouver Island in British Columbia, Canada. Ferries usually operate in areas where time can be saved by transporting automobiles across the water instead of driving around the coastal areas.

Other inland water transporting vehicles

Other forms of water vehicles are often found in smaller lakes and rivers. Such vehicles are most often used for recreational purposes. Sailing and wind surfing are a very big sport along the coastal areas and northern lakes. Sailboats are a common water transporting vehicle. Jet skiing has become a popular past time on the water. A jet ski is similar to a motorcycle. Speed boats, canoes, rafts, and paddle boats are some other examples of water

vehicles that are most often used for leisure, Fig. 12-18. Can you think of any other recreational water vehicles?

Transocean

Transocean is another mode of water transportation. *Transocean* means traveling across the ocean. Many vessels are designed for travel across the ocean. Some of the vessels carry cargo and others carry people. As mentioned earlier, vessels that travel across the ocean follow sea-lanes (established routes). They stay within the designated sea-lanes by being navigated. Some transocean vessels are oceanliners, freighters, tankers, container ships, aircraft carriers, and submarines.

Ocean liners

Ocean liners are basically for luxury use. Ocean liners or cruise ships can carry thousands of passengers. Most people travel on ocean liners for a relaxing vacation. Ocean liners are very large and often have several decks. Decks may include bedrooms, swimming pools, restaurants, and game rooms. One of the most famous ocean liners is the Queen Elizabeth II from England.

Bulk-cargo freighters

Bulk-cargo freighters are ships that are deigned to carry very large quantities of cargo. Freighters usually have a series of holds below the main deck, Fig. 12-19. Several different kinds of cargo can be carried, each in a different hold. Freighters carry such goods as coal, ore, oil, grain, sugar, cotton, and cement. The cargo is referred to as dry bulk or liquid bulk. An OBO freighter (Ore, Bulk-cargO) carries coal, grain, ore, and oil. An advantage to such a vessel is its ability to carry several

Fig. 12-17. This ferry carries passengers and vehicles between Victoria, Vancouver Island, Canada and Port Angeles, Washington.

Fig. 12-18. Recreational boats are also a form of water transportation. (Bayliner Marine Corp.)

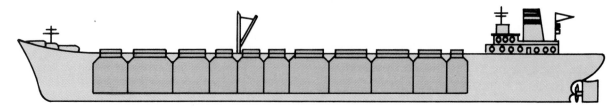

Fig. 12-19. A bulk cargo carrier has a series of holds that look very like containers. The are also called OBO ships because they carry ore, bulk cargo, and oil.

types of cargo at one time. As it unloads a hold at one port, it can fill that hold up with something else and continue on its route.

Tankers

A tanker is a vessel designed to carry liquids. A tanker has tank-shaped holds (sections) for carrying oil, petroleum products, chemicals, wine and even molasses. The most common tanker is that for transporting oil. A tanker is constructed with two or three long tanks which are divided into sections. By dividing the tanks in sections, the liquid won't move so much during transport. This makes the ship easier to handle and less likely to capsize (rollover). Because the cargo on a tanker is liquid, large pumps and hoses are used for loading and unloading. Large ocean tankers can carry up to 2 million barrels of oil.

Container ships

Container ships are very large and carry cargo stored in a container before loading. If you took several milk cartons and stacked them in a rowboat you would have the same concept as a container ship. The containers usually carry dry bulk cargo. They are airtight, permanent, reusable, weathertight and fitted with at least one door on the end. Some containers are made of steel but most are made of aluminum because it's a lighter metal that does not rust. The containers vary in length. Some are the size of a semi-trailer. Container ships save time and money in the loading and unloading of cargo.

Other transocean vessels

Submarines and aircraft carriers are other large ocean vessels. Usually they are used by the military. Submarines are vessels that can submerge and travel underwater. They are used to explore the ocean and are also useful for military purposes. They can stay below the surface because their weight is greater than the weight of the water they displace. By filling the tanks with water to increase the weight, the submarine sinks. Replacing the water in the tanks with air, lightens the submarine allowing it it to rise.

Aircraft carriers carry fighter jets for the air force. An aircraft carrier is a very large ship with a pad-like deck. The large deck allows the jets to take off and land, Fig. 12-20.

SUPPORT SYSTEMS

Water transportation is made possible through its support facilities. Support facilities aid in keeping vessels maintained and operating. Vessels need a place to be repaired, refueled, loaded and unloaded. Harbors, docks, ports, and locks are all support systems. Without them ships couldn't operate effectively. Terminals are also a physical facility used to house passengers and cargo.

Harbors, Ports, and Docks

A *harbor* is a point along the coast where the water is deep enough for the vessel to come very close to shore, Fig. 12-21. The main purpose of a harbor is to get the vessels in close to land. The *port* is a place where vessels load and unload cargo or passengers. There are many ports located along sea coasts, lake fronts, and rivers. Ports also have means for fueling and repair. They offer many other services to a vessel. Located at the port are docks. A dock is an area that is totally closed in by piers. A ship usually is not docked long at a port.

Fig. 12-20. Aircraft carriers have a large deck so that planes can take off and land on them. It is a ''floating airport!'' (U.S. Navy)

Fig. 12-21. Aerial view of a harbor. Water is deep enough for large ships to dock. (Norfolk Southern Corp.)

They must get loaded or unloaded and continue on their journey to another port.

Locks

Locks are used in the inland waterways. A *lock* is a chamberlike facility constructed in a canal between two different water levels. A lock is made up of gates, pumps, and filling and draining valves, Fig. 12-22.

As the vessel enters the upper level, the lock chamber is already filled to the same level by the filling valve, Fig. 12-22A. When the gates close behind the vessel, the drain valve opens to lower the water level, Fig. 12-22B. The water will now be level with the lower level. The gate will open and the vessel will be on its way out, Fig. 12-22C. Locks work similar to elevators. Where elevators move people from one floor to another, a lock moves a vessel from one water level to another.

Maneuvering vessels through a lock requires great skill. Once a vessel is seen coming towards the lock, the traffic control center is contacted by radiotelephone. Permission is given to begin the locking process. It takes about 10 minutes to raise and lower the water in the lock chamber. The average time for a vessel to move from entry to exit through a lock is 30 minutes.

Terminals

Terminals are a physical facility, a building. In land transportation there are train terminals, bus terminals, and trucking terminals. The same are needed for water transportation. A terminal is needed to load and unload passengers. In passenger terminals, there are restaurants, waiting areas, and shops of various kinds.

Another kind of terminal is a cargo terminal. Its main purpose is cargo storage. Cargo is unloaded

at the port and stored. It is later loaded onto another vessel and/or reshipped by rail, air, or highway transport.

SUMMARY

Transporting of people and cargo by water has been around for thousands of years. The water transportation system is an efficient form of transportation. Water transportation vehicles are called vessels. Vessels travel in one of the two modes of water transportation: on inland waterways or across the ocean. Traveling across the ocean, a vessel follows a pathway or route called a sea-lane. Sea-lanes are comparable to highways on land.

Vessels can carry passengers or cargo. Passenger vessels that are on inland waterways include ferries, hovercraft, and hydrofoils. Passenger vessels

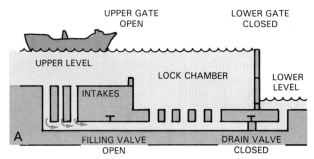

1. THE LOCK CHAMBER IS FILLED TO THE SAME LEVEL AS THE UPPER LEVEL. THE UPPER GATE OPENS AND THE VESSEL ENTERS THE LOCK CHAMBER.

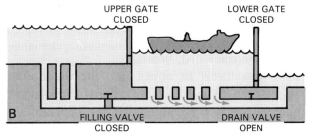

2. THE UPPER GATE IS CLOSED. THE WATER IN THE LOCK CHAMBER IS ALLOWED TO DRAIN.

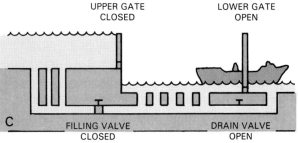

3. WHEN THE WATER DRAINS TO THE SAME LEVEL AS THE LOWER LEVEL, THE LOWER GATE OPENS AND THE VESSEL MOVES OUT OF THE LOCK.

Fig. 12-22. Operation of a lock. Different water levels float ships up or down.

named the plane "Flyer." In 1903, at Kitty Hawk, North Carolina, Orville Wright made the world's first powered, sustained, and controlled flight. He was airborne for 12 seconds. Since 1906, the pace of air transportation has accelerated. People from all over the world experimented with different airplane designs. Flight time was increasing. Time in the air and the distance the plane flew continued to increase. The development, in a short year, went from 200 ft. to 62 miles, and from 36 1/2 minutes across the English Channel to 1 1/2 hours in flight. The military soon adopted the airplane when World War I began in 1914. Air transportation has been the fastest growing transportation system, Fig. 13-2.

ROUTES

Just as water transportation has no highways on the water, there are no highways in the air. There are *airways*, however. Airways are paths or routes that airplanes follow. Since there are no highways in the air with speed limits and other such regulations, the airways are controlled by the FAA (Federal Aviation Administration). Planes can fly anywhere in the air. For the safety of flying and carrying passengers and cargo, planes must be kept apart from one another. This is done through maintaining distance or airspace from one another. The airway is made up of zones and routes for aircraft (air transportation vehicles) to fly in. There are different routes and zones for different air vehicles such as military, commercial, and private. The airways are set up in layers.

Air layers are designed to keep the skies safe from accidents. There are three main layers from the ground level up to 75,000 ft. Each of these layers is further divided into smaller layers and each layer is numbered according to its height, Fig. 13-3. All even numbered layers are for planes flying west. All odd numbered layers are for planes flying east, Fig 13-4. There should always be 1000 ft. of airspace between planes and 10 minutes of flying time in front and in back of a plane. Airplane pilots

Fig. 13-2. Air transportation has grown very rapidly over a few years. The advancement in technology, design, and knowledge have aided this advancement. (United Airlines)

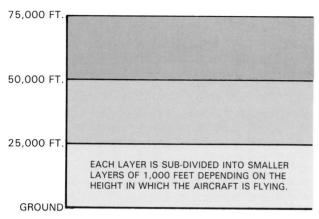

75,000 FT.

50,000 FT.

25,000 FT.

EACH LAYER IS SUB-DIVIDED INTO SMALLER LAYERS OF 1,000 FEET DEPENDING ON THE HEIGHT IN WHICH THE AIRCRAFT IS FLYING.

GROUND

Fig. 13-3. Airways divide up the sky into layers so that air collisions are avoided. Craft are assigned layers according to direction of flight and type of aircraft.

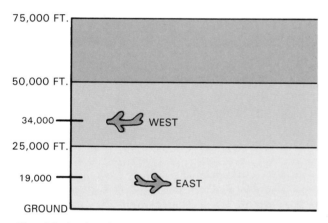

75,000 FT.

50,000 FT.

34,000 — WEST

25,000 FT.

19,000 — EAST

GROUND

Fig. 13-4. In all even-numbered layers, the aircraft flies in a westerly direction. In all odd-numbered layers, the aircraft flies in an easterly direction.

need to be well versed on the regulations for flying an aircraft.

MODES OF TRANSPORTATION

As with any other transportation system, people and cargo are moved by a transporting vehicle. In the air transportation system, vehicles that transport through the air are called *aircraft*. An aircraft is a vehicle designed for navigation in the air. An aircraft is also supported by the air against its surfaces. Aircraft are of two modes; lighter-than-air (LTA) and heavier-than-air (HTA).

Lighter-than-air craft are known as balloons and dirigibles (blimps). Lighter-than-air craft rise and float. Wind, in the case of a balloon, is the only means of propulsion (power).

Heavier-than-air craft are airplanes, helicopters, and gliders. This type of craft requires power to

maintain its speed, thus, creating lift. Lift occurs as the air creates a high pressure under the wing. At the same time the air pressure above the wing is reduced. This situation lifts the plane off the ground and keeps it in the air as long as the craft maintains sufficient air speed.

Lighter-Than-Air

Once the subject of much experimentation, lighter-than-air craft are more energy efficient than heavier-than-air craft. Where HTA craft require heavy use of energy to keep them in the air, LTAs are held aloft by their captive gases.

Balloons

The invention of balloons dates back to the 1700s. It happened at a time when people were curious about the upper atmosphere. Courageous experiments were carried out. The first experimenters used hot air to give the balloon lift. Then, after a short period of successful hot-air flights, new experiments proved that hydrogen (light gas) gave more lift than hot air.

The two balloon technologies of that day are still in use. Balloons are still filled with hot air or a gas such as hydrogen or helium, Fig. 13-5. The first balloon passengers were a duck, a rooster, and a sheep. They were hoisted up in a cage attached to the balloon. Their flight lasted eight minutes and they traveled two miles.

Balloons were periodically called upon for military duties all over the world. Their main use

Fig. 13-5. Since they cannot be steered, hot-air balloons need plenty of space for landing.

in warfare was to drop bombs. The military soon decided that a balloon was not the best device for dropping bombs. Being uncontrollable, balloons tended to overshoot their targets.

Balloon Structure

Balloons today, as well as in their early history, have little in the way of structure. The envelope (balloon portion) is filled with a gas or hot air. Shroud lines attach a basket (car) to the balloon for passengers to ride in. The wind provides the only means of propulsion. For example, if the wind is blowing to the east, then you will travel to the east. Today, balloons are mainly used as sport or for recreational purposes, Fig. 13-6.

A balloon floats in the air under the same principle as a boat floating in the water. Just as objects in water have buoyancy, objects in the air have *lift*. Lift is the upward pressure equal to or greater than the air displaced by the object. A balloon or any other object that floats in the air must weigh less than the air that has been displaced (pushed aside).

Dirigibles

In the late 1800s and early 1900s, large LTA ships were being built. They were designed to carry cargo and passengers around the world. These airships were called *dirigibles*. (In French the word dirigible means steerable.) A big difference between a balloon and a dirigible is that the latter is steerable.

This type of airship was built with a rigid frame made of metal. The experimentation with dirigibles was far more hazardous than that of balloons. The main hazard was the use of hydrogen for the lighter-than-air gas. Hydrogen is very combustible. It burns very rapidly when it is ignited. Many dirigibles were spectacular sights to see, but unfortunately, nearly all of them met tragic ends. The greatest of the old dirigible airships was the Hindenburg, Fig. 13-7. It measured 800 feet in length and could carry 100 people on long trips. On May 6, 1937, the Hindenburg made its last flight. It was docking in New Jersey after a trans-Atlantic flight when the hydrogen gas caught fire. The Hindenburg burst into flames and was destroyed.

Fig. 13-7. The German airship Hindenburg flying over New York City in the 1930s. (Smithsonian Institute)

Fig. 13-6. Balloons are mainly used for recreational purposes today.

Blimps

Today, LTA ships are used that are similar to the dirigibles of the early 1900s. They are not as rigid in construction, however. These ships are called *blimps*. They use helium instead of hydrogen to provide lift. Helium is a heavier gas but much safer because it does not burn. Mainly, blimps provide a platform for observation cameras and aerial views. They are also used for advertising and for some cargo lifting. The most famous is the Goodyear blimp which is used as a form of advertising for Goodyear tires, Fig. 13-8.

Heavier-Than-Air

Craft that are heavier than the air that must support them in flight are far more numerous. Although more energy must be expended to keep them in the air, they are usually much easier to control than LTAs. The heavier-than-air craft are: gliders, planes, and helicopters.

Gliders

After the development of balloons and dirigibles, people were still brave, curious, and often foolhardy. There began an era of great inventions. Sir George Cayley's was the first. He envisioned a fixed-wing aircraft. The design was soon developed. A craft made of light wood, stable wings, but no power source was the result. It was known as the *glider*. Several other people attempted to develop a glider that could sustain flight for a long period. The Wright brothers had experimented with many gliders. They soon concluded it needed a source of power, so they added a 12 horsepower engine. The engine drove two propellers. This time success was

in the air! The Wrights made a short airborne flight of 120 feet (36.6 meters). The age of the airplane had begun!

Many of the early planes had two or three wings to increase lift. With the development of bigger engines came the construction of stronger and heavier aircraft.

Airplanes

Since 1900, the plane has progressed very rapidly in design and construction, Fig. 13-9. There are many types of airplanes. They are used for business, personal, sport, agricultural, and commercial activities.

Planes have advanced in design from a two-wing (bi-plane) to a supersonic transport that can travel at speeds of 1550 mph (2494 km/h). The supersonic transport travels over twice the speed of sound, which is known as mach 2. There are many supersonic aircraft in the military but only one in commercial use. It is known as the Concorde. The Concorde can carry passengers from New York to Europe in 3 1/2 hours.

An airplane is carefully designed using strong but lightweight material. The material is made from special metal alloys. Aircraft engines must be powerful enough to withstand gravity, wind, and pressures from the air. The basic parts of an airplane are the fuselage, cockpit, wings, tail

Fig. 13-9. Comparison of old and new aircraft shows how aircraft design has advanced. (United Airlines, America West Airlines)

Fig. 13-8. The most famous of modern blimps is this one which advertises a brand of tires. (Goodyear Tire & Rubber Co.)

assembly, and power plant (engine). See Fig. 13-10.

The *fuselage* is the body of an airplane. It supports all other parts. The fuselage's size varies according to the type of plane. In bigger planes, the fuselage also holds the passengers and cargo. Also included in the fuselage is the *cockpit*. It includes space for the plane's instruments and controls. The pilot and the co-pilot operate the plane from the cockpit.

The wings of an aircraft are attached to the fuselage. They provide the lift necessary to keep the aircraft airborne. The pilot has control over the plane's movement through use of flaps and spoilers which are movable parts of the wings and tail section. Both are used to help control the plane's ascent or descent. The *tail assembly* is connected to the back of the fuselage. It is made of a vertical stabilizer or fin and a horizontal stabilizer, Fig. 13-11. A movable part of the fin is called the rudder. It assists the plane in making turns. Movable sections on the horizontal stabilizer help control up and down movement of the plane. The tail is needed to keep the plane stable and controllable.

Aircraft propulsion is needed to give the aircraft thrust. Propellers and engines provide propulsion. Propellers are common on small, piston engine planes. When propellers are driven by a jet engine, they become a turboprop propulsion system. A turboprop develops much more thrust at take-off which enables the engines to lift heavily loaded carriers.

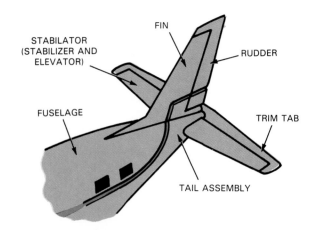

Fig. 13-11. The tail assembly of an airplane keeps the craft stable in the air and more controllable.

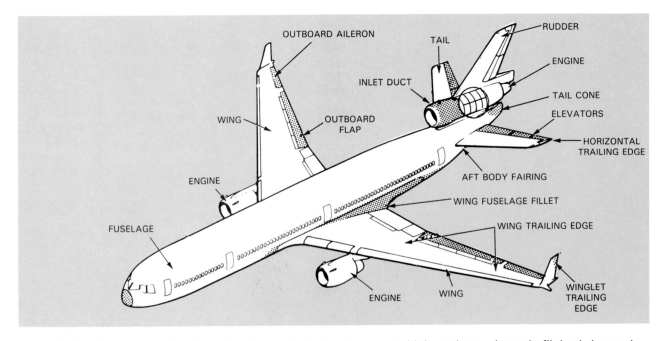

Fig. 13-10. Main parts of a plane. Not shown is the landing gear which, on large planes in flight, is housed in the underside of the fuselage. (McDonnell-Douglas)

The jet engine draws in air through an intake. Once the air is drawn in, a compressor compresses it to a high pressure. Then, fuel is added to the compressed air and ignited. Burning the fuel produces a hot gas flowing at high speed. It flows through and drives a turbine with part of its pressure. The turbine drives the compressor. The rest of the energy in the expanding gases provides thrust as it escapes at high speed through the engine's exhaust nozzle, Fig. 13-12

The flight of an aircraft is made possible by the engine and wings. Because planes are heavier than air, they must rely on their engines to provide the power and on their wings to give them a lift. Without both the engine and the wings working together, the plane would not stay in the air.

Four forces affect the flying of a plane. They are *lift, weight, thrust,* and *drag.* Flight depends on these forces being balanced, Fig. 13-13. Wings have a special shape called an *airfoil*. This airfoil supports the airplane in flight by reacting with the airflow. Due to the shape of the wing, the air over the top of the wing is moving faster than the air on the underside of the wing. As a result, there is less air pressure on the top of the wing. Thus the higher pressure below the wing creates an upward force we call lift, Fig. 13-14.

Planes are constructed using a smooth-surfaced material and are shaped in a way that reduces drag. Drag is the resistance of the air to the plane flying through it. The weight of the plane must be balanced out by the lift, drag, and thrust. The weight of the plane varies according to the type of plane. The weight includes not only the weight of the plane itself, but the fuel, the cargo and the passengers. The plane is moved forward through the air by thrust. Thrust is produced by propulsion. A plane is propelled by a propeller or by heated gases at high speed escaping from the exhaust. This provides the thrust or forward motion.

Aircraft are also used for aerial views and for photography. Crop dusting also employs an airplane. Still another use of airplanes is to help advertise businesses through flying a banner.

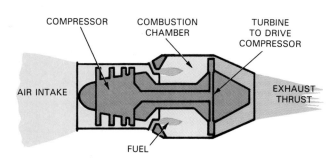

Fig. 13-12. The propulsion unit (engine) of a modern airplane. A jet engine depends on the exhaust thrust to move the craft through the air.

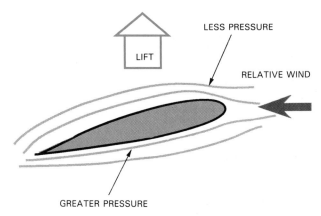

Fig. 13-I4. An airplane wing is an airfoil designed to provide lift to counteract gravity when there is sufficient airspeed.

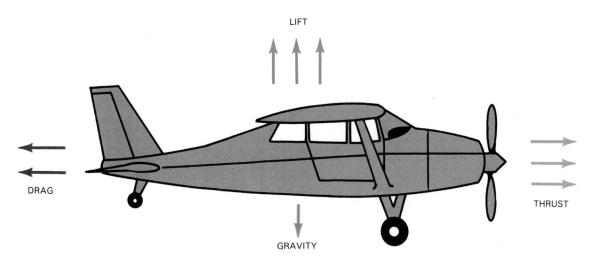

Fig. 13-13. For an airplane to fly lift and thrust must be great enough to overcome gravity and drag.

Helicopters

Helicopters are used to transport people and cargo to places that are hard to reach by other transportation vehicles, Fig. 13-15. Helicopters are used to rescue people. News reports are often gathered by way of helicopter. Farmers often sow seed, such as wheat or rye, from a helicopter. A unique quality of the helicopter is that it can take off and land in vertical flight. In other words, it takes off and lands in a straight up or down flight pattern, Fig. 13-16. Helicopters can hover (stay in one place) in the air. They can also change direction of flight very quickly.

Helicopters fly a little differently than an airplane. A helicopter has rotating wings to make it fly, whereas, a plane has stationary wings. The rotating wings, also known as *rotor blades*, provide lift in the same way that a wing does on a plane. The helicopter has become a popular means of air transportation for short trips.

Fig. 13-15. Because it requires no runway and can hover in the air, the helicopter is useful for performing tasks impossible for other transportation means. (Bell Helicopter Textron)

Fig. 13-16. Helicopters are able to land and take off without a runway as they can move vertically at will. (Bell Helicopter Textron)

Recreational

Some types of air transportation vehicles are used only for recreation or for sport. Hang gliding is done mainly for recreation. Para-planing, parachuting, and ballooning are done for either sport or recreation, Fig. 13-17.

GENERAL, COMMERCIAL, AND MILITARY AVIATION

Aviation describes all air transportation activities that are performed. There are three categories of aviation:
- General aviation.
- Commercial aviation.
- Military aviation.

General Aviation

General aviation consists of privately owned planes that are used for a wide variety of tasks. General aviation usually includes the use of smaller aircraft as opposed to commercial aviation using very large aircraft. General aviation is used to transport fewer people over short distances. Some services that general aviation offers is to the farmer, the community, the business person, and the individual. To the farmer, general aviation performs such tasks as planting, spraying, and fertilizing crops. See Fig. 13-18. To the individual, general

Fig. 13-17. Hang gliding is a type of air transport done for recreation.

Fig. 13-18. General aviation aircraft are smaller and can be used for recreation, business flying, and for agricultural tasks such as crop dusting.

aviation provides a form of recreation and personal transportation. For businesses, general aviation offers fast and efficient transportation and communication. To the community, general aviation offers mail services, fire fighting, aerial mapping, and photography.

The aircraft used in general aviation have a wide range of size. Some are small single engine craft and some are small jet engine luxury craft. The most common craft flown in general aviation is the single-engine aircraft. Many individuals own their own planes. These airplanes can take off and land on small runways at small airports.

Commercial Aviation

When air transportation is mentioned, you probably envision commercial aviation. Any scheduled airline flights are examples of commercial aviation. Such commercial airlines receive money for the travel service that they offer, Fig. 13-19.

Commercial airlines offer four types of services.

They are commuter airline service, international airline service, domestic airline service, and regional airline service. *Commuter service* transports people from several small airports to a major airport in a major city. *Regional airline service* involves the transport from small airports to major airports within a specific region. *International airline service* is simply a service that provides travel between countries. *Domestic airline service* is the transport by way of air to and from major airports within a country. Airports handle all of these services for people. The three busiest airports in the United States are O'Hare International in Chicago, Los Angeles International, and Hartsfield International in Atlanta.

Commercial aviation offers scheduled services all around the world. Travel from place to place by air is often expensive; however, when great distances are involved, it is the fastest and safest way to travel.

Military Aviation

Military aviation consists of air activity performed by the military. The maneuvering of military aircraft is used to perform military operations, Fig. 13-20.

SUPPORT SYSTEMS OF AIR TRANSPORTATION

As with any other transportation system, air transportation also has support systems to assure accurate, safe, and efficient operation. Air transportation has several support vehicles and facilities. Ground support vehicles are needed to service the aircraft. For example, a baggage truck is needed to load all the luggage onto the aircraft, Fig. 13-21. Tank trucks carry jet fuel to the plane.

Fig. 13-19. A commercial airliner carries hundreds of air travelers across the skies to various distant destinations. (United Airlines)

Fig. 13-20. Military aviation requires special types of aircraft. (Grumman Corp.)

Fig. 13-22. Without an airport, air transportation would be neither efficient nor effective. (United Airlines)

Fig. 13-21. Baggage trucks are needed to transport cargo to and from the aircraft. (United Airlines)

Fig. 13-23. Maintenance on an aircraft is done in a hangar.

How does the food get on a plane that is served to the passengers? A food service truck brings the food to the craft and unloads. A sanitary truck is needed to empty the waste water from the storage tanks on the plane.

The airport includes passenger terminals, gates for loading and unloading, runways, taxiways, and control towers, Fig. 13-22. Hangars are also support buildings and garages for the airplane. This is where they are serviced, Fig. 13-23. For more detail see Chapter 22.

SUMMARY

Many attempts to fly have been made by humans throughout the centuries. The development of air transportation has progressed rapidly since the early 1900s. The Wright brothers have been recognized throughout history for their accomplishments in airplane design. They were the first to achieve powered flight. Their first recorded flight time was 12 seconds.

The pace of development for air transportation has been accelerating since 1906. Inventors all over the world contributed their ideas to new designs. In one year, flight distance grew from 200 ft. to 62 miles. By 1914 flying had moved beyond being a novelty as the military adopted the airplane.

The airways are the routes in which airplanes travel. They are the highways of the skies. Airways are set up in layers. These air layers are designed to keep the skies safe from accidents.

There are two different modes of air transportation. They are heavier-than-air and lighter-than-air. Lighter-than-air includes balloons and dirigibles and blimps. Heavier-than-air include gliders, airplanes, and helicopters.

Commercial and general aviation are two types of services offered by the airlines. Privately owned aircraft are known as general aviation. Commercial aviation consists of those scheduled airline businesses that make a profit on their services.

KEY WORDS

All of the following words have been used in this chapter. Do you know their meaning?

Air foil	Glider
Aircraft	International airline
Airways	service
Blimps	Lift
Cockpit	Military aviation
Commuter service	Regional airline service
Dirigibles	Rotor blades
Domestic airline service	Tail assembly
Drag	Thrust
Fuselage	Weight

TEST YOUR KNOWLEDGE

Write your answers on a separate sheet of paper. Do not write in this book.

Short answer:
1. Define aircraft.
2. Define lift.

Fill in the blank:
3. The main reason for airways (routes) is for _____.

4. The word dirigible means _____ in French.

True or False:
5. A hot-air balloon is a heavier-than-air vehicle. True or False?
6. The flight of an aircraft is made possible by the engine and wings. True or False?

Multiple choice:
7. A commercial aviation service that transports to and from major airports within a country is:
   A. Domestic airline service.
   B. Commuter service.
   C. Regional airline service.

ACTIVITIES

1. Construct a model of a heavier-than-air aircraft.
2. If a wind tunnel is available, test the aircraft in the wind tunnel.
3. Construct a model of a hot air balloon and test it.

The space age was launched in 1926 when the first liquid-fueled rocket was fired by Goddard. Who could have predicted that humans would walk on the moon 43 years later? (NASA)

Chapter 14
SPACE TRANSPORTATION SYSTEMS

After studying this chapter, you will be able to:
☐ Define spacecraft.
☐ Describe the space environment.
☐ Identify the two types of space transportation modes.
☐ Identify the different space vehicles.
☐ Discuss what makes a spacecraft fly.
☐ Describe orbiting.

SPACE TRANSPORTATION

Space transportation is the use of rockets and orbiting vehicles to explore the regions beyond the limits of the atmosphere. The space beyond the atmosphere extending from 50 miles to 10,000 miles is known as near space. Beyond 10,000 miles is outer space.

HISTORY OF SPACE TRANSPORTATION

The space transportation age has been a time of dreams coming true. The dream of manned space flight is as old as astronomy itself. The pioneering of space travel came around the turn of the 20th century. Three men, living in different countries, came up with the same conclusions to space travel around the same time. They concluded that a multistage liquid fuel rocket would be the most effective means of escaping the earth's gravitational pull.

These men were a Russian teacher, Konstantin E. Tsiolkovsky, an American professor, Robert H. Goddard, and a German experimentalist, Herman Oberth. Tsiolkovsky had the practical possibilities in mind and a theory of how things would work. In 1926, Goddard launched the world's first liquid-fuel rocket, Fig. 14-1. He also demonstrated how

Fig. 14-1. Dr. Robert H. Goddard was a pioneer of American rocketry. He is shown with his first liquid fuel rocket which he launched at Auburn, Massachusetts, March 16, 1926. (NASA)

rockets could carry scientific instruments into the upper atmosphere. Goddard paved the way for manned and unmanned space vehicles. After World War 1, Oberth was at work in Germany on the development and testing of rockets. The discoveries of these three men became the basis for all later space transportation developments. The first successful space flight came in 1957.

October 4, 1957, was not just another day but the beginning of a new age, a new dimension in transportation and exploration. The bulletins were flashed around the world carried by radio, newspapers, and television. The Soviet Union had just launched and placed in orbit around the earth the first successful artificial satellite, Fig. 14-2. The satellite was called Sputnik 1, Fig. 14-3. The word Sputnik means "the simplest."

This event came as a surprise to many nations including the United States. Reacting to a deep concern that Russia was taking the lead in the exploration of space, the U.S. federal government mobilized a "crash" program in rocket development. The race into space had begun!

The United States' response was to put their first satellite, Explorer 1, into orbit. The year was 1958. For several years a contest was waged with the U.S. and the Soviet Union vying with each other in putting new satellites into earth orbit.

Then, on April 12, 1961, the Soviet Union amazed the world by announcing that it had just put a man into earth orbit. At this time, the United

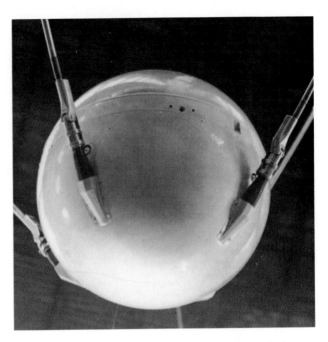

Fig. 14-3. This full-scale mock-up of Sputnik 1 was placed on display in the Soviet pavilion at the Paris air show.

States, feeling very much in second place because of the Soviets accomplishments, set a much more difficult goal: placing a human being on the moon! John F. Kennedy, then president of the United States, placed a high priority on the project and set it in motion. After some eight years of intensive planning and work, the United States launched the first manned flight to the moon. The success of the space flight depended on the advanced technology employed to effect a lunar landing and then return the space travelers safely to earth, Fig. 14-4.

In the early 1960s, the United States considered other space developments. America had resolved to equal or surpass the Soviets accomplishments. This same attitude was encouraged by President Kennedy and a program of space activity and experiments was carried forward.

Then, as is true today, the primary organization in charge of the United States space program was the National Aeronautics and Space Administration (NASA). The main goal of NASA was to expand space technology. Another task given NASA was to take this knowledge and expand it into beneficial and practical uses for our society as a whole.

Some of the major programs set up were the Mercury, Gemini, and Apollo projects. All of these projects consisted of a one or two manned flights into space. A space-based workshop program was one of the most important projects developed by NASA.

Fig. 14-2. Russia amazed the world when it launched the first satellite and placed it in orbit around the earth.

Fig. 14-4. Photograph shows historic moon landing in 1969. Astronaut, David Scott, commander of the mission stands beside the U.S. flag at the landing site. Lunar module, Falcon, is at the right.   (NASA)

Skylab

On May 14, 1973, this space workshop or laboratory was launched into orbit. It was known as *Skylab*, Fig. 14-5. Skylab was used to support scientific experiments and studies. Throughout the six years that Skylab was orbiting the earth, three different manned crews were launched to work in its laboratories performing experiments. The final launch was the longest mission, lasting 84 days. This mission was a great success.

During this time many studies were made leading to important discoveries. Over the six years, this pioneer space station had compiled some very important and impressive statistics and records.

Eventually, Skylab drifted down into a denser part of the atmosphere. Here, heat and friction caused it to break up and fall to earth.

Fig. 14-5. This photograph of Skylab was taken from the command/service module during the final "fly-around" inspection.   (NASA)

Skylab was a great contribution to our understanding of the space environment. It set the pace for the future programs in space.

THE SPACE ENVIRONMENT

The atmosphere of the earth has several characteristics that are important to space travel. First, let us take a look at the different regions of the earth's atmosphere, Fig. 14-6. The different regions include the troposphere, stratosphere, mesosphere, thermosphere, and exosphere.

Atmospheric Regions

The *troposphere* is about six miles from the earth's surface. Most clouds appear in this region. The temperature is approximately -70°F. The farther a region is from the earth, the lower the atmospheric pressure.

The next region, the *stratosphere,* ranges from 7 to 22 miles above the earth's surface. In this region, there is an absence of water vapor and clouds. About 50 miles above the earth's surface is a region known as the *mesosphere.* This region contains an ozone layer that helps absorb ultra-violet radiation from the sun. This ozone layer shields the earth from much of this ultraviolet radiation.

The next region is a layer that extends from about 50 miles to about 300 miles out. This layer is known as the *thermosphere*. In this region, the atmosphere is so thin that no sound is transmitted. It has, however, intense electrical activity. Many satellites orbit the earth in this region.

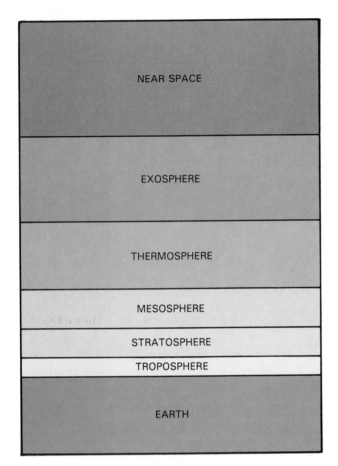

Fig. 14-6. There are six different layers in the space environment surrounding the earth. The closest, the troposphere, is six miles from earth's surface. The farthest, the exosphere, is 500 miles from earth.

At about 75 miles from the earth, radio communication waves bounce back to the earth. Very little friction takes place in this layer. That's why it is good to orbit satellites at this particular level of the atmosphere.

The extreme outer region of the atmosphere, before getting to outer space, is a region known as the *exosphere*. This region is located about 500 miles to 1000 miles from the surface of the earth. Beyond this limit is outer space.

No one is exactly sure how far away *outer space* is. Some estimates place it about 10,000 miles above the earth's surface.

Space Environment and Design

Space environment characteristics affect the design and development of a spacecraft. Among the most important characteristics are the extremes of temperature and radiation levels. These have a direct affect on the material used in the construction of space vehicles. Radiation is a vital factor in the design and development of space vehicles.

Besides the affect it would have on the craft itself, there is also a concern for the health of personnel on manned space flights. Radiation can seriously affect health if precautions are not taken.

Vacuum must also be considered in the design of a space vehicle. Where there is a vacuum, there is no sound.

Another very important characteristic of space is weightlessness. *Weightlessness* occurs due to the forces around bodies in space. Both a pull and push effect takes place. Gravitational forces pull the body toward the earth and a centrifugal force pulls the body away. When gravitational forces are equal to a centrifugal force, weightlessness occurs. When you are jumping up and away from a diving board, you experience weightlessness as you reach the height of your jump, Fig. 14-7.

Weightlessness has always appeared to be fun as we see films of the astronauts in space or read about their experiences. Fun it could be for a time. It can also become frustrating as astronauts go about their daily routines. For instance, drinking liquid and taking a shower are problems.

Fig. 14-7. Divers experience weightlessness at the point where their bodies lose upward momentum a fraction of a second before they begin to fall.

WHAT MAKES A SPACECRAFT FLY

Many inputs are needed in the launching of a spacecraft. Tools, energy, materials, money, and people are all needed to begin the process. However, once the spacecraft is on the launching pad, *thrust* produces lift-off. Thrust is a force that produces motion in a body. Thrust is measured in pounds or newtons. Have you ever blown up a balloon and pinched the end so the air won't leak out? When you let go of the balloon what happened? The balloon moves upward or away because of the pressure being released from within the balloon. That is how thrust works. The pressure inside a rocket engine is created by the burning of fuel. As the fuel burns, the pressure increases, causing a great pressure buildup within the engine. The exhaust of the engine allows for the release of pressure so that there is higher pressure at the front of the rocket engine than at the tail. When the pressure within a rocket engine is unequal, the rocket will move in the direction of the higher pressure. If the rocket is aimed skyward, an upward motion is the reaction to such a force, Fig. 14-8. Once this upward force ceases, gravitational forces will cause it to fall back to earth. Therefore, the spacecraft needs to achieve a very high speed so it can escape the earth's gravitational pull. At this time, the gravitational forces and the centrifugal forces are equal. As a result, the spacecraft will stay in orbit.

What Is Orbiting?

To *orbit* is simply to stay in a path that circles the earth. If the spacecraft were to increase its speed while in orbit, a greater centrifugal force would result and the spacecraft could possibly be slung out of orbit into space. If it loses speed, then the centrifugal force would decrease and the spacecraft would achieve a lower orbit or re-entry into the earth's atmosphere. The concept of orbiting is like swinging a ball on a string. You can demonstrate this by taking a small ball tied to a string about 3 ft. long and, while holding the end of the string in your hand, begin to whirl the ball around. As you whirl the ball around slowly, with the string extended to its full length, you can understand what a satellite in orbit experiences. You have two forces acting, a centrifugal force (circular motion) and the gravitational pull. If you decreased the speed of the ball moving in its circular path, it would fall out of its orbit (the path in which it was travelling). If you increased the speed of the ball's orbit, the centrifugal force would be greater and you would probably lose control of the ball on the string. Thus, it would fly away from you at a rapid speed. Like a satellite, it would fly out of orbit if travelling at too great a speed. Can you see how satellites travelling at too high a speed will spin away out of orbit and into outer space?

When any space vehicle is in orbit around the earth, it follows an elliptical path, Fig. 14-9. The highest point of the path is the farthest away from earth. This point is called the *apogee*. The point that is the closest to the earth is called the *perigee*.

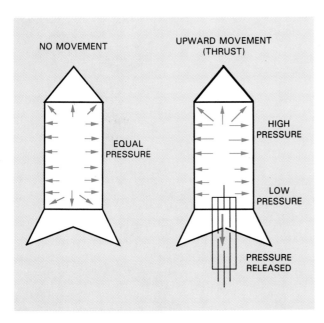

Fig. 14-8. The unequal pressure inside a rocket engine propels it forward.

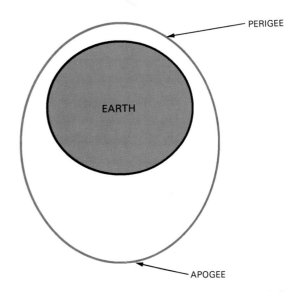

Fig. 14-9. Most satellites and space craft follow elliptical orbits. The apogee is the point farthest from the earth. The perigee is the point closest to earth.

UNMANNED AND MANNED VEHICLES

Two modes of space transportation are manned vehicles and unmanned vehicles. A space vehicle is called a *spacecraft*. The spacecraft is that part of the space vehicle that actually travels into space. The launch vehicle which is made up of a rocket engine is separated from the craft when it leaves the earth's atmosphere. Spacecraft include sounding rockets, satellites, space probes, and space shuttles. Spacecraft differ greatly in size, shape, and purpose. Another manned transporting unit is a jet pack. A jet pack is strapped to the back of the astronaut. Some spacecraft are actually operated by a human being and some are not. Therefore, some are manned and some are unmanned.

Unmanned Vehicles

Unmanned vehicles include satellites, space probes, and sounding rockets. These unmanned space vehicles have been used for space exploration. The following paragraphs will briefly introduce you to the different unmanned spacecraft.

Satellites

Satellites are of many designs and purposes. Satellites may weigh from 100 lb. to thousands of pounds. A satellite is launched into orbit and it usually has a specific task it is to accomplish. There are communication satellites that bounce telephone, television, and radio waves from one transmitter on earth to another. For instance, because of satellites, a live report from Seoul, Korea, can be seen and heard in Indianapolis, Indiana, Fig. 14-10. Weather satellites are also launched into space to monitor the weather conditions. The monitoring is done by using a television camera. This satellite helps to forecast the weather conditions around the world. Satellites are also used for scientific research. A research satellite may be launched to take pictures of the moon, other planets, or landing sites for astronauts, Fig. 14-11. Satellites are also used for military and navigational purposes.

Space probes

Space probes are launched very high above the earth where they can escape the earth's gravitational attraction. Space probes are used for research purposes. They are sent to explore outer space. Probes are equipped with photographic instruments and radio transmitters. NASA has launched various types of space probes.

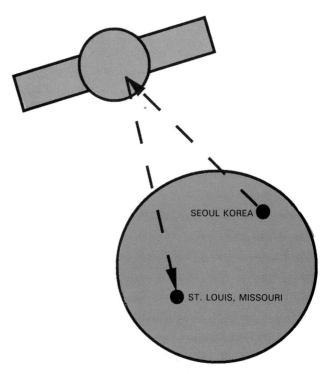

Fig. 14-10. Because of satellites we can have instant communication around the world. A signal from St. Louis, bounced off the satellite, can be picked up almost instantaneously in Seoul, South Korea.

Fig. 14-11. This is a model of a satellite meant to be inhabited. Two center modules are habitable. Two solar panels are designed to supply electrical power. (NASA)

This equipment sends results back to earth where scientists can research this data more in depth. Space probes help us to understand what's out there in the space beyond our atmosphere.

Space probes are classified as three types: lunar, planetary, and deep space.

Lunar probes had been sent to the moon several times to see what the landing surface of the moon was like. Until this time, no one knew if the moon had soft, spongy surface, a dusty surface, or a hard rocklike surface. Information was gathered and sent back to earth. After studying this data, scientists concluded that the moon had a hard landing surface.

Planetary probes are sent to other planets in the solar system. Once there they collect data for study of the planets, comets, and asteroids of the solar system.

Deep space probes explore the outer planets. They are long-distance probes sent on fly-by missions past Jupiter, Mars, and Saturn. Exploration of the outer planets by probes also includes examination of the asteroids and comets.

Sounding rockets

Sounding rockets gather information about the sun and stars. They use electronic devices to retrieve information. Sounding rockets can measure temperatures, take photographs, and record important data. Information about the sun's radiation and solar activity is also gathered by a sounding rocket. A sounding rocket has collected some very valuable information about space that has aided scientists in new discoveries.

Manned Space Vehicles

Manned vehicles are those vehicles sent to space with a crew in them. In the late 1950s and early 1960s, several manned spacecraft flights were tested. A space project known as Project Mercury tested several manned space flights. Until 1963, none of the previous flights made it to orbit. They were tested to give humans a feel for space and for operating and controlling a spacecraft. In May of 1963, the first successful manned flight was put into orbit, bringing Project Mercury to an end. It had accomplished its goals of orbiting the earth, giving humans a chance to test their ability to function in space, and returning both man and spacecraft safely to earth. Project Gemini was the second of the projects for manned flights. Project Gemini's main purpose was to continue exploration of space and resolve some other technological problems before attempting to land anyone on the moon. On July 20, 1969, after centuries of dreaming of setting foot on the moon, a dream came true. Three Americans, Neil Armstrong, Michael Collins, and Edwin Aldrin were aboard Apollo 11 as it landed on the lunar surface. They spent 21.6 hours on the moon before returning safely to earth, Fig. 14-12.

Space shuttle

In 1981, the first reusable space transportation vehicle was put in use. This vehicle is known as the space shuttle. The space shuttle was developed primarily to be a reliable and reusable means of space transportation. At present, the main purpose is that of transporting data-gathering equipment into space. However, in flights to come, the space shuttle may be used to transport materials to construct buildings, to transport products, and to carry people to and from earth.

A

B

Fig. 14-12. The manned spacecraft, Apollo 11, landed on the moon in July, 1969. A—The crew, left to right, Neil Armstrong, commander; Michael Collins, command module pilot; and Erwin Aldrin, Jr., lunar module pilow. B—Aldrin descends the steps of the lunar module ladder in preparation for a walk on the moon. (NASA)

A space shuttle is made up of two booster rockets, an external fuel tank, and an orbiter, Fig. 14-13. At lift-off, the rocket engines ignite at the same time. Two minutes after lift-off the rockets separate from the space shuttle. A parachute opens and the rockets slowly drop into the ocean where tugboats collect them. Eight minutes into flight and just prior to entering orbit, the shuttle's external fuel tank separates. As it re-enters the earth's atmosphere, it burns up. One hour after the initial countdown, the orbiter achieves orbit, Fig. 14-14.

It's now time for the astronauts to begin their studies and experiments in space. The shuttle can remain in orbit for about 30 days before re-entering the atmosphere. During re-entry, intense heat of 2500°F envelopes the front and bottom of the shuttle. Very thick tiles are attached to protect the space shuttle from such intense heat. Once it is back in the atmosphere, the space shuttle acts like a big glider. It glides through the atmosphere without power. It lands on a runway just like a jet. A space shuttle acts like a rocket during lift-off, like a spacecraft during orbiting, and like an airplane during landing.

In the 1980s, the shuttle Challenger made several flights. In 1985, there were nine successful flights in the shuttle. The tragedy came the following year when the Challenger burst into flames just seconds after lift-off. A nation looked on in horror as this tragic accident killed all seven crew members, Fig.

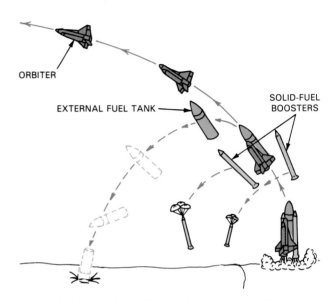

Fig. 14-14. A launch of the shuttle. Solid fuel booster tanks are parachuted to a water landing. The external fuel tank burns upon re-entry into earth's atmosphere.

14-15. The following year, 1987, America sent no astronaut into space. The program was grounded while NASA examined, researched, and retested space shuttle transportation. The shuttle has provided many opportunities and benefits to scientists, engineers, and researchers in the discoveries of the future of space.

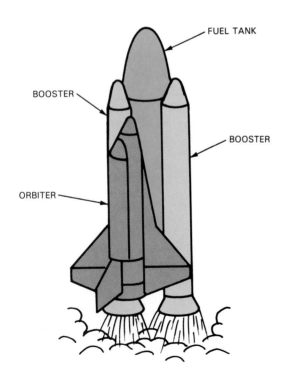

Fig. 14-13. The space shuttle consists of two booster rockets, an external fuel tank, and an orbiter.

Fig. 14-15. Actual launching of the space shuttle Challenger on January 28, 1986. An accident 73 seconds after lift off claimed both vehicle and crew. (NASA)

Manned maneuvering unit

In the early 1980s, two astronauts strapped back packs on their backs. This device was known as a *jet pack*. A jet pack or a Manned Maneuvering Unit (MMU) allows for mobility of an astronaut outside the space shuttle without a tether line, Fig. 14-16. The astronauts are able to move around in the MMU by releasing bursts of compressed nitrogen gas which is shot through tiny thrusters. This has become the first human spaceship.

SUPPORT SYSTEMS OF SPACE TRANSPORTATION

Like all transportation systems, space transportation also has some support systems. Some examples of space transportation support systems are the control centers. Control centers control the missions and the launches. The mission control center is located at the Johnson Space Center. The launch control center is at the Kennedy Space Center in Florida. The Centers themselves support certain functions of space transportation. Computerized operation of the space vehicle is supported by the Centers, Fig. 14-17. Another support system is the *launching pad* and vehicle, Fig. 14-18. Launch vehicles are rocket engines that provide the power

Fig. 14-16. A jet pack or a Manned Maneuvering Unit allows an astronaut to move around outside the space shuttle without a tether line.

Fig. 14-17. An aerial view of the Johnson Space Center at Houston, Texas. Computers here support the control of space flights. (NASA)

Fig. 14-18. Kennedy Space Center, Florida, is the launch site for the U.S. space program.   (NASA)

lift off for the space vehicle. Without the launch vehicle, the space transportation system could not function. In fact, it could not get off the ground!

SUMMARY

Space transportation has been a time when humans' dreams came true. For centuries humans have dreamed of a manned flight to the moon. This dream moved a step closer to reality in 1957 when Russia launched its first successful satellite into orbit. They named it Sputnik. That day in October added a new dimension to space transportation and exploration.

Galvanized into action, the United States soon had a space program underway to research and develop space technology. The program then as now was controlled by NASA. The U.S. successfully placed its first satellite in orbit in 1958 and 11 years later placed a manned spaceship on the moon. In 1973, NASA launched Skylab, a workshop in space. It remained in orbit for six years.

The two types of space transportation modes are manned and unmanned vehicles. Unmanned space vehicles are satellites, space probes, and sounding rockets. Manned vehicles are space shuttles and jet packs. Both modes of space transportation are used to research, experiment, and explore space. They represent the future of our travel into space.

KEY WORDS

All of the following words have been used in this chapter. Do you know their meaning?

Apogee	Perigee
Exosphere	Skylab
Jet pack	Spacecraft
Launching pad	Stratosphere
Manned vehicles	Thermosphere
Mesosphere	Thrust
Orbit	Troposphere
Outer space	Unmanned vehicles
	Weightlessness

TEST YOUR KNOWLEDGE

Write your answers on a separate sheet of paper. Do not write in this book.

Short answer:
1. What was the name of the first successful satellite to orbit the earth?
2. When is a spacecraft said to be in orbit?
3. What is the main purpose for a space probe?

Multiple choice:
4. A workshop in space is known as _____.
   A. Sky shop.
   B. Skylab
   C. Space shop.

True or False:

5. The farthest point away from the earth in the elliptical path of orbit is known as a perigee. True or False?

Matching:

6. __ Troposphere.
7. __ Stratosphere.
8. __ Mesosphere.
9. __ Thermosphere.
10. __ Exosphere.
11. __ Outer space.

A. A region that contains an ozone layer.
B. Six miles from the earth's surface.
C. An absence of water vapor and clouds.
D. A region beyond the atmosphere.
E. No sound is transmitted.
F. Outer region of the atmosphere before outer space.

ACTIVITIES

1. Design and construct your own version of "Skylab." Check with your resource center for books and other materials on its design.
2. If your class has access to a model rocket kit, construct and launch a rocket with your instructor's assistance. This can be a class project or a team project. Prepare a report on what you did and what you observed.
3. Construct a model of a satellite and display it.

Fig. 15-1. Intermodal transportation is the use of several different methods of transport to move people or cargo to a new location.

Chapter 15
INTERMODAL TRANSPORTATION SYSTEMS

After studying this chapter, you will be able to:
☐ Define intermodal transportation.
☐ Describe passenger and cargo intermodal transportation.
☐ Identify and discuss the advantages of intermodal transportation.
☐ Describe the importance of containerization.
☐ Understand the importance of intermodal transportation in our society.

In an earlier chapter, modes of transportation were discussed. As you learned, a mode of transportation is simply the method. Land, air, water, and space transport are all modes or different systems for moving cargo or people to a new location. Now we are going to discuss transportation in which we use several modes of transport to relocate the same cargo or the same people. The term for this is *intermodal transportation.* The term,"inter" comes from the Latin language and means "between." Thus, intermodal means between several modes or involving more than one mode.

INTERMODAL TRANSPORTATION

Over the past few decades, intermodal transportation has become very common and more efficient in transporting people and goods. Today, railroad companies may also own and operate trucklines and shipping services. Airline companies may not only own the airline but also cars rentals, shipping, and trucklines. Likewise, shipping companies may also own trucking lines and railroads. See how all transportation systems have intermixed with other modes of transportation? Years ago, an airline, for instance, owned no other mode of transportation but its own. Since different transportation companies have become more dependent on each other, our transportation systems have been more economical and better coordinated (made to work together more smoothly).

Intermodal transportation, as we have just said, uses more than one mode of transportation in the process of transporting either passengers or cargo, Fig. 15-1. Intermodal systems involve less material handling which also results in less damage and loss of goods. Intermodal transportation has also cut down on shipping time and costs.

Intermodal transportation takes time to plan and organize. This type of transportation system depends on each mode working to a timetable. Service can easily break down if all modes do not stay on schedule. If one mode doesn't pick up where the other one ends, the process is slowed down. There are delays and confusion. Both timing and planning are vital to intermodal transportation.

Since the intermodal transportation system has grown, special shipping containers and transport vehicles have been developed.

Intermodal transportation can be broken into two categories: *intermodal cargo transportation* and *intermodal passenger transportation.* Both of these will be discussed in the following paragraphs.

Intermodal Cargo Transportation

Transporting cargo from one point to another may be done by using several different modes of transportation. For example, the shipping of grain from the United States to Russia may go something like this:

- The grain is first harvested by the farmer and brought out of the fields in trucks or wagons, Fig. 15-2.
- The farmer then sells it and hauls it to a grain elevator.
- The grain is then loaded into railroad cars or semi-trucks and transported to a port.
- Here the grain is loaded onto a ship that carries it across the ocean.
- Once it arrives in Russia, it must then be unloaded and distributed by way of land vehicles to various places of use.

There are a few different ways in which to ship cargo by intermodal transport. They are mentioned in the following paragraphs.

Containerized shipping

Containerization is a method of handling goods by packing many smaller packages in a large container. This eliminates handling of many small packages going to a common destination. Another advantage is that less handling of individual packages cuts down on accidentally-damaged goods and theft. This method of packing is making intermodal transportation more efficient. At the same time, transport of cargo is easier when using different modes of transportation.

Fig. 15-2. The first intermodal transport step following the harvest of this shelled corn is to haul it by truck to a grain elevator. It might travel by train, barge, and ship before it reaches its final destination.

Remember, containerized shipping is an efficient method of transporting goods. It is not a form of intermodal transportation.

Most shipping containers are very convenient and versatile. They can be moved and carried in many different ways. The containers can be hoisted onto railroad cars. They can be put on wheels and pulled by trucks or semi-tractors. Large shipping containers can also be swiftly loaded onto ships with the aid of cranes. After transport across the ocean, other cranes remove the containers from the ship, Fig.15-3. The same crane will move them to storage or to other modes of transportation. Moved to a central distributing point, they are opened and contents sent on to their final destination.

The container is a large metal box. A standard size is eight feet wide, eight feet high, and forty feet long. This standard container is used by highway, rail, and water transporting vehicles. A smaller container is used in air transportation.

When using a highway mode, the container is lifted onto a frame that has eight wheels, Fig. 15-4.

Fig. 15-3. Containerized shipping. Large metal containers, filled with goods, are loaded onto flat rail cars to be transported. (CSX Creative Services)

Fig. 15-4. Often, containers are loaded onto a trailer frame and hauled away by a tractor. (CSX Creative Services)

It can now be pulled by a truck tractor or the semi-trailer can be lifted onto a rail car and carried piggy-back. *Piggyback* is the carrying of truck trailers on railroad flatcars.

Carrying the containers can also be done by railroad flatcars. The containers can be lifted directly onto the flatcar and transported to their destination by way of rails, Fig. 15-5. Once they arrive at their destination, the trailer is ready to be hooked up to a truck and transported across the land. This method of transporting a container on a railroad flatcar is referred to as *COFC*. It means *Container On Flat Car*.

Transporting the containers across the ocean on barges and ships is done quite often. The ships are designed to carry these standard containers. The ships are referred to as *containerships.*

Transporting of containers by air is another way to ship goods. The containers used in aircraft are lighter and smaller than the standard. The containers are custom made to fit different models of aircraft. Special equipment loads the containers into the cargo hatch.

The biggest advantage of containerization is the reduction of material handling time. By using a container on different modes of transporting vehicles, a great amount of labor and money can be saved. Containerization has become a popular method of transporting cargo in the intermodal system.

Trailer on flat car

TOFC (Trailer on Flat Car) is another method of intermodal transportation. TOFCs are trailers full of cargo carried on a rail flatcar, Fig. 15-6.

Moving cargo from one point to another using TOFC is very interesting. A trucking company may send tractors to pick up semi-trailers loaded with cargo. The tractors take them to a railroad yard. At this point, the trailers are detached from the tractor and loaded onto a flat car. The flat cars are then hooked together in a train. A locomotive hauls the railroad cars to another railroad yard. This railroad yard is close to the final destination of the cargo. The trailers are unloaded and hooked to a tractor and then travel over the highways to their customers.

Fig. 15-6. Once the containers in Fig. 15-5 reach their destination they are unloaded and once more placed on trailer frames so they can be pulled down the highway by a tractor.

Fig. 15-5. Rail transport. These containers have been loaded onto flat cars to be transported part way to their final destination.   (Norfolk Southern Corp.)

Other forms of intermodal cargo transportation

Liquids and mined materials are also transported by using several different methods. Liquids such as oil, milk, inks, and chemicals are transported through pipelines. For instance, oil is transported to the terminal through pipelines and then pumped into a tank truck and hauled to its destination, Fig. 15-7. So it is with milk coming off a dairy farm. The milk is taken from the cow and is transported through the pipelines and then pumped into a tank truck and hauled to a dairy for processing. So the liquids are being transported through pipelines into trucks or rail tank cars and hauled over the highway or railways. This, too, is an example of intermodal transportation.

Mined materials such as coal, ore, and various stones are first transported by way of conveyor out of the ground. Then from the stationary conveyor they are loaded into trucks or hopper railroad cars. The railroad car or truck hauls the materials to their final destination.

The transporting of cargo using the intermodal method is very efficient. It allows for faster delivery of cargo. By using intermodal transportation, there is less material handling which cuts back on theft and damage to the cargo.

Intermodal Passenger Transportation

People like you and I also use intermodal transportation. Often we use it several times a day without realizing it. How do you get to school? If you ride your bike to your friends house and your friend's mother takes you to school in the car, then you've just experienced intermodal transportation. Where would you like to go if you could go anywhere in the world? How would you get to that place? Let's say you have just won a trip to Maui, one of the Hawaiian Islands. You live in Boston, Massachusetts. What modes of transportation would you use to get there? You would probably get to the airport by way of a bus or car. Then you could catch a plane to San Francisco, California, Fig. 15-8. Once you are in California, you have to change planes. So you get on the moving sidewalk that goes through the airport and you board the next plane, Fig. 15-9. You then fly to Honolulu, Hawaii. Once you are there, you take a taxi to board a ferry that will take you to the island of Maui, Fig. 15-10. Do you see all the modes of transportation you used to get to your destination? You have just experienced intermodal passenger transportation. You used a combination of land, air, and water transportation. See the importance of intermodal transportation! Without this system, it would not have been possible to get there.

Fig. 15-8. Airplanes are often part of an intermodal transportation system.   (United Airlines)

Fig. 15-9. A moving sidewalk may be part of an intermodal transportation system.

Fig. 15-7. Some tractor-trailers, called tankers, haul liquids.   (Freightliner Corp.)

Fig. 15-10. A tourist to Maui, Hawaii, may change forms of transportation as often as six times before arriving.

SUMMARY

Intermodal transportation is using a combination of several modes of transportation to get from one place to another. Cargo as well as passengers use intermodal transportation. Intermodal transportation is an efficient system of transportation. Containerization is a very popular method to use which makes intermodal transportation so effective. Using containers is effective because it cuts back on material handling and it also saves on labor costs. Containers can be loaded onto ships, flat railroad cars, and airplanes. Carrying a trailer or a container on wheels on a flat railroad car is referred to as piggyback.

Passengers also use intermodal transportation. To get from one place to another, several modes of transportation are usually used. When traveling, a combination of land, water, and air transportation may be used. This is intermodal transportation.

KEY WORDS

All of the following words have been used in this chapter. Do you know their meaning?
Containerization
COFC (Container On Flat Car)
Containerships
Intermodal cargo transportation
Intermodal passenger transportation
Intermodal transportation
Piggyback
TOFC (Trailer On Flat Car)

TEST YOUR KNOWLEDGE

Please do not write in this text. Place your answers on a separate sheet.
Short answer:
1. Define intermodal transportation.
2. List the two categories of intermodal transportation.
3. What does TOFC stand for?

True or False:
4. Containerization is an efficient method of handling cargo. True or False?
5. Travelers hardly ever use intermodal transportation systems. True or False?

Multiple choice:
6. Carrying truck trailers on the back of railroad cars is known as:
   A. Hauling
   B. Container ship.
   C. Piggyback.
   D. Trailer on flat car.

SUGGESTED ACTIVITIES

1. Design and build a scale model of a transportation system with two modes.
2. Invite a speaker to talk about scheduling of intermodal transportation.
3. As a class project, develop a proposal for an intermodal transportation system to relieve traffic congestion in a major city with a population of 2 million people.

Section V
VEHICULAR SYSTEMS

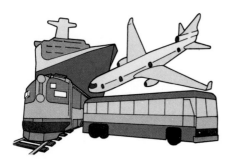

Chapter 16

WHAT IS A VEHICULAR SYSTEM?

After studying this chapter, you will be able to:
☐ List various types of vehicles used in transportation systems.
☐ Identify the six separate systems that make up a vehicular system.
☐ Define each of the six technical components of vehicular systems.
☐ Describe safety factors in the design and operation of vehicular systems.

Vehicles are the "machines" that are the basis of our transportation systems. Everyone recognizes that trains are the vehicles used by the railroad industry to transport passengers and cargo. Airplanes are the vehicles employed to move things by companies involved in the air transportation industry. Ships are used for pleasure cruises, as well as transportation of large quantities of cargo over waterways both large and small. Fig. 16-1, as well as many other photographs in this book, illustrates many types of vehicles.

The *vehicular system* is a collection of separate systems that allow that machine to move through its environment safely and efficiently. These systems are usually part of the vehicle itself, but may be external depending on their purpose. The following is a list of the technical components that make up vehicular systems:
• Propulsion systems.
• Guidance systems.
• Control systems.
• Suspension systems.
• Structural systems.

• Support systems.
These systems will be defined here but explained with further detail in later chapters.

PROPULSION SYSTEMS

Propulsion systems provide a method to use energy for propelling, or moving the vehicle. Energy sources may be converted and transmitted through various methods in propulsion systems. The most familiar propulsion unit is the automobile engine, Fig. 16-2. This device normally uses gasoline as the energy source. Then it mechanically transmits that energy to the wheels in order to drive the vehicle. Other propulsion systems include humans, jet engines, and electric motors. Can you think of vehicles that use these propulsion systems? Fig. 16-3 shows various types of propulsion systems in action.

GUIDANCE SYSTEMS

Guidance systems provide information required by a vehicle to make it follow a particular path or perform a certain task. These systems are read by the vehicle operator, who then controls her or his vehicle according to the information given. For example, the pilot of an airplane uses radar to detect obstacles like other aircraft.

Have you ever read road maps or road signs on a family vacation? These are other examples of guidance systems. Look at Fig. 16-4 for examples

Fig. 16-1. Many different vehicles are necessary to transport people and goods through the four environments. (AMTRAK, Greyhound, BC Transit, Carnival Cruise Lines, Kawasaki, and Delta Airlines)

Fig. 16-2. Propulsion systems use energy to provide force that moves vehicles. The automobile and the gasoline engine are popular as a means of transportation in North America.

Fig. 16-3. Propulsion systems in action. If you ride your bicycle to school you are the propulsion system!

Fig. 16-4. Guidance systems may be part of the vehicle or separate. Various gauges in an airplane cockpit provide guidance for the pilot. Road signs, and maps are other guidance systems we use every day. A control tower is a guidance system for aircraft.   (U.S. Navy and U.S. Air Force)

of guidance systems. Can you tell where they might be used?

CONTROL SYSTEMS

Control systems include the parts of vehicles that enable it to change direction and speed. See Fig. 16-5. These systems are normally controlled by the vehicle operator, but may be automatic. Such is the case with cruise control on an automobile or automatic pilot in an airplane. Control systems are very important for the safe operation of vehicles. Have you ever felt the uneasiness of being "out of control" on a bicycle? It is not very comfortable. Can you name the control systems on a bicycle? How about an automobile?

SUSPENSION SYSTEMS

Suspension systems on vehicles are designed to suspend or hold up the vehicle in or on its given environment. It should be easy to see that the suspension systems for vehicles that fly through the air are completely different from the systems that are used on cars and trucks, Fig.16-6. Suspension systems also provide a method to smooth the ride for passengers and cargo. Modern automobiles often have special suspension systems so that the ride in them is very comfortable. This can be very

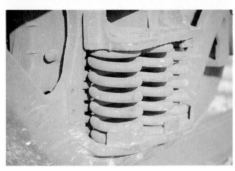

Fig. 16-6. Suspension systems support all vehicles and smooth the ride on land-based vehicles.

A

B

C

Fig. 16-5. Control systems provide a means of changing the speed or direction of a vehicle. Do you see how steering wheels and brake pedals are part of a control system? A—Steering wheel on a tractor. B—Steering wheel and disc-based navigation system on an experimental car. (GM) C—An engine order telegraph controls engine speed on a ship. (U.S. Coast Guard)

important if you drive long distances on the roads humans have built.

STRUCTURAL SYSTEMS

Structural systems determine the shape of the vehicle, Fig. 16-7. They include the framework of the vehicle that contains many of the other systems, as well as the vehicle "skin" that protects the systems, passengers, and cargo from the environment. Most vehicle structures are made of steel and other metal alloys so that they are very strong and

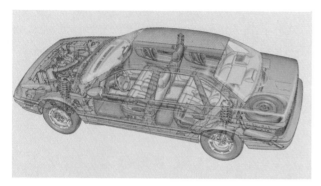

Fig. 16-7. Structural systems provide a "body" or support for all other vehicular systems. They also protect cargo and travelers.

durable. Plastics and composite materials have also been used by the industry to save weight and enhance the beauty of some vehicles. Advancements in structural designs have made vehicles safer and more efficient. Why is this important for our society?

SUPPORT SYSTEMS

Support systems include all of the external operations that maintain transportation systems. These include maintenance, life support, economic support, and even legal support. Fig. 16-8 shows a variety of support systems for transportation technology.

Transportation industries would not be able to survive or compete without support services. People would not be able to own or operate automobiles without support services. Vehicles and their systems are only a part of the whole transportation story. Support systems include all the parts of society that are devoted to sustaining transportation technology, and the ability of people to use it. Although support systems are not a direct part of the vehicles themselves or of the vehicle system, they are so important that they should always be discussed along with vehicular systems.

Fig. 16-8. Support systems provide protection, services, and repair facilities for vehicular systems. A— Quick-change oil station. B—Rail car repair. (AMTRAK) C—Gas stations allow vehicles to refuel. D—An airport provides transfer for passengers and protects them from the environment. E—Ports provide facilities for loading and unloading ships as well as storage for goods. (Port of Long Beach) F—Repair equipment keep roadways in good condition.

SAFETY IN VEHICULAR SYSTEMS

People naturally place a high value on human life. Because of this we tend to be very careful when designing advanced technological machines. Vehicular systems have evolved with more and more emphasis on built-in safety. We are constantly improving every aspect of the vehicle from car windshields and chassis configurations to the flame-retardant materials used in airplane upholstery. Vehicle designers study the results of crash tests as well as actual accidents to determine better ways of constructing vehicular systems. Fig. 16-9 shows one method of testing vehicular safety.

Government agencies have been developed to study the effects of transportation systems on our society. The National Transportation Safety Board and the Federal Aviation Administration are two such agencies. Investigators from these agencies study crash tests and vehicle disasters, as well as normal transportation operations to determine legislative (law) changes for transportation systems. Industry regulations and limitations are set and enforced by these agencies.

SUMMARY

Vehicles can be considered the most important part of transportation in our society. Without them, fast, safe, and efficient movement of people and cargo would not be possible. Vehicular systems are a series of separate, but interrelated systems. The separate components of a vehicular system include propulsion, guidance, control, suspension, structure, and support systems. Many of these components are a part of the vehicle itself,

although some are not. Support systems include a broad range of facilities and services that are very important to transportation technology in our society.

Through the actions of the transportation industry and government agencies, transportation and vehicular systems are constantly improved so that they will be safer for the public. Careful monitoring and studies by these groups ensure the steady progress of transportation technology while maintaining a high respect for human life.

KEY WORDS

All of the following words have been used in this chapter. Do you know their meaning?

Control system

Guidance system

Propulsion system

Structural system

Support system

Suspension system

Vehicular system

TEST YOUR KNOWLEDGE

Write your answers on a separate sheet of paper. Do not write in this book.

Short answer:
1. List five different kinds of vehicles that you have seen, and describe the environment for which they were designed.

Matching:
2. __ Propulsion systems.

3. __ Guidance systems.

4. __ Control systems.

A. Parts of vehicles that provide methods for changing speed and direction.

B. Systems that provide a smooth ride for pas-

A

B

Fig. 16-9. A—Automobile manufacturers conduct crash tests to determine the structural safety of their vehicles. (GM) B—Aircraft are crash tested to learn how fabrics and other materials resist burning. (NASA)

5. __ Suspension systems.
6. __ Structural systems.
7. __ Support systems.

sengers and cargo.
C. Vehicle components that provide methods for using energy to propel vehicles.
D. Includes all external operations that maintain vehicle and transportation systems.
E. Includes parts of vehicle that contain other systems and protect passengers and cargo.
F. Provide information required by a vehicle to make it follow a certain path.

Fill in the blank:

8. _____ are the machines that transportation systems use to move passengers and cargo safely, swiftly, and efficiently.
9. _____ systems are not a direct part of vehicles but are so important that without them industry and citizens could not utilize vehicles for transportation.
10. _____ and _____ are two government agencies that have been established to study vehicular systems so they will be safe.

ACTIVITIES

1. Secure a picture of a lawn mower and then draw arrows to its different parts. Label each part with its proper name. Then write after the name of the part what subsystem of the vehicular system it is.
2. On a sheet of paper list all of the propulsion systems you can. Then, after each system write down the environment (land, water, air, or space) for which it is suited.
3. Design and construct a working model of a land vehicle that includes all or as many subsystems as you can devise.

Fig. 17-1. Steam engines were developed long before other types of heat engines. They were popular for propulsion units in both land and water vehicles. Shown is an old "stern wheeler" that still steams on the Mississippi River as an excursion boat. (Delta Queen Steamboat Co.)

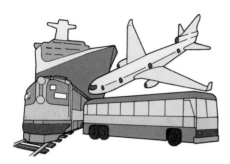

Chapter 17
PROPULSION OF A VEHICLE

After studying this chapter, you will be able to:
☐ Explain the purpose of propulsion systems in transportation technology.
☐ List the major propulsion systems used in transportation vehicles.
☐ Describe the operation of a basic four-stroke engine.
☐ List and explain the operation of jet airplane engines.
☐ Explain the operation of rocket engines.
☐ Describe how electrically powered vehicles receive their energy.

No transportation vehicle could move without a means of propulsion. The components of a vehicle's system of motion are called a propulsion system.

WHAT ARE PROPULSION SYSTEMS?

Propulsion systems are the parts of vehicles that convert energy to produce power that propels (moves) a vehicle. The energy source that people commonly rely on is gasoline. It is converted by heat engines to move cars, trucks, and many other types of vehicles. Many different types of propulsion systems have been used and developed throughout history. Some are as useful today as when they were first tried. Others are no longer used for one reason or another. Not efficient, unreliable, and unsafe are just a few reasons why some propulsion systems have been shelved.

Systems studied in this chapter will include everything from early steam engines through some complex systems used in the modern vehicles designed for various transportation modes.

HEAT ENGINES

The conversion of chemical energy to heat energy is common in many propulsion systems. Remember from Chapter 9 that this conversion is called combustion. *Heat engines* are those that use combustion to move mechanical power systems. For this reason, heat engines are also called combustion engines. There are two different types of combustion engines: external and internal. The difference between the two is in where the heat is produced to move the mechanical parts. Let us look at these systems more closely.

External Combustion Engines

External combustion engines are heat engines that burn their fuel outside of the engine itself. Essentially they are steam engines. Since the steam is produced outside the cylinder, the name external combustion makes sense for these devices. These are the workhorses that powered old steam locomotives, tractors, and boats, as well as industrial equipment. See Fig. 17-1. Steam is produced by heating water in a boiler that is attached to a cylinder and piston arrangement, Fig. 17-2. Wood or coal is usually burned to create the heat. The steam is allowed to expand into the cylinder.

Fig. 17-2. An old-time steam engine usually used to operate threshing machines on farms. The boiler is the drum-shaped portion. The engine is located at the back after the boiler.

This forces the piston to move away from the steam inlet. The steam actually pushes the piston. At the end of the piston stroke, steam is let into the cylinder on the opposite end so that it pushes the piston back. This action makes the piston reciprocate (move back) in the cylinder. Reciprocating motion of the piston is usually changed to rotary motion of wheels, Fig. 17-3.

A British inventor named Richard Trevithick developed a steam-powered vehicle that traveled at a top speed of 20 mph (32 km/h). It traveled on rails. Therefore, Trevithick was credited with being the designer of the first steam locomotive. Soon after that, American inventors started producing their own steam locomotives. In 1830, Peter Cooper introduced the "Tom Thumb" which was put to use for the Baltimore and Ohio Railroad Company.

Steam engines were also being put to use on water. Robert Fulton created a steamboat which worked so well it could be used to run a regular passenger service. He named the boat "Clermont" and established a profitable transportation line on the Hudson River in New York. The time was the early 1800s.

Steam turbines are another type of external combustion engine. They are able to produce power continuously. As the name suggests, pressure of steam is used as power. Look at Fig. 17-4 for an illustration of a steam turbine. Steam is produced in a boiler, then directed toward the blades of a turbine.

The turbine is basically a wheel with blades fixed around the outside. It is similar to a fan, except that it has many more blades. As the steam hits the turbine it pushes on the blades, producing

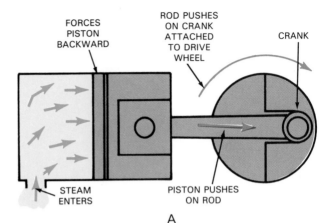

A

Fig. 17-3. Steam engines sent power to the drive wheels directly from the piston of the engine. A—Schematic shows how steam engines drove locomotive wheels. B—Drive wheel and crank of an old-time steam locomotive.

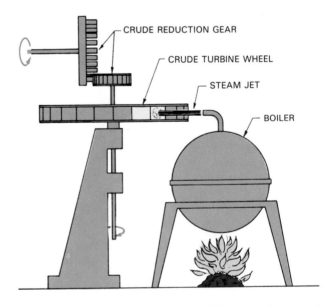

Fig. 17-4. The first practical turbine was invented in 1629 by an Italian engineer, Giovanni Branca. A continuous jet of steam was directed against the turbine wheel. An arrangement of crude gears transferred the turning force to provide power where it was needed. It was considered a curiosity and was never put to practical use.

rotary motion. This motion can then be used to move the vehicle on land or in water, depending on the vehicle. Steam turbines are also used to run generators in electric power plants.

Internal Combustion Engines

External combustion engines create heat on the outside of the engine. Can you guess how *internal combustion engines* get their name? It is because the heat is created inside the engines' combustion chambers. The engines used in automobiles and the engines used on jet airplanes, though much different in operation, are of this type.

While both types create heat inside the engine to power them, they do not work alike. Automobile engines use the heat to move pistons inside cylinders. Jet engines force heat out the rear of the engine. This makes the engine move forward.

We will study the type of engine used in cars, trucks, tractors, boats, and other vehicles first. Jet engines will be studied in more detail later.

Piston engine components

Piston engine components are similar in all engines, although they may be set up a number of different ways. There are two different cycles on which piston engines can run: four-stroke cycle and two-stroke cycle. The *four-stroke cycle engine* is so called because it requires two upward movements of the piston and two downward movements to complete a cycle. This is accomplished in two revolutions of the engine. The *two-stroke cycle engine* completes a cycle in just one downward and one upward movement of the piston. Both types contain similar parts, but they are set up differently in each.

The main parts of the four-stroke cycle engine are illustrated in Fig. 17-5. The engine block is the main part of the engine. Holes called cylinders are bored into the engine block, Fig. 17-6. Each cylinder contains a piston. There are usually four, six, eight, or sometimes twelve pistons used in the engines of automobiles produced today.

Each piston is connected to a central crankshaft. (Refer, once more, to Fig. 17-5.) The crankshaft is important because it converts reciprocating piston motion to the rotary motion which can be used to turn the wheels. Since all the pistons are connected to the same crankshaft, they all contribute to the power that is generated.

The tops of the cylinders are enclosed by the cylinder head. The space in the cylinder between the head and the piston is called the combustion chamber. Each cylinder in a four-stroke cycle has two valves. They let fuel in and let the exhaust (burnt gases) out. The valves are opened and closed by a camshaft. The camshaft is driven by the crankshaft, usually through a belt or chain. This allows each cylinder to go through its cycle correctly.

Each cylinder also has a spark plug at the top of the combustion chamber. It provides the spark that ignites the fuel. The spark plug is part of a vehicle's electrical system. Its timing in the four-stroke cycle is also very important. A spark must be delivered to each cylinder as its piston is at or near the top of its compression stroke. This produces the power stroke that follows.

You must realize that the action that goes on in a cylinder is very quick. Each cycle repeats many times each second. Let us now study the cycle and how the internal combustion engine really works.

Four-stroke cycle

This type of engine is used in most gasoline powered, internal combustion engine vehicles. It can be found in the vehicle your parents drive as well as the school bus in which you ride. The four-stroke cycle gets its name from the number of times the piston moves in the cylinder each cycle. Each time the piston goes up or down it is called a stroke. The four strokes, in the order they happen, are:

1. Intake stroke.
2. Compression stroke.
3. Power stroke.
4. Exhaust stroke.

Intake stroke. Look at Fig. 17-7 for a description of the intake stroke in a four-stroke cycle engine. In this stroke, the piston is moving down. The intake valve is open and the exhaust valve is closed. The downward movement of the piston creates a suction. This draws a fuel/air mixture into the combustion chamber.

When the piston is at the lowest point in its stroke, the intake valve closes. The lowest point is called *bottom dead center* (BDC). As the intake valve closes, the piston starts to move upward into the next stroke.

Compression stroke. Fig. 17-8 shows the action of the compression stroke. Notice that both the intake and exhaust valves are closed. The piston is moving up, and the fuel/air mixture is in the combustion chamber. As the combustion chamber is made smaller, the fuel mixture is compressed (squeezed) into a smaller area. By compressing the fuel, then igniting it, more power can be generated in the next stroke.

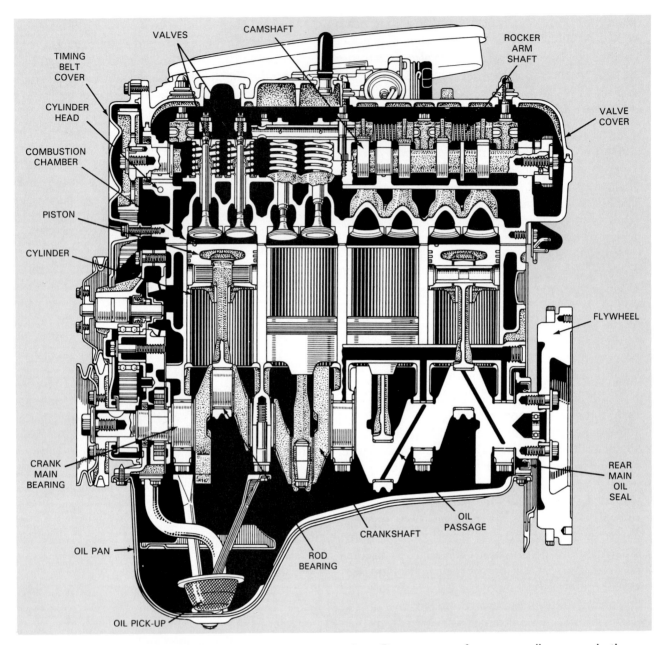

VALVES
CAMSHAFT
ROCKER
ARM
SHAFT
TIMING
BELT
COVER
CYLINDER
HEAD
VALVE
COVER
COMBUSTION
CHAMBER
PISTON
CYLINDER
FLYWHEEL
CRANK
MAIN
BEARING
REAR
MAIN
OIL
SEAL
OIL PAN
OIL
PASSAGE
CRANKSHAFT
ROD
BEARING
OIL PICK-UP

Fig. 17-5. Modern internal combustion engine cutaway view. Power comes from expanding gases in the combustion chamber pushing on the piston and turning the engine crankshaft.   (Chrysler)

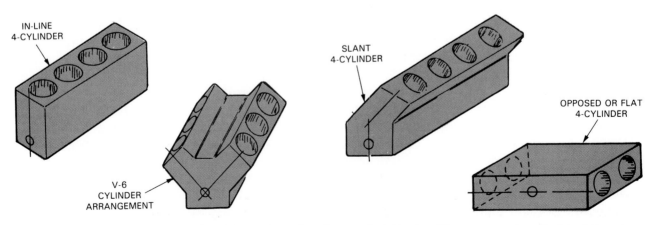

IN-LINE
4-CYLINDER
SLANT
4-CYLINDER
OPPOSED OR FLAT
4-CYLINDER
V-6
CYLINDER
ARRANGEMENT

Fig. 17-6. Four different shapes of internal combustion engine blocks. They are cast out of metal and cylinders are bored out to receive the pistons.

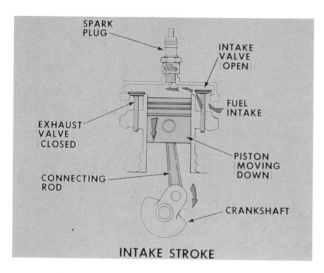

Fig. 17-7. Intake stroke of an internal combustion engine draws in fuel vapor. (Kohler)

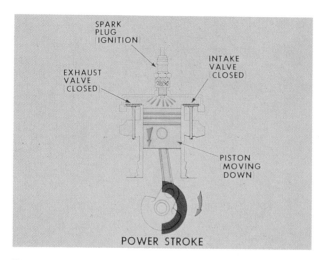

Fig. 17-9. Power stroke results from rapid burning of the air-fuel mixture. The piston is driven down rapidly, creating power. (Kohler)

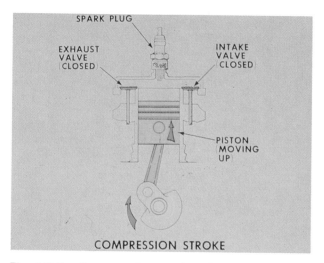

Fig. 17-8. Compression stroke of an internal combustion engine compresses the fuel vapor in preparation for burning the fuel mixture. (Kohler)

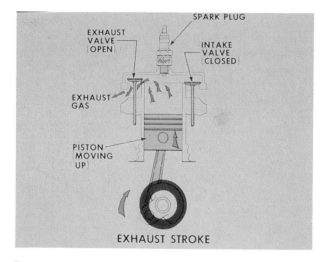

Fig. 17-10. Spent fuel is forced from the combustion chamber during the exhaust stroke. (Kohler)

Power stroke. The power stroke, Fig. 17-9, is where the engine converts heat energy to mechanical energy. As the piston reaches *top dead center* (TDC) in the compression stroke, the spark plug ignites the compressed fuel/air mixture. The explosion in the combustion chamber forces the piston down in the cylinder. This is the energy that turns the crankshaft. Eventually this power also turns the wheels, track, or propeller of the vehicle. Both valves are closed in the power stroke so none of the energy from the explosion escapes from the top of the cylinder.

Exhaust stroke. After the fuel is burned in the cylinder, there is a lot of smoke and dirt left from the combustion process. This matter is called exhaust. In the exhaust stroke, Fig. 17-10, the piston moves up. The exhaust valve is open and the in-

take valve remains closed. The piston forces the exhaust from the combustion chamber as it moves to TDC. When the piston reaches TDC, the exhaust valve closes and, at this point, the whole cycle starts over again.

Two-stroke cycle engine

Gasoline engines using the two-stroke cycle perform all the steps of a four-stroke engine, except it does them with fewer piston movements. The two-stroke completes its cycle in one revolution of the crankshaft. These are small, high-revolution engines that are used in chain saws, outboard motors, and many lawn mowers.

Fig. 17-11 is an illustration of a two-stroke engine. Notice that instead of valves, it has holes (ports) drilled in the cylinder walls. One lets in fuel,

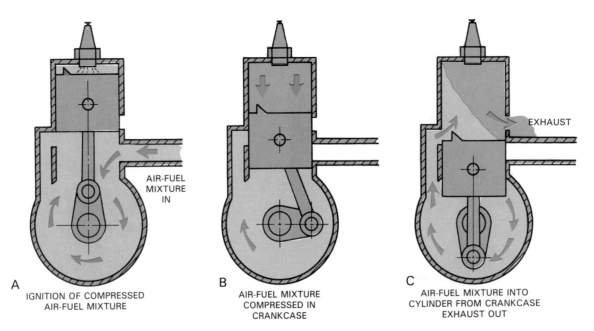

A
IGNITION OF COMPRESSED
AIR-FUEL MIXTURE

B
AIR-FUEL MIXTURE
COMPRESSED IN
CRANKCASE

C
AIR-FUEL MIXTURE INTO
CYLINDER FROM CRANKCASE
EXHAUST OUT

Fig. 17-11. Diagram of a two-stroke cycle engine. In this design, the piston's position controls the exhaust, intake, and transfer ports. One complete cycle is shown. A—Intake stroke is completed and spark has ignited to begin a power stroke. All ports are closed except the intake port. Vacuum in the crankcase pulls in air-fuel mixture. B—Expanding gases push the piston down in a power stroke. The air-fuel mixture in the crankcase is compressed. All ports are closed. C—At bottom of power stroke, compressed air-fuel mixture enters the combustion chamber through the transfer port, replacing exhaust gases leaving through the exhaust port. Now the cycle is repeated.

and the other allows exhaust to leave. The piston acts as a valve. When it moves up and down it either opens or closes the ports.

Two-stroke cycle operation

Normally gasoline and lubricating oil are premixed in the two-stroke engine. The fuel/air mixture is allowed to enter the crankcase, below the pistons through a reed valve. Here it lubricates the moving engine parts as it awaits entry into the combustion chamber. There is a passage that leads directly from the crankcase to the intake port. The reed valve is in place to ensure that the fuel mixture can enter the crankcase. At the same time, it closes should any mixture attempt to leave. It is a one-way valve that is able to hold the pressures generated inside the engine during operation.

Look at Fig. 17-12 for the order of events in a two-stroke cycle. Notice that when the piston is at BDC, a charge of fuel/air mixture enters the combustion chamber. As the piston moves up, it closes off the intake and exhaust ports. It keeps moving up to compress the mixture, similar to the compression stroke in the four-stroke cycle. While the piston moves up, it also creates a vacuum beneath it. This opens the reed valve and draws more air/fuel mixture into the crankcase.

As the piston reaches TDC, the spark plug ignites and forces the piston down into the power

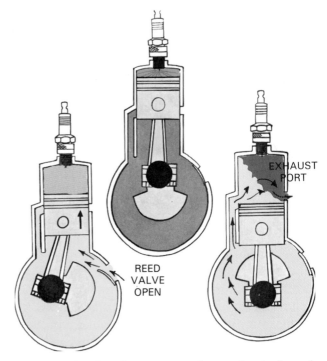

Fig. 17-12. Another two-stroke cycle design. A reed valve controls air-fuel entry into the crankcase. The piston controls the transfer and exhaust ports. (Kohler Co.)

stroke of the cycle. Remember, this is the point at which mechanical energy is sent to the crankshaft to move the vehicle. The crankshaft converts reciprocating motion into rotary motion.

When the piston travels past the exhaust port, the port is opened and the exhaust gases leave the combustion chamber. Before the piston reaches BDC, it passes the intake port which is usually located just below the exhaust port. The downward moving piston is compressing the mixture in the crankcase, and when the intake port is opened, that mixture rushes into the combustion chamber. This way, the engine sets itself up for the next cycle with a fresh charge of fuel.

Advantages and disadvantages

The two-stroke engine is popular for small engine applications for a number of reasons.

- Because it has no valves, valve train, or camshaft, the two-stroke cycle engine is lighter and can be more compact. This is advantageous for use in smaller vehicles like lawn mowers, go-carts, outboard motor boats.
- Having fewer parts reduces machining costs making two-stroke cycle engines cheaper to manufacture.
- The absence of a valve train makes it possible for two-stroke engines to run at a very high speed. The higher revving characteristic is useful in many small engine applications like chain saws.
- Because it supplies power on every downward stroke, it is efficient in power-to-weight ratio.

On the downside, some of the power produced is lost by compressing the fuel mixture in the crankcase. Therefore, it is not as efficient as a four-stroke cycle engine of the same size. It is also not as fuel efficient. This is because some of the intake fuel can be lost through the exhaust port before the piston closes it off.

You will find many two-stroke engines being used in spite of these obvious disadvantages.

Diesel Engines

Diesel engines are internal combustion engines that use heat and pressure to ignite their fuel. They were developed by Rudolph Diesel, a German automotive engineer. These engines follow the same basic power cycle as the other internal combustion engines that we have discussed so far.

Diesel engines are different from gasoline engines in several ways. For one thing, they have no spark plugs. They rely on the extreme heat of the compressed air to supply the ignition. When diesel fuel is injected into the combustion chamber, the hot compressed air causes the fuel to burn with explosive force.

Another point of difference is the high compression ratio of the diesel when compared to gasoline engine ratios. *Compression ratio* is the difference in the volume of the combustion chamber when the piston is at bottom dead center compared to the volume at top dead center. Fig. 17-13 compares two cylinders, one from a diesel and one from a gasoline engine. Notice that when the pistons are at BDC, the diesel chamber is larger than the gasoline chamber. This allows a greater compression ratio. Compression ratio is a comparison of the size of the combustion chamber when the piston is at BDC and TDC. Compression ratios for diesel engines may be about 18:1, while those of gas engines are usually around 10:1. The larger amount of fuel allows the high temperature needed to ignite the compressed mixture.

Still another difference in the diesel is that it is built much stronger than the gasoline engine. This added strength is necessary because of the stress the higher compression ratio places on the engine parts, especially the pistons, rods, and crankshaft.

Diesels use a glow plug for starting a cold engine. This creates enough heat for the first ignitings to take place in the cylinder. The additional heat is not needed after the engine heats up and is underway. Because the diesel engine relies on heated compressed air for ignition, it is called a *compression-ignition engine.*

ROTARY ENGINES

Rotary engines are internal combustion engines that use rotors in place of pistons. They are usually called Wankel rotary piston engines. The name comes from their German inventor, Dr. Felix

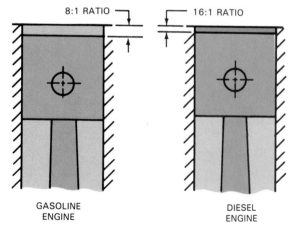

Fig. 17-13. Diesel engines have a much higher compression ratio than gasoline engines.

Wankel. The engine is small, lightweight, powerful, and smooth running. The smoothness comes from the use of rotary rather than reciprocal (up and down) movement of a piston. The rotor turns inside a specially shaped housing. It lets fuel and air in, compresses it, burns it, then releases the exhaust all in one smooth rotation.

Because rotors replace the pistons, we classify these engines differently. Where we refer to four, six, or eight cylinders in traditional piston engines, we call out the number of rotors in the Wankel engine. Generally, one-rotor Wankel engines are used in smaller applications like lawn mowers. Two-rotor Wankel engines are used for automobiles. Experimental engines with more than two rotors have been developed but are not yet commonly used.

Rotary Engine Operation

Fig. 17-14 shows the parts of a Wankel rotary engine in an exploded, cutaway view. The rotor has the shape of a slightly rounded equilateral (having three equal angles) triangle. It is attached to an eccentric (off center) shaft which comes through the center of the housing. The special shape of the housing is very critical. It is somewhat like a large figure "8." This shape is called an *epitrochoidal curve*. It allows the tips of the rotor to ride against the housing as the rotor revolves. Special replaceable tips maintain a tight seal between the two. If the seal were not kept tight, the engine would have a great loss of power.

Intake and exhaust ports are located in the epitrochoidal housing. They are placed so that they take advantage of the expanding and contracting spaces made by the spinning rotor. Fig. 17-15 il-

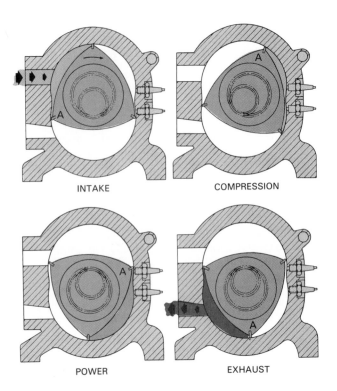

INTAKE   COMPRESSION

POWER   EXHAUST

Fig. 17-15. The combustion cycle of the Wankel engine. Each lobe (point) of the rotor goes through four phases during one revolution.

lustrates how the spinning rotor creates the combustion chamber. Study the steps that it follows. Can you see how the intake, compression, power and exhaust stages all take place in one revolution of the rotor?

REACTION ENGINES

At the beginning of this chapter, we briefly compared two major types of internal combustion engines. We called them automobile engines and jet engines.

We will now study the types of engines used on jet airplanes and rockets. These are classified as *reaction engines.* They operate on the principle defined in Isaac Newton's Third Law of Motion. This states that "for every action, there is an equal and opposite reaction."

Have you ever blown up a balloon, then let it go? What happens? If you didn't tie the opening shut, all the air rushed out. It left with such a force that it moved the balloon in the opposite direction, Fig. 17-16. This is one example of Newton's Third Law in action. Can you think of any more? How about pushing yourself along on a skateboard?

Basically, reaction engines force hot gases from the rear of the engine. This is called thrust. It may appear that thrust is the rapidly exhausting gases

Fig. 17-14. A Wankel engine uses spinning rotors instead of pistons to convert heat energy to power. Note the shape of the rotors and the combustion chambers.

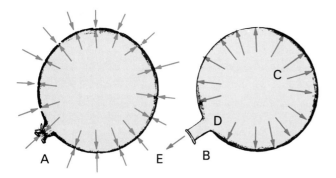

Fig. 17-16. If an inflated balloon is tied shut, nothing happens. If left untied, the air escapes. If not held, the balloon reacts by moving in the opposite direction from the opening.

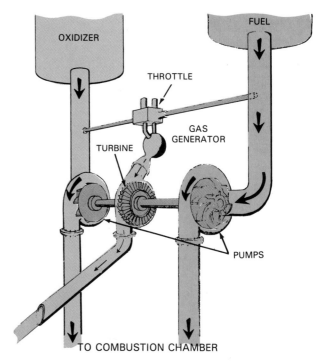

Fig. 17-17. Diagram of a fuel mixture control in a model rocket. Oxidizer and fuel are mixed as they are used. (Estes)

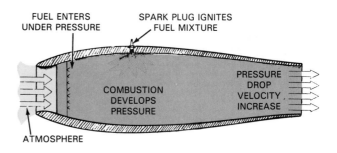

Fig. 17-18. A ramjet engine has no moving parts and has no device for drawing in air. It can operate only when moving at a high rate of speed. As in all reaction engines, unequal pressure between the front of the engine and the back, propels it forward. (Estes)

pushing against the air that is behind the engine, propelling the engine forward. Actually, what is happening is that unequal pressure in the engine causes the reaction that moves the engine. Greater pressure, being at the front of the engine, causes the engine to move in that direction. Can you see how this is similar to the air escaping from the balloon?

We can classify reaction engines in two categories: *air stream reaction engines*, and *rocket engines*. Air stream reaction engines are those that are used on vehicles that fly through our atmosphere. Jet engines in airplanes are an example. These use the oxygen found in our atmosphere to mix with the fuel. Rocket engines need to carry their own oxidizer (air) because there is no oxygen in the vacuum of space. See Fig. 17-17.

Air Stream Reaction Engines

Our discussion of air stream reaction engines will explore five different types. They are:
• Ramjet engines.
• Turbojet engines.
• Turbofan engines.
• Turboprop engines.
• Experimental engines.

You will see that the five operate on the same principle (action-reaction). They are only different in how they produce thrust.

Ramjet Engines

Ramjet engines are the simplest type of all reaction engines. They have no moving parts. Fig. 17-18 shows a cross section of a ramjet engine. Air enters the front of the engine as the vehicle is moving at a high rate of speed. The internal shape of the engine causes the air to be compressed. When this

happens, fuel is sprayed into the combustion area so that it mixes with the compressed air. This mixture is then ignited. It expands rapidly as it burns, and is forced out the back of the engine as thrust.

Ramjets can only operate at high speeds because of the way air enters the engine. They cannot be used for takeoffs and will not work at low speeds.

Other types of reaction engines are used to give ramjets their initial speed. When the vehicle is moving fast enough, ramjets take over to produce a great amount of added thrust. This type of engine is often used on missiles and other weapons that can be fired from moving aircraft.

Turbojet Engines

These are commonly used on commercial aviation vehicles. Unlike the ramjet, turbojets are used in all aspects of powered flight, from takeoff to landing. Fig. 17-19 shows a vehicle that uses a turbojet engine.

Fig. 17-20 illustrates a cross section of a turbojet engine. Notice that it has internal parts that rotate on a shaft. Arrows show airflow from the front of the engine through the back. At the front, there is a compressor section. The compressor is used to pack air into the combustion chamber for the same reason we need a compression stage in a four-cycle engine. It gives the combustion process more force.

The air is packed into a combustion chamber in the middle of the engine. Here, fuel is injected so that it may mix with the compressed air. The engine's operation is similar to the ramjet. After mixing, the fuel and air are burned and forced toward the back of the engine. Once ignition has started, it becomes a continuous process inside the engine.

Before the hot gases leave the rear as thrust, they pass through a turbine section. The gases spin the turbine blades at high speed.

There are two functions the turbine must perform. One is to power the compressor section at the front of the engine. The compressor section is attached to the shaft that runs through the center of the engine. The second function is to add to the thrust provided by the hot gases leaving the rear of the engine.

Turbofan Engines

Turbofan engines are sometimes called fanjets or bypass engines. They are similar in operation to turbojet engines. The difference is the addition of turbofans at the front of the engine. Look at Fig. 17-21. The turbofan is powered by the turbine section at the rear of the engine. Basically, the action caused by the engine supplies power in addition to thrust. Turbofan engines use compressors and combustion chambers like turbojets.

Engine designers started to work with turbofan engines after they realized that a large amount of slower moving air produced more thrust than a small amount of high speed air. Turbojets produced the small stream of fast air. Turbofans utilize a large amount of slower-moving air.

The addition of the turbofan does two things for the engine.

- It brings more air to the compressor section. This allows for a more efficient combustion process.
- The fan forces air around the outside of the engine. This adds to the total thrust put out by the engine.

Turbofan engines are widely used on commercial passenger airplanes because they are efficient as well as powerful at low speeds. Fig. 17-22 shows a commercial airliner with turbofan engines.

Fig. 17-19. Military aircraft are one of the users of the turbojet reaction engine. Unlike the ramjet, it is able to develop full power for takeoff as well as when moving rapidly through the air.   (U.S. Navy)

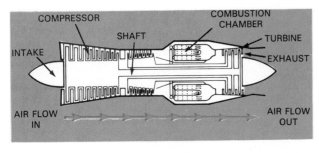

Fig. 17-20. A cross section of a turbojet engine. As in other engines of this type airflow and combustion are continuous.   (Pratt and Whitney, Canada)

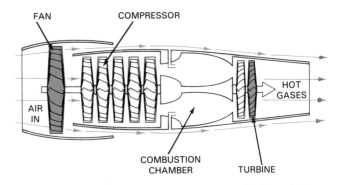

Fig. 17-21. A turbofan engine is a variation of the turbojet engine. A fan has been placed in front the compressor section. The fan is driven by a separate turbine located in the path of the hot exhaust gases.

Fig. 17-22. A Boeing 727 on takeoff. Powerful turbofan engines move it quickly to cruising altitude. (Delta Airlines)

Turboprop Engines

Turboprop engines are basically turbojets that have a propeller mounted on the front. These engines use the product of the combustion to turn the propeller. Thrust from the rear of the engine is not relied on as propulsion. It is used to turn the propeller which, in turn, moves the vehicle forward.

Fig. 17-23 illustrates a cross section of a turboprop engine. Notice the gear section between the propeller shaft and the main engine shaft. It is used to multiply the energy between the engine and the propeller.

Experimental Engines

Several leading manufacturers of aircraft power plants are working on an engine which is a takeoff of a turbofan. General Electric calls their version an "Unducted Fan," while others call them propfans.

Fig. 17-23. A cutaway drawing of a turboprop engine. A gear assembly connects the turbines (at right) to the propeller shaft (at left).
(Allied Signal Aerospace, Garrett Engine Division)

This engine uses a combustion process similar to other air stream reaction engines. It produces thrust by turning modified propeller blades around the outside of the engine. Look at Fig. 17-24.

A

B

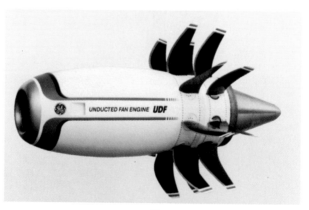

C

Fig. 17-24. These are examples of experimental reaction engines. A—An advanced turboprop design. B—The design shown in A under test in a jetliner. (NASA) C—An "unducted fan" experimental engine. Propeller blades on the outside of the engine are thought to produce more thrust. (General Electric Co.)

This engine is based on the premise that large amounts of air produce more thrust than small streams of air. The propeller blades are efficiently designed so that they will work well at high speeds. There is also less vibration than occurs in other propeller-driven aircraft.

Rocket Engines

As was mentioned earlier, rocket engines also work according to the principle of Newton's Third Law of Motion. They are, by far, the most powerful type of internal combustion engines. The tremendous power is needed to lift heavy space vehicles away from the pull of earth's gravity.

Air stream reaction engines use the oxygen in the atmosphere for combustion. Because rocket engines need to work outside our atmosphere, they need to carry their own oxidizer. An *oxidizer* is a chemical substance that mixes with fuel to allow combustion.

Rocket engines are classified by the type of propellant (fuel) they use. There are two types: solid-fuel and liquid-fuel.

Solid-fuel rocket engines

Of the two types of rocket engines, this one is the simplest. It is so simple, in fact, that it is used in model rockets, Fig. 17-25. It contains solid fuel and oxidizers, usually packed into a cylindrical container. There is usually more oxidizer than fuel in the propellant mixture. When ready for use, the propellant is ignited at the bottom. As this fuel burns, thrust is produced from the bottom of the engine. See Fig. 17-26.

Once the combustion process is started it cannot be stopped. The engine will burn its fuel until

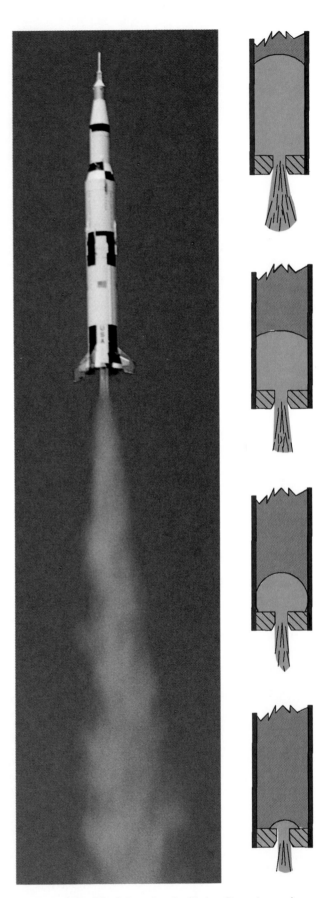

Fig. 17-26. Model rocket in flight. Drawings show the burning of the solid fuel as the flight continues. Solid-fuel rockets continue the burn until fuel is exhausted.

Fig. 17-25. A model solid-fuel rocket is launched as a school technology education activity.

it is all gone. This is why liquid-fuel rockets are considered safer than solid-fuel rockets. There is also less control over the power in solid-fuel engines. The propellant burns at a fixed rate, producing a fixed amount of thrust. You cannot change the thrust produced by a solid-fuel rocket engine.

Liquid-fuel rocket engines

Space exploration vehicles use liquid-fuel rocket engines. As you have just learned, they are safer than solid-fuel engines. They also offer control over power output. Fig. 17-27 shows some space exploration vehicles that use liquid-fuel engines.

The two propellants are kept in separate tanks inside the vehicle. They are pumped to a combustion chamber where they are mixed and burned. Fig. 17-28 illustrates the inside of a simple liquid-fuel rocket engine. As propellant is burned in the combustion chamber, it leaves the bottom of the engine as thrust.

Fuels that are often used include liquid hydrogen and kerosene. Oxidizer is often in the form of liquid oxygen. Propellants must be put into the rocket shortly before they are to be used. Space exploration vehicles are never left for long with liquid propellants in them.

Inert gas jets

Some specialized space vehicles use inert gas jets to propel them while they are in space. Manned Maneuvering Units or MMUs, developed by NASA are one example. See Fig. 17-29. These use small jets that emit nitrogen gas. The escaping gas pro-

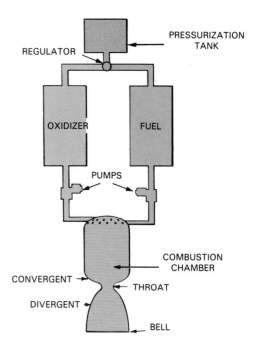

Fig. 17-28. This is a diagram of the liquid propellant system in a model rocket. (Estes)

vides the action that causes a reaction in the opposite direction. When the operator wants to move in a certain direction, she or he activates the jet nozzle that will produce movement in that direction.

Gas turbines

Gas turbine engines have been successfully used in aircraft and heavy trucks. This type of engine is relatively simple. Fig. 17-30 illustrates a cross section of a gas turbine engine.

Air enters the engine in the front where a compressor packs it into a combustion chamber. There

Fig. 17-27. Liquid-fueled rockets at lift off. This type is controllable and much safer than solid-fuel rockets. (NASA)

Fig. 17-33. "Maglev" trains float along suspended above the track by magnetic levitation. It works on the principle that like magnetic poles repel each other. Magnetism also pulls the train along at high speed. This train is in operation in Germany. (Transrapid International)

however, also be used to run electric generators. The generators are then used to run powerful electric motors. The motors provide power to turn the drive train.

Diesel-electric propulsion systems are most commonly found in train engines. Fig. 17-34 shows a diesel-electric locomotive.

NUCLEAR PROPULSION

Some vehicles, especially military ships and submarines, use nuclear propulsion, Fig. 17-35. These

Fig. 17-34. Modern locomotives employ diesel engines to generate electric power to operate electric drive motors. (Santa Fe Railroad)

Fig. 17-35. Some naval ships use nuclear propulsion units. (U.S. Navy)

vehicles carry small nuclear fission reactors. They are similar to the ones used in electric generating stations. These reactors generate intense amounts of heat which is used to create steam. The steam is then used to turn steam turbines, which turn the propeller shafts. Geared transmissions are needed to control the power put out by the turbines.

SOLAR PROPULSION

Vehicles that operate using the power of the sun are electrically powered vehicles. They utilize photovoltaic cells to convert light energy to electrical energy. That energy is put into storage batteries where it can be used to run electric motors.

Fig. 17-36 shows the GM Sunraycer. It is a solar-powered vehicle designed and built to participate in a "solar challenge" race in Australia. The Sunraycer proved to be a good design as it won the race. It made good use of lightweight materials, and efficiently harnessed the sun's energy.

Fig. 17-36. This solar-powered vehicle was built to compete in a "solar challenge" race in Australia. It made good use of lightweight materials along with good design and won the race. (GM-Hughes)

SUMMARY

Propulsion systems are the parts of vehicles that convert energy to produce power for moving a vehicle. Very early transportation systems relied on the power of wind, water, and animals for propulsion. Other early systems used external combustion engines, such as steam engines. Modern transportation vehicles use either internal combustion engines or electric motors.

Internal combustion engines may be classified as either piston engines or reaction engines. Four-stroke and two-stroke cycles are common piston engines. These engines perform basically the same steps. They take in fuel and air, compress it, burn it, then release the exhaust gases. Power is produced when the fuel and air is burned.

Reaction engines operate on Newton's action-reaction law. It states that for every action there is an equal and opposite reaction. Two types of reaction engines are air stream reaction engines and rocket engines. Air stream reaction engines burn the oxygen found in our atmosphere. Rocket engines need to carry their own oxidizer because there is no oxygen in the vacuum of outer space.

Vehicles that use electric motors for propulsion systems get their energy through a variety of ways. Some get it from overhead lines or tracks. Other vehicles carry their own electric generators. Diesel-electric locomotives, and nuclear-powered submarines are two examples.

Newer, exploratory propulsion systems include solar-powered vehicles and electromagnetic propulsion systems. Only the future will tell if we can rely on these systems.

KEY WORDS

All of the following words have been used in this chapter. Do you know their meaning?

Air stream reaction engine
Bottom dead center
Compression ratio
Compression-ignition engine
Diesel engines
Epitrochoidal curve
External combustion engines
Four-stroke cycle engine
Heat engines

Internal combustion engines
Magnetic levitation systems
Oxidizer
Propulsion system
Reaction engines
Rocket engines
Steam turbines
Storage batteries
Top dead center
Two-stroke cycle engine

TEST YOUR KNOWLEDGE

Write your answers on a separate sheet of paper. Do not write in this book.

Fill in the blanks:
1. _____ combustion engines create heat on the inside of the engine.
2. _____ combustion engines are the type used in automobiles and jet airplanes.
3. The four steps in a four-stroke cycle engine are _____, _____, _____, and _____.
4. In a piston engine, TDC stands for _____.
5. _____ engines are internal combustion engines that need to carry their own oxidizer into space.

Matching:
6. __ Crankshaft.
7. __ Turbine.
8. __ Combustion chamber.
9. __ Compression.
10. __ Exhaust.
11. __ BDC.
12. __ Valves.
13. __ Wankel engine.
14. __ Thrust.
15. __ Propellant.

A. Fuel intake and exhaust outlet devices on four-stroke engines.
B. Packs air into combustion chamber.
C. Rotary piston engine.
D. Used to drive compressors on a turbojet.
E. Converts reciprocal to rotary motion.
F. Burnt gases.
G. Fuel used in rockets.
H. Place in internal combustion engine where fuel is burned.
I. Bottom Dead Center.
J. Force that moves true reaction engines.

Short answer:
16. Describe the four strokes of a four-stroke cycle engine.
17. How is a four-stroke different from a two-stroke engine?
18. How do diesel engines ignite their fuel/air mixture?
19. Name four types of air stream reaction engines, and describe how one of them works.
20. How are rocket engines different from air stream reaction engines?
21. What type of propulsion device do electrical powered vehicles use?

ACTIVITIES

1. Prepare a display (drawings or mock-up) showing either of the following:

A. Four-stroke cycle engine's combustion cycle.
B. Combustion cycle of a two-stroke cycle engine.
C. Combustion cycle of a Wankel rotary engine.
D. Cutaway view of a jet engine during combustion.

2. Organize a model rocket launch using a commercially available model rocket or one designed and built under your instructor's supervision.

3. Organize a rocket payload contest in which contestants will launch a raw egg. Winner is the contestant whose egg is safely returned.

4. Construct a model of a turbojet engine.

5. Construct and operate a balloon-powered vehicle to demonstrate the principle of the jet engine.

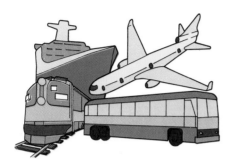

Chapter 18
GUIDANCE OF A VEHICLE

After studying this chapter, you will be able to:
☐ Explain the purpose of guidance systems in transportation technology.
☐ Describe how guidance systems communicate information.
☐ Read and locate coordinates on maps and charts.
☐ Define navigation and describe basic examples.
☐ List and describe electronic navigation equipment involved in transportation technology.

No vehicle can be operated unless certain conditions about the vehicle and the environment are known. Without information about the vehicle's condition, the operator might cause damage to it without knowing. Furthermore, what would the operator do if she or he received no information about routes to take to a destination? What if there was no information to direct surface traffic? The information required is provided by guidance systems.

GUIDANCE SYSTEMS

Guidance systems provide information required by a vehicle to follow a particular path or perform a certain task. Messages provided by these systems are read and interpreted by the vehicle operator. The operator can then control the vehicle according to the information given.

A simple example will help explain guidance systems and how they might work: You are riding your bicycle to the store, and a sign tells you that there is construction ahead. The path you were going to take has been closed, Fig. 18-1. No vehicle can pass, not even a bicycle. In your mind you quickly review the options you have. Which will you choose: detour a block to the right or left, go to a different store, or even try to ride your bicycle closer to the construction work because you are curious?

Whatever way you decide, you have used a guidance device. It was the "road closed" sign. As the operator of your vehicle, you had to interpret the sign, then decide how to control your bicycle.

This is essentially the function of guidance systems. They give information. Can you see the importance of vehicle operators knowing how to use guidance systems properly?

Fig. 18-1. "Road closed" signs may be used to warn vehicle operators to take an alternate route.

You will recall that an earlier chapter discussed the degrees of freedom. Each direction a vehicle can travel is a degree. Depending on the freedom your vehicle has (one, two, or three degrees), guidance systems may be simple or very complex. This chapter will focus on the types of guidance systems used by various transportation systems. They are important to understand because, many times, safety hinges on where a vehicle travels.

TYPES OF GUIDANCE INFORMATION

Suppose you were asked, "What types of information does a vehicle operator need?" You would probably say direction of travel, speed, and location of destination, Fig. 18-2. These are all correct answers. Location and direction of travel are the most required information by vehicle operators. How would you be able to drive a car, or fly an airplane to Washington D.C., or anywhere, if you had no idea where it was? It sounds impossible without proper guidance information. Speed of vehicles also plays an important part in guidance, as you will soon see.

NAVIGATION

Navigation is a word used to describe the act of guiding a vehicle. It usually refers to the guidance of a ship or airplane, but it may also be used for land transportation vehicles. Navigation has its roots in the Latin words "navis," which means ship, and "agere," which means to drive.

Maps and Charts

Maps are graphic representations of features on the surface of the earth. They are drawn to scale. Scale is the relationship between the actual size of an object, and its size on a drawing such as a map. For example, 1:63,360 means one inch equals one mile. This can be compared to a common architectural scale where 1/4" equals 1 foot.

As the second number (the denominator) in the ratio increases, more area can be fit onto the map. A ratio of 1:250,000 is equal to about 4 sq. miles. This can be seen further when you understand that a scale of 1:1,000,000 will show more area, and less detail, than a map the same size with a scale of 1:1000. Maps usually have a linear, or bar scale on them to help determine distances between points on the map, Fig. 18-3.

The term, maps, refers to the general category of graphic representations. *Chart* is a term given to marine and air maps that are designed for navigation purposes. Those that are typically used for transportation are road maps, aeronautical charts, and nautical (marine) charts. Maps are usually flat so that they are easy to carry and use.

You might have used road maps on a family vacation. These are detailed drawings of all the roads, highways, topographical (land) features, landmarks, etc., in a certain area. See Fig. 18-4. There are a large variety of road maps. Some show all the major highways between cities in a coun-

Fig. 18-3. A bar scale is found on road maps to indicate how to compute the distance between points on the map.

Fig. 18-4. A typical road map. It guides motorist traveling unfamiliar areas of a country. It shows expressways, state highways, rivers, rail lines, and other features.

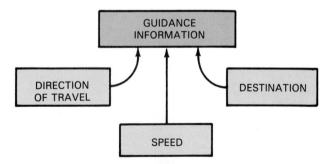

Fig. 18-2. Before operating a transportation vehicle, the operator must have these three kinds of information.

try, while others show all the streets and alleys in a small town or large city.

Road maps use different symbols to denote different types of roads. These symbols can be found in the legend located on the map. It describes the type of roads, how landmarks are represented, and the scale of the map. Usually, the linear scale is located on the legend also.

Aeronautical charts

Aeronautical charts are those that provide important data for airplane pilots and navigators, Fig. 18-5. These are basically topographic maps on which special guidance information has been added. Aeronautical charts show elevations of hills and mountains, as well as the locations of airports and other landing areas. They have special markings which locate prohibited areas where aircraft cannot fly legally, such as around military installations. Other areas are labeled as restricted. These are not prohibited but areas that could be dangerous for air safety. Artillery ranges are marked as restricted areas.

Landmarks that are easily visible from the air are shown on aeronautical charts. The locations of radio transmitters are another important feature on these charts. Radio transmitters are vital for airplane navigation.

When plotting a course for an aircraft, the pilot or navigator uses a navigation plotter. It is made from clear plastic, and combines a protractor with a straight edge that is marked with different scales. The plotter is used to measure distances as well as directions when placed on top of an aeronautical chart.

Nautical charts

Nautical charts are maps that show coastal waters, rivers, and other marine areas, Fig. 18-6. They are specially designed to show information for navigating waterways. The charts are marked with special symbols that represent depths of water, channel markers, buoys, underwater phone and electric lines, wrecks, etc. Coastal features that can aid in navigation also appear on nautical charts. These include lighthouses, church steeples, and water towers.

Ships use maps on the open sea to plot their own position and, possibly, that of other craft in the area. See Fig. 18-7.

Maps and charts that are used for guidance and navigation purposes need to be updated constant-

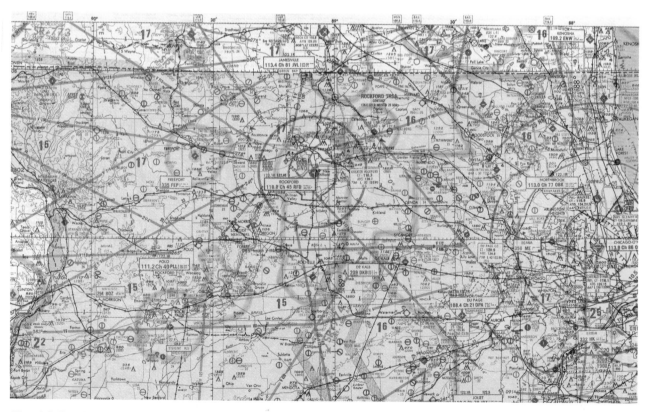

Fig. 18-5. An aeronautical map has guidance information useful and necessary to pilots who are using ground navigation.

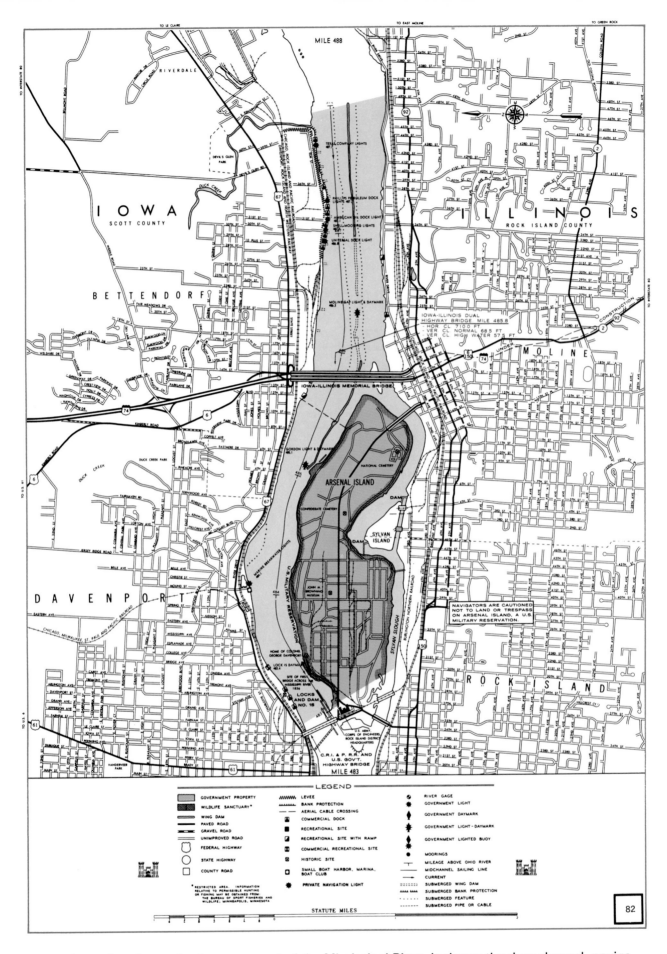

Fig. 18-6. A chart for navigating a segment of the Mississippi River. It shows the river channel, navigational aids, islands, and other features. (US Army Corps of Engineers)

Fig. 18-7. Ship's navigators plot courses and positions on nautical maps. Here a crew member of the USS Curts, a guided missile frigate, plots ship movements. (US Navy)

ly. New construction of highways, bridges, and tunnels has to be identified on road maps. What would happen if these items were not included? Do you suppose you would be able to plan the best route if you did not have accurate information? Nautical and aeronautical charts are also constantly updated to show new facilities, restricted areas, and newly submerged wrecks in the case of marine navigation.

LONGITUDE AND LATITUDE

To accurately pinpoint a location on a map, there needs to be a definite reference system. For this we use imaginary lines that run vertically and horizontally over the entire world. They are marked with degrees so that each one is identifiable. Fig. 18-8 shows a *globe*, which is a spherical map. It is used here to illustrate latitudes and longitudes. Globes are not very practical for navigation purposes, but they are useful when you want to see a graphic representation of the entire world.

The equator is an imaginary line that runs around the middle of the earth from east to west. It divides the earth into northern and southern hemispheres, Fig. 18-9. The equator, and the lines that run parallel to it, are called latitudes. The reference number given to the equator is 0 degrees. Latitudes to the north of the equator are numbered from 0 to 90 degrees north. Latitudes to the south are numbered from 0 to 90 degrees south.

Lines that run from north pole to south pole are called longitudes. The 0 degree reference longitude is called the "prime meridian." Because the earth is round there are 360 longitudinal degrees. Longitudes that lie to the east of the prime meridian are

Fig. 18-8. Globe of the world is not useful for navigation, but it shows the relationship of continents and regions of the world.

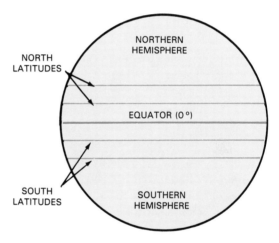

Fig. 18-9. Midway between the north and south poles there is a dividing line separating the northern hemisphere from the southern hemisphere. It is known as the equator. Parallel lines north and south of the equator are called lines of latitude. They are numbered from 0 degrees (equator) to 90 degrees in either direction.

numbered from 0 to 180 degrees east. Longitudes that lie to the west of the prime meridian are numbered from 0 to 180 degrees west, Fig. 18-10.

When locating a fixed position on a chart, the numbers of the closest latitude and longitude are used. These numbers together are called coordinates. If the location is not on an intersection of coordinates, we use minutes. Minutes make up the spaces between longitudes and latitudes. Each space

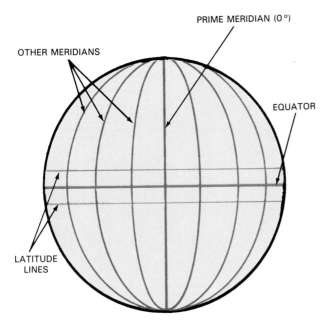

Fig. 18-10. For purpose of navigation, the world is also divided up by lines of longitude that run from north to south from pole to pole. Water and airborne vehicles use coordinates to establish their position. One coordinate is the latitude; the other is the longitude.

between longitudes or latitudes is divided into 60 minutes. This can be compared to inches being the spaces between foot marks, except there are only 12 inches for each foot.

For an example of coordinates, look at Fig. 18-4 again. It shows an airport which is located somewhere on the northern hemisphere. By studying the numbers, you can tell that its coordinates are 30 degrees, 15 minutes north, and 60 degrees, 18 minutes west. By using this system, we can accurately locate positions on the earth's surface.

DETERMINING SPEED

As mentioned earlier, the speed of the vehicle is required information for navigators. Speed indicators have different names depending on the vehicle that is using them.

Airplanes use *airspeed indicators*. These instruments measure the difference between two pressures acting on an aircraft. When an airplane is at rest on the ground, the two pressures are equal. As the plane starts flying, air rushes into a small tube on the outside of the aircraft. This increases the pressure in that tube. There is another tube inside the plane's fuselage. Both tubes lead to the airspeed indicator. The difference in pressure activates a small diaphragm. Its motion is read on

the face of the instrument. The face is marked in miles per hour, and knots. A knot is the unit used to describe a nautical mile. It is equal to about 1.15 statute miles.

Land transportation vehicles use *speedometers*. They are hooked up to the rotating wheels, or other parts of the drive train. Speedometers tell how fast a vehicle is moving in miles (or kilometers) per hour.

Speed indicators aboard marine transportation vehicles are called *logs*. They determine how fast the ship is moving in knots. Logs work similar to airspeed indicators, except that they use water pressure to activate the instrument. Some logs also have markings that show miles per hour.

DETERMINING LOCATION AND DIRECTION

There are many ways in which navigators have determined the position and heading (direction) of their vehicles. Most of these devices and practices are used by the navigators of sea and air vehicles. However, land vehicle operators have also found some of these useful.

Compasses are simple devices for determining which direction is north. Once you know which direction is north, you can compare it to the direction you are traveling. Simple compasses use a free-floating, magnetized needle that spins on an axis. It will always point north (unless it is placed near a magnetic field). Because compasses are based on magnetic fields, they will point to what is known as magnetic north.

Gyrocompasses are more complex devices that point the direction of true north, Fig. 18-11. It uses a gyroscope, which consists of a wheel rotating so that its axis may point in any direction. Gyrocompasses are usually used on larger vehicles that have a need for extremely accurate direction finding. Usually, ordinary magnetic compasses are used as a simple guidance system.

Compasses and gyrocompasses locate two different north poles. The true north found by gyrocompasses is the point about which the earth would seem to rotate if you were looking at it from space. Magnetic north, as found by compasses, is located about 1000 miles south of true north. It can be found on Prince of Wales Island, in Canada. The only problem as far as navigation is concerned, is allowing for the variation when charts use true north as a reference, and your compass points to magnetic north.

Fig. 18-11. The gyrocompass is one of many navigation and control instruments used by pilots of large aircraft. A digital readout shows direction. (McDonnell Douglas)

Sextants are a very old tool used to determine the position of ships, and planes, Fig. 18-12. Using it, a navigator measures the altitudes of stars and other celestial bodies from the horizon. By comparing these findings with recorded data, positions of the vehicles may be found.

Modern technology has brought about *radio sextants*. These are sensitive electronic devices that receive radio waves given off by the sun to determine position of the vehicle. They do this by continuously measuring the position of the sun in the sky. An advantage of a radio sextant is that it can track the sun in all weather conditions.

Fig. 18-12. A crew member uses a sextant to take a reading for determining a ship's position.

TYPES OF NAVIGATION

You learned earlier that navigation is the act of guiding a vehicle. For this, operators or navigators need to know their present location and their intended destination. There are several ways to navigate a vehicle. Some are relatively simple, requiring only basic equipment. Others are more complex, using sophisticated electronic equipment some of which have just been discussed.

Dead reckoning is a term used to describe a frequently used type of navigation. It is an old form of navigation which has not always proved to be accurate. Because of this, dead reckoning is usually used along with other types of navigation to improve accuracy.

Dead reckoning navigation determines a vehicle's position by figuring how far and in what direction it has come from its last known position. A known position is called a *fix*. The direction of travel can be found with a compass. The distance of travel can be found by multiplying the time of travel by the speed of the vehicle. These numbers are used to draw lines on a chart which will show the vehicle's new fix. This is not very accurate because it does not take into account wind speed, currents, steering errors, or any number of other variables.

Piloting is a more accurate and common method of navigation. It is used around coastal areas, or when land is in sight. Basically, piloting determines the bearing (position based upon the compass angle) of a vehicle by the use of landmarks. A navigator sights one or more distinct features of a coastline or shoreline. Then she or he lays out the same headings on a chart. By looking at where the various headings converge, Fig. 18-13, the navigator can tell the position of the vehicle. Obviously, charts must be used that are current.

Navigational Markers

When you drive down any road it is possible to see hundreds of navigational markers. Road signs of all types are placed so that they warn of dangerous conditions, mark routes, and give traffic signals or traffic information. See Fig. 18-14. Highways that are built for high-speed travel are well marked to indicate the directions and destinations of roads that lead from them. This makes it easier for drivers to find the right road, and exit or enter the highway with plenty of time to be safe.

Waterways that lead in and out of harbors and waterways that are inland shipping channels, are marked with special types of markers. Buoys, like

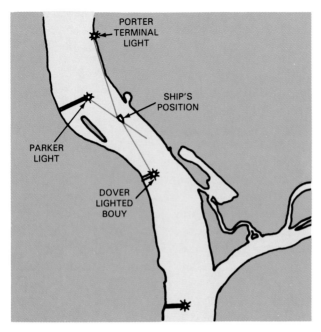

Fig. 18-13. By taking bearings on several landmarks, a navigator can fix the position of her or his ship. The ship is always at the point where the bearing lines intersect.

Fig. 18-15. A red buoy marks the channel limit in the Illinois River. North- or east-bound traffic must keep the buoy to starboard (right side).

the one in Fig. 18-15, are painted markers that are anchored in a body of water to guide water vehicles. Their color has significant meaning to boat pilots. Red buoys mark the right side of a channel as the boat is coming into port. Green buoys mark the left side. Safe water is marked by buoys painted in red and white bands. Orange diamonds painted on buoys mark dangerous water and should be avoided. Some buoys have messages marked on them so their meaning is clear. An example of this is a buoy marked 'No Wake' which is placed near docks or boat ramps. Only a boat traveling slowly will not produce a wake.

Many buoys have lights so that they can be seen easily at night. Navigators can tell what each lighted buoy means by the color of its light, and the length of its flashes. Some buoys are fitted with bells so that they can be heard in extremely foggy weather.

Fig. 18-14. Roadways are the paths used by some types of land vehicles. The more heavily a pathway is traveled, the more markers and signs guide the vehicle operators. Parking lots, too, have to assist parking of vehicles.

ELECTRONIC NAVIGATION EQUIPMENT

Since technology has produced vehicles that move with three degrees of freedom, we have extended our range of travel. This has also brought about the need for guidance equipment that is both accurate and useful over long ranges.

Electronic guidance equipment fills this need. It is based on the use of radio waves. Radio transmitting stations used for guidance are usually land-based. They are mostly government-owned and operated.

Radio waves are distinguished by their frequencies. High frequency waves are very accurate for navigation, but they cannot travel past the horizon. Low frequency waves are still accurate, and their signals carry for thousands of miles.

The type of frequency used is determined by the function of the transmitting station. If it is for short range only, high frequencies are employed. If the waves are to be sent over very long distances, lower frequencies are then used.

Radio Direction Finding

Radio direction finding is one of the early methods for guiding airplanes and ships. Electronic equipment aboard the vehicle receives transmissions sent by radio transmitters (beacons). The navigator adjusts the antenna until it signals that it is locked onto the direction of the incoming signals. The course of the vehicle can then be adjusted according to the position of the beacon.

VOR Navigation System

VOR navigation was developed in the 1940s. It means very high frequency omnidirectional range. This is a commonly used guidance system for air transportation. There are presently hundreds of VOR transmitting stations in the United States.

Each VOR station transmits a series of beams in all directions. The beams of radio waves are called *radials*, Fig. 18-16. Each radial is different from the others so that they may be kept apart and identified. The airplane has a VOR detecting device which locks onto the signals, and tells the pilot or navigator which radial it is following.

The radials are numbered in degrees with the 0 degree beam heading toward magnetic north. This makes it possible for the equipment and navigator to tell exactly which radial it is receiving.

VOR navigation systems have many advantages. Because the systems send out signals in all directions, pilots can navigate in any one of 360 verified (known) directions toward or away from the VOR transmitter. VOR signals are not affected by storms

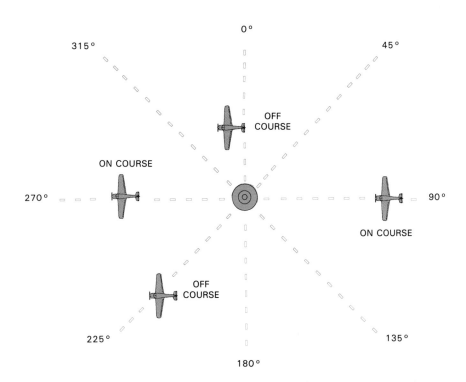

Fig. 18-16. A VOR station sends out radio signals in all directions for aircraft to "home in" on. A pilot selects a signal, also called a radial and locks onto it. The plane's VOR equipment can then tell whether the pilot is on course or not.

or other static-causing conditions. The signals used are also very accurate. It is difficult for an experienced pilot to fly off course when following a VOR signal.

Loran

Loran stands for long-range navigation. It is widely used in the United States to guide ships and planes that are approaching the coast. Loran navigation makes use of multiple transmitting stations. Usually there is one master and two slave stations.

Electronic equipment on board the vehicle receives frequencies transmitted by the loran stations. The system then compares the frequencies, and locates the position of the vehicle accordingly. Positions found by using the loran system are usually accurate to within 1/4 mile.

Omega

The *omega* navigational system is similar to Loran except it is a worldwide system. Because of the nature of this system, international cooperation is necessary for its success. There are eight omega transmitting stations on the earth. Signals from any two transmitters are used to locate the position of a vehicle.

Again, sophisticated electronic equipment is needed on board the vehicle to use the omega system.

NAVSAT

The United States Navy developed the *NAVSAT* system to guide ships and submarines. The name stands for navigation satellite system. It employs up to five satellites. They circle the earth in orbits that are very far away from each other.

Transmissions sent toward earth from the satellites tell their relative positions. Equipment aboard ships receives the transmissions and gives it to computers. The computers then measure the Doppler effect of the signal. The **Doppler effect** is the apparent change in frequency of a wavelength as it travels toward or away from an observer. Information from the measurements is then used to determine the bearing of the vehicle.

On Board Electronic Navigation Equipment

Some guidance systems are designed to be located on the vehicle itself. The transmitters and receivers are on the vehicle. There is no need for

external transmitting stations. These systems are commonly referred to as radar and sonar.

Radar stands for radio detection and ranging. It uses radio signals that are sent from equipment on board the vehicle. Basically, signals are sent out in all directions. As they strike objects the signals are reflected to a receiver and create images on a viewing screen. The images show the direction and distance of the objects from the transmitter.

Radar systems are useful in locating hazards that may not be visible to a person because of distance or weather conditions. They are relied on at airports to help direct pilots to runways and prevent collisions, Fig. 18-17. Radar systems can be used effectively at night and in bad weather.

Sonar stands for sound navigation and ranging. Its operation is similar to radar, except it uses sound waves instead of radio waves. Sonar was developed for underwater use. If you have ever seen or used a depth finder on a fishing boat, you have used a sonar guidance system.

Fig. 18-18 illustrates how a sonar system operates. Pulses of sound energy are sent through the water. As the pulses reflect off objects, they are "echoed" back to the receiver. These images are then recorded on paper or a viewing screen, Fig. 18-19. Developments in sonar technology have made it possible to distinguish even the size of fish within the range of sonar devices.

SUMMARY

Guidance systems are those that provide information required by a vehicle to follow a certain path, or perform a certain task. The information provided by the systems is read and interpreted by

Fig. 18-17. Radar control room in an airport control tower. Controllers rely on radar to keep track of planes. (United Airlines)

Fig. 18-18. Ships use sonar to detect objects submerged in the water. (General Electric)

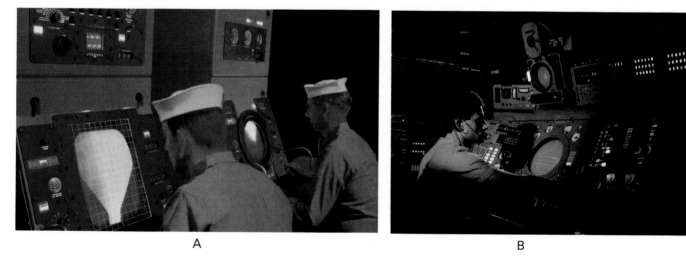

A   B

Fig. 18-19. Naval sonar operators "read" echoes off sonar screens. A—On a mine sweeper. (GE Ocean Systems) B—On an aircraft carrier. (U.S. Navy)

the operator of the vehicle. The act of guiding a vehicle to a destination is known as navigation. Navigators need to be concerned with speed, location, and direction of a vehicle. These are the types of information most frequently provided by guidance systems.

Maps and charts are useful guidance tools. They are graphic representations that show sections of the earth's surface. Road maps have clearly marked highways and landmarks to aid in navigation. Aeronautical and nautical charts are usually marked off with lines for longitudes and latitudes. Exact positions can be located on these charts by the use of coordinates.

Many devices are used for determining the speed of moving vehicles. They are called different names depending on the vehicle on which they are used.

Compasses and gyrocompasses are used to determine a vehicle's direction. Sextants are devices that can be used to determine the altitude of celestial bodies from the horizon. By comparing these altitudes with data on charts, navigators can determine the position and direction of their vehicles.

Electronic navigation devices are widely used guidance systems today. There are many types of systems based on the use of radio waves. VOR, loran, omega, and NAVSAT are all electronic systems that are mostly used to provide guidance information for airplanes and ships. Radar and sonar are guidance systems that are contained on board their respective vehicles. They are used to help prevent collisions with unseen obstacles and other vehicles.

KEY WORDS

All of the following words have been used in this chapter. Do you know their meaning?

Aeronautical charts	Loran
Airspeed indicators	Nautical charts
Chart	NAVSAT
Compasses	Omega
Dead reckoning	Piloting
Doppler effect	Radar
Fix	Radials
Globe	Radio sextants
Guidance systems	Sextants
Gyrocompasses	Sonar
Logs	Speedometers

TEST YOUR KNOWLEDGE

Write your answers on a separate sheet of paper. Do not write in this book.

Fill in the blank:

1. Guidance systems provide _____ for the operators of transportation vehicles.
2. The three most important pieces of guidance information are _____, _____, and _____.
3. _____ lines are those that run between the earth's poles on navigational charts.
4. _____ lines are those that run east/west around a globe.
5. _____ stands for radio detection and ranging.

Matching:

6. __ Compass.
7. __ Minutes
8. __ Sonar.
9. __ Airspeed indicator.
10. __ VOR.
11. __ Piloting.
12. __ Globe.
13. __ Log.
14. __ Omega.
15. __ Gyrocompass.

A. Chronometer for a ship or submarine.
B. Worldwide electronic guidance system.
C. Chronometer for an airplane.
D. Units into which latitudinal and longitudinal spaces are divided.
E. Common, basic method of navigation.
F. Device that locates magnetic north.
G. Sound detection and ranging.
H. Very high frequency omnidirectional range.
I. Spherical map of the earth.
J. Device that locates true north.

Short answer:

16. What kind of information is found on a map's legend?
17. What types of information are found on a nautical chart?
18. Explain how VOR navigation systems work.
19. What is dead reckoning, and how is it accomplished?
20. List 10 navigational markers used for land transportation vehicles.

ACTIVITIES

1. On a map of a coastal area or of a section of a navigable river, plot the position of craft from bearings given you by your instructor.
2. Demonstrate the use of a magnetic compass.
3. Secure a speaker on aeronautical or nautical navigation.

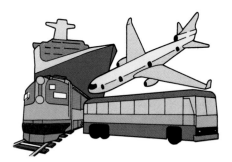

Chapter 19
CONTROL
OF A VEHICLE

After studying this chapter, you will be able to:
☐ Explain the need for control systems on transportation vehicles.
☐ Determine degrees of freedom for transportation vehicles.
☐ Describe how various transportation vehicles control speed.
☐ Explain how various transportation vehicles control direction.
☐ List and describe parts of control systems.

Control systems are the parts of vehicles that are used to change a vehicle's direction and speed. Obviously, different vehicles have different abilities regarding the number of directions in which they can be controlled. For example, a train can only move forward and backward on its tracks, while a helicopter has much more freedom. It can move forward and backward, left and right, and up and down. The number of changes in direction a vehicle is allowed is called *degrees of freedom*. The train has one degree of freedom, and the helicopter has three. Can you think of other vehicles that have one, two, or three degrees of freedom? Look at Fig. 19-1.

Do you think you would be able to safely operate a vehicle if it had no method of slowing down? Could you operate one if it had no method of increasing speed? It is necessary to be able to do these things if a vehicle is to be operated on our roads, or in the waterways and skies that surround us.

You should be able to see that there are a wide range of control systems needed to safely operate modern transportation vehicles. This chapter will focus on the various types of systems which give us control of our vehicles' speed and direction.

CONTROLLING SPEED

Various components are needed to transmit and control power provided by the propulsion system. Collectively, these components are known as the *drive system.* It takes in clutches, drive shafts, transmissions, speed controls, and brakes.

Drive Systems

When we have a propulsion system that is running and providing constant power, it is necessary to transmit that power to the parts of the vehicle that cause movement. Automobiles send this constant power through transmissions, drive shafts, universal joints, differentials, axles, and wheels to create movement of the vehicle, Fig. 19-2. Helicopter engines drive rotors through a gearbox which provides power for main and tail rotors, as well as accessories inside the vehicle, Fig. 19-3.

Clutches

Many times, however, it is necessary to disconnect the drive system from the power system. *Clutches* are mechanical devices that provide control for the separation of power and drive systems. These allow us to:
• Start the vehicle moving smoothly.
• Shift gears.

Fig. 19-1. Transportation vehicles have various degrees of freedom. A—This people mover was in use at the Vancouver, Canada Exposition. It has one degree of movement, forward and back. (French Technology Press Office) B—A motorcycle, like all steerable vehicles, has two degrees of freedom. (Harley-Davidson International) C—How many degrees of freedom does a hot-air balloon have—two or three?

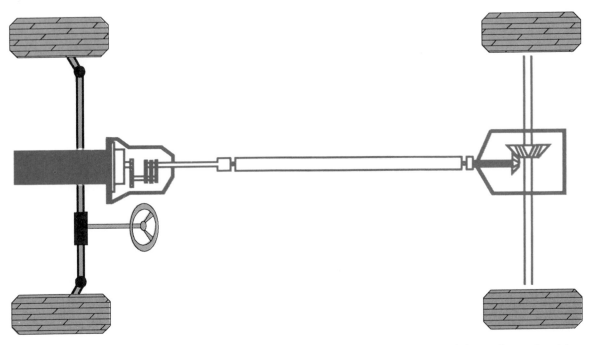

Fig. 19-2. A drive system, made up of many parts, transmits power from a vehicle's engine to its drive wheels.

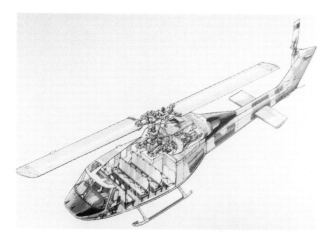

Fig. 19-3. A phantom view of a helicopter shows how power is transmitted from the engine to the rotor. (Bell Helicopter Textron, Inc.)

- Stop the movement of the vehicle, allowing it to stand still with the power source still running.

A popular type of clutch, widely used in vehicles with manually operated transmissions, is called a friction clutch, Fig. 19-4.

It uses a friction disk that is attached to a pressure plate on the drive shaft. The vehicle operator disengages the clutch by pressing on a foot pedal. The friction disk is moved away from the flywheel by the series of levers and springs that make up the clutch mechanism, Fig. 19-4A. When the clutch is disengaged, no power is transmitted between the power system and the drive system.

When the clutch is engaged, the vehicle moves because a heavy spring pushes the friction disk against the rotating flywheel that is powered by the engine, Fig. 19-4B.

Many types of clutches have been designed and built by vehicle manufacturers. Friction clutches are the choice that dominates the technology because of their versatility and smooth operation. Depending on the type and weight of the vehicle, variations of the basic friction clutch are used.

Transmission Systems

Without being geared up or down, internal combustion engines used to power many transportation vehicles today would be able to move a vehicle only on level surfaces, and at a moderate speed. The engines used to power earth-moving, and other heavy equipment would be able to lift and move only relatively small, light loads. When we want to climb a steep hill in a car, or move a very heavy load with a bulldozer, the power supplied by the engine must be modified (changed). *Transmission*

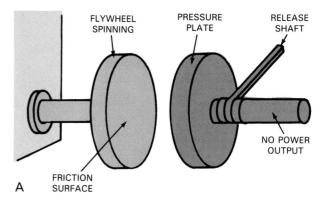

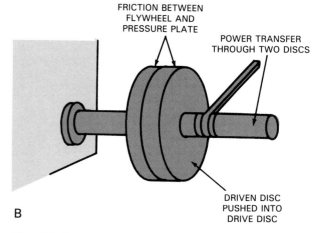

Fig. 19-4. A simplified drawing of a clutch shows how a manual transmission works. A—When the clutch is disengaged, the driven wheel, represented by the pressure plate, does not spin. B—When the clutch is engaged, the pressure plate is pressed against the flywheel. Power is transferred from the pressure plate to the wheels.

systems are the devices that provide for multiplying, dividing, or reversing the mechanical power coming from the engine. The power produced by the engine is in the form of torque. This means that energy in the engine is carried by a spinning crankshaft, Fig. 19-5.

Multiplying Torque

Can you imagine trying to open a door latch that had no knob? It would be very difficult because you cannot apply enough twisting force to the latch. By adding a doorknob, you are able to apply force as with a lever. This enables you to turn the latch easily, Fig. 19-6. The doorknob actually multiplies the force you exert and transfers that power to the latch.

Transmission systems combine different sizes of gears to multiply force. Their effect is much the same as the effect of a doorknob on a latch. Fig. 19-7 illustrates how gears mesh and work together to multiply torque. For every three rotations of the small

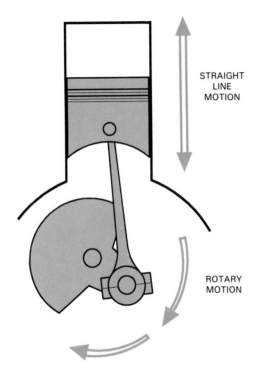

Fig. 19-5. As this simplified drawing shows, an engine piston transmits its downward motion to a crankshaft which, in turn, changes the motion to rotary motion or torque.

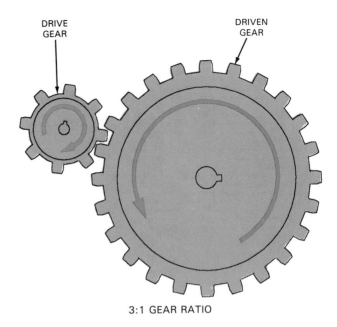

3:1 GEAR RATIO

Fig. 19-7. How a pair of gears multiply force. The left-hand gear is the drive gear and the right hand gear is the driven gear. Think of the right hand gear as a lever with the fulcrum (pivot) at the hub. Then think of the small gear as the force moving the larger gear.

Fig. 19-6. A door knob is a good example of how torque can be multiplied. The knob is actually an application of the lever.   (Kwikset Lock)

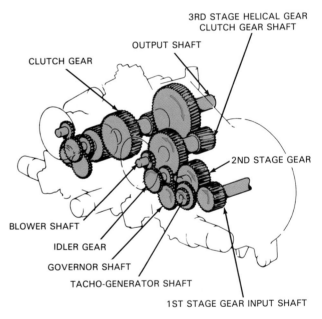

Fig. 19-8. Typical reduction gearbox of a helicopter makes intensive use of spur gears. This design provides a 5:1 reduction of the power turbine speed. (Bell Helicopter Textron)

drive gear, the larger driven gear rotates only once.

Gears used in transmissions are made of high quality steel, and are designed to be tough and durable. Two basic types of transmission gears use different arrangements of gear teeth. These arrangements are spur gears, Fig. 19-8, and helical gears, Fig. 19-9. Helical arrangements are preferred because of their great strength and smooth operation.

Manual Transmissions

Manual transmissions are totally controlled by the operator of the vehicle. He or she uses a clutch to disconnect the power source. A lever called a stick-shift, Fig. 19-10, controls and engages dif-

Fig. 19-9. Helical gears are usually favored because of their strength.

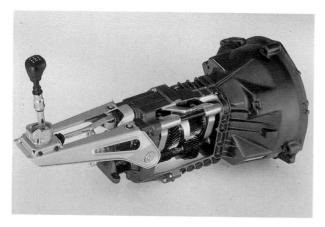

Fig. 19-10. A cutaway of a five-speed manual transmission. The clutch is contained in the "bell" housing at the front end of the transmission.

ferent combinations of gears. Thus, the driver can change speed and power according to road or environmental conditions.

Automatic Transmissions

Automatic transmissions also change the torque between the power and drive systems, but are not dependent on the vehicle operator for control. There is no need for a clutch with an automatic transmission because it uses a fluid coupling to receive power from the engine. These transmissions can produce an unlimited number of torque ratios. They do so automatically once the vehicle operator has selected a range suitable to road conditions. See Fig. 19-11.

Acceleration

Acceleration means changing the speed of a vehicle so that it moves faster. The method of acceleration depends on the type of propulsion system used

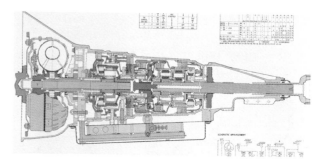

Fig. 19-11. Cutaway drawing of an automatic transmission. Fluids circulating in the transmission automatically change the ratio of engine torque to torque delivered to the drive wheels of the vehicle. (Ford Motor Co.)

by the vehicle. Those using internal combustion engines, accelerate by forcing more fuel into the engine through a throttle system. This system includes the carburetor or fuel injectors, Fig. 19-12. Giving the engine more fuel produces more rpm (revolutions per minute) from the engine.

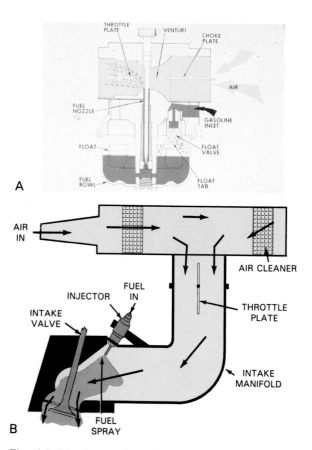

Fig. 19-12. Internal combustion engines accelerate as more fuel is delivered to an engine through its carburetor or fuel injection system. A—Simplified cutaway drawing of a carburetor. B—Cutaway drawing showing how air and fuel are drawn into the combustion chamber of an engine that has a fuel injection system.

The drive components receive the extra power and use it to produce an increase in speed. Fig. 19-13 is a phantom view of a semi-tractor showing the engine and various drive components. Can you tell how drive trains move the vehicles to which they are attached?

Rockets and other vehicles that have reaction engines use similar methods of acceleration. Extra fuel is forced into the propulsion system by a throttle.

In the jet engines of flying vehicles, the burning of extra fuel causes an increase in the speed of the gases leaving from the rear of the engine. This action causes an increase in the reaction that pushes the vehicle through its environment, Fig. 19-14.

Marine vehicles that employ jet propulsion accelerate in a similar way. Opening a throttle adds more fuel to the propulsion system. This causes an increase in the speed of the drive components. The volume and speed of the water that is moved through the system increases. The water that is pushed out the rear of the system will accelerate the vehicle significantly, Fig. 19-15.

Vehicles that use *electromagnetic levitation* for propulsion, like the Maglev system, are locked into a "wave" that travels through coils in a guideway. As the operator increases the frequency of the wave, she or he increases the speed of the vehicle, Fig. 19-16. Refer to Chapter 11 for an explanation of the propulsion systems for electromagnetic levitation vehicles.

Deceleration

To be safe, vehicles that are able to speed up must be able to slow down. *Deceleration* is slowing down or braking a vehicle. Manufacturers design vehicles so that they can decelerate gradually. This provides safety for the passengers and cargo on board. Many types of braking systems have been developed for use on a variety of land vehicles. These systems are also used on air and space vehicles, but are only applied when the vehicle is landing.

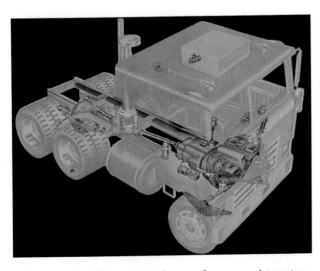

Fig. 19-13. Phantom view of a semi-tractor. Transmission and shift lever are shown in blue while the drivetrain is shown in brown. (Hayes-Dana, Inc.)

Fig. 19-14. Concept drawing of a supersonic aircraft. Four reaction engines would propel it at speeds well above the speed of sound. (Boeing Airplane Co.)

Fig. 19-15. Jet powered boat uses reaction engine principles to propel the boat.

Fig. 19-16. A "Maglev" train uses no wheels. It is suspended by the repulsion action of magnetism. (HSST)

Hydraulic Braking Systems

The *hydraulic braking systems* used on modern, wheeled vehicles link a master cylinder to a brake pedal and to one or two brake cylinders at each wheel. The cylinders are connected to the master cylinder with steel tubing. The tubing carries and contains the flow of hydraulic fluid through the system, Fig. 19-17. When the vehicle operator steps on the brake pedal she or he activates the master cylinder. Force produced at the master cylinder is transmitted to each wheel cylinder by the hydraulic fluid. The wheel cylinders expand to activate the vehicle's brakes. In this way, each wheel receives an equal amount of force to decelerate the car evenly. Refer to Chapter 4 for a review of the operation of hydraulic cylinders.

There are various types of mechanical brakes powered by the individual wheel cylinders. *Drum brakes* and *disc brakes* are the devices which use friction to physically slow the vehicle.

Drum Brakes

The drum brake uses two brake shoes that are shaped to fit the inside of the brake drum. They are held close to the inside of the brake drum but are not touching it. The brake drum is attached to the wheel of the vehicle, and rotates freely around the brake shoes while the vehicle is moving. As the brake pedal is depressed, the hydraulic cylinders activate the wheel cylinders. They push the brake shoes outward against the rotating brake drum. The two surfaces rub against each other. The friction from this contact slows the vehicle.

Disc Brakes

Disc brakes are another commonly used brake device. Instead of a drum, a steel disc, called a *rotor* is mounted to the wheel assembly so that it spins freely. See Fig. 19-18 for an example. A brake caliper straddles the rotating disc, but does not touch it. When the disc brake is activated through the hydraulic brake system, the caliper is squeezed against both sides of the disc. The disc is slowed by the friction of the rubbing surfaces. This, in turn, slows the wheel.

Brake Protection

Because of the heat generated in a brake device, the metal brake parts must be protected. Brake shoes and calipers are fitted with linings made of special asbestos compounds. The materials are

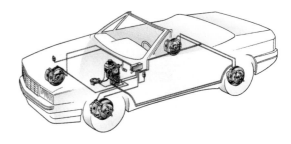

Fig. 19-18. An artist's drawing shows a phantom view of an automobile's disc brake system. Tubing shown delivers braking power to the wheels. Friction on the rotors stops the vehicle. The system shown also has a computer-controlled traction system. (GM-Cadillac Motor Car Div.)

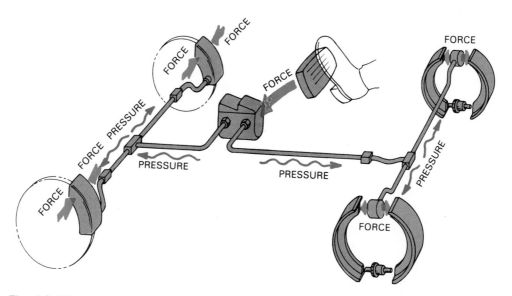

Fig. 19-17. A piston in the master cylinder forces fluid to wheel cylinders where it forces brake shoes and pads against rotating wheels to reduce vehicle speed.

strong and resist heat very well. The asbestos parts eventually wear, and may be cleaned, ground, or replaced. When mechanics work on brake devices, they must be very careful not to inhale the dust created. Asbestos is carcinogenic. This means it can cause cancer. See Fig. 19-19.

Power Brakes

Power brakes are found on many modern automobiles. This brake system adds a vacuum control valve between the brake pedal and the master cylinder. When the brake is pushed the vacuum unit uses the vacuum created by the propulsion system to activate the master cylinder. The balance between vacuum pressure and atmospheric pressure is controlled in the unit. As a result, vacuum exerts the major force on the master cylinder. This allows the driver to use less foot pressure. At the same time, the brake pedal may be positioned more comfortably.

Anti-Lock Braking Systems

Recently, to improve braking systems, manufacturers have installed sensors that monitor vehicle speed. When wheels are braked, the sensors activate an electronic controller which applies and releases brake pressure to prevent brake lockup. These systems improve the safety of the vehicles. Avoiding skids during braking is important for adequate control over the speed of a vehicle.

CONTROLLING DIRECTION

You can readily see that if there were no way of steering a vehicle, that vehicle would be unsafe. Drivers, pilots, and other vehicle operators would have no way of avoiding obstacles. Additionally, vehicles would be almost useless; while they could move easily, they would never arrive at the desired destination. Can you imagine running a transportation system with vehicles that couldn't be kept on the pathway?

Vehicles on Rails and Guideways

Railroad trains, electromagnetic levitation vehicles, monorails, and vehicles that travel through tubes and pipes, as well as escalators, elevators, and moving sidewalks all have one degree of freedom. See Fig. 19-20. This means that they can only move

A

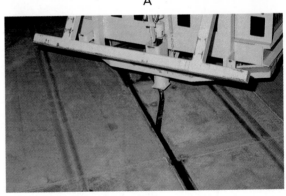

B

Fig. 19-20. An on-site transport system with one degree of freedom. A—Like a train, this towline cart system moves materials around in a factory. B—Towline connects carts to recessed tow chain. (SI Handling Systems Inc.)

Fig. 19-19. An auto mechanic uses proper protective equipment during brake repair to avoid breathing asbestos-laden dust. (Nilfisk of America, Inc.)

forward or backward in or on their guideways. The control of direction is mostly done automatically by the arrangement of vehicle and guideway. Wherever the guideway goes, the vehicle must go.

Built-In Railroad Steering

Train wheels are ground at a slight angle and fit on the tracks so that there is a gap between the wheel flange and the inside of the tracks, Fig. 19-21. When the train approaches a turn in the track, the whole vehicle shifts over slightly so that the outside wheel has to turn more revolutions than the inside wheel. This helps the vehicle to follow the track. Just as important, it prevents the wheels from skidding or derailing. Skid prevention also means less wear on the metal parts of the vehicle and track, Fig. 19-22.

Fig. 19-21. Flanges on wheels of railroad cars allow track to provide control of train's direction of travel. The flange keeps the wheel on the rail.

Fig. 19-22. Flanges on the wheel keep train on the track as tracks change direction. (Norfolk Southern Corp.)

Steering Wheeled Land Vehicles

There are four basic systems for controlling the direction of wheeled vehicles. Front steer, rear steer, front and rear steer, and crab steer are illustrated in Fig. 19-23. These are the movements that are allowed by the wheels to control the direction of the vehicles. Most automobiles rely on front steering for control, Fig. 19-24. Both front wheels act instantly with the movement of a steering wheel.

Forklifts, some street-cleaning machines, and other small vehicles that need to have a tight turning radius are designed with rear wheel steering, Fig. 19-25. These vehicles can turn around in a very small space. Can you think of other vehicles that use rear steering?

Recent improvements in the control of automobiles, and trucks with oversized tires have led to all-wheel steering. This system uses the steering wheel to operate the front and rear wheels at the same time. However, front and rear turn in opposite directions from each other. Both front wheels act together, and both rear wheels act together. This setup allows for a tighter turning radius. Crab steer is used by some automobiles when cruising at highway speeds. All four wheels are allowed to move slightly in the same direction. This allows for very quick steering from side to side. The wheels do not need to turn very far to steer the automobile at highway speeds. Can you see a problem with the wheels oversteering at high speeds?

Wheel Positioning

The rolling wheels that pivot to steer vehicles must be positioned with attention to caster and camber. *Caster* is positioning the wheel so that where it contacts the road is actually behind the

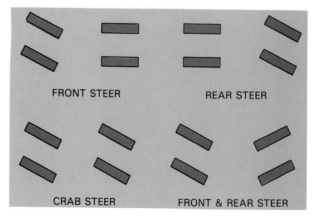

Fig. 19-23. Four basic systems control the movement of wheeled land vehicles.

A   B

Fig. 19-24. A—Passenger cars and many other steerable land vehicles are controlled by front-steering wheels. B—Farm tractors use a combination of front-steering wheels and braking of drive wheels to allow sharp turns. (John Deere)

Fig. 19-25. A fork truck, because it is steered with the rear wheel or wheels has a small turning radius. (Caterpillar Inc.)

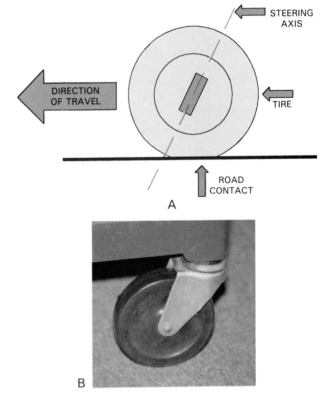

A

B

Fig. 19-26. The meaning of the term, caster. A— If you were to continue the centerline of the pivot point (where wheel is attached to the axle), the line would end ahead of the point where the tire touched the road. B—A wheel on a piece of furniture is also called a "caster." It is a simple illustration of what caster does for a vehicle's front wheel. It tends to keep it moving in the line of travel, making steering much easier.

centerline of the steering axis, Fig. 19-26A. *Camber* is a tilting of the front wheels slightly off the vertical.

Caster may be easier to understand if you were to examine the casters on furniture or shopping carts. Have you ever watched a piece of furniture or office equipment rolling on casters? The wheels always align themselves with the path of the furniture. This is because the steering axis of the caster is in front of the point where the wheel meets the floor. The car tire, like the caster wheel, Fig. 19-26B, naturally follows the line of travel of the vehicle.

Positive camber is also very important in controlling the direction of a vehicle. Positive camber is achieved by tipping the tops of the front wheels outward, Fig. 19-27.

When the bottoms of the wheels are farther apart than the tops, the wheels have negative camber, Fig. 19-28. By adding positive camber, the weight of the vehicle does not force the wheels out, avoiding stress on the wheel bearings and axles. Car builders are able to lessen the road effects on the steering system in this way. Most modern automobiles use a small degree of positive camber.

Articulated Frame Steering

Some vehicles designed for mass transit, farm operation, and construction have an **articulated** (hinged) section in the middle of the vehicle, Fig. 19-29. Steering is then controlled by swiveling the trailing wheels along with the front wheels. This system allows a small turning radius on very long vehicles.

Steering Tracked Land Vehicles

Tanks, bulldozers, some logging equipment, and other off-road vehicles use tracks. The tracks im-

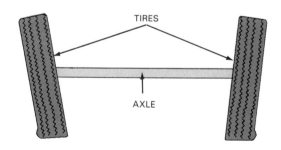

Fig. 19-27. This drawing shows a pair of wheels that have positive camber.

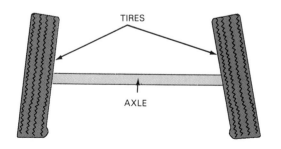

Fig. 19-28. These wheels show negative camber.

Fig. 19-29. An articulated mass transit "Megabus." It is "hinged" or articulated at two places along its length to allow a shorter turning radius. (French Technology Press Office)

prove traction on difficult terrain. To change the direction of such a vehicle, the operator must vary the speed of one of the tracks. By decelerating one track and accelerating the other, she or he can pivot the vehicle. See Fig. 19-30. Tracked vehicles are able to turn around in one spot by moving one track forward and one track backward. Can you explain why certain types of vehicles or machines would need this capability?

STEERING MARINE VEHICLES

Vehicles that move through fluid environments, like water, often use *rudders* for control, Fig. 19-31.

Fig. 19-30. A bulldozer uses tracks instead of wheels. Control of direction is possible by varying the speed of one or the other of the tracks. (Caterpillar Inc.)

Control of a Vehicle 213

Fig. 19-31. A rudder on a vessel uses water's resistance to compression to control the vessel's direction of travel.

Rudders are hinged vertical surfaces on water vehicles. Usually located near the output of the propulsion source, they are part of the steering mechanism.

They act to change the direction of water pressure against the vessel. Because of the change in pressure, vessel's heading is changed. When the vessel is on its new heading, the propulsion system will move it in that direction. Rudders control the stern (rear) of most marine vehicles. This is similar to rear-steered land vehicles.

Air-cushioned marine vehicles, also known as *Hovercraft®* or ground-effects machine, have the rudders behind the propulsion fans that move air, Fig. 19-32. The rudders or vanes use the airflow

Fig. 19-32. An "airboat" is propelled by twin propellers. Vanes behind the props help steer it. (Freuhof)

to change the vehicle's direction of travel. Airboats used in swampy areas also use this method of directional control, Fig. 19-33.

Jet propelled marine vehicles do not need rudders. Their operators change the position of the jet nozzles to change the direction of thrust. The stern of jet-propelled marine vehicles will move in the opposite direction of the thrust. Fig. 19-34 shows a recreational vehicle that uses this method of steering.

Directional Control of Lighter-Than-Air Vehicles

The amount of directional control of lighter-than-air vehicles depends entirely on the type of vehicle. *Hot air balloons* can only control vertical flight by controlling the amount of hot air in the vehicle, Fig. 19-35. County fairs, festivals, and

Fig. 19-33. An airboat in the Everglades. Vehicles of this type use airflow for steering control. (National Park Service.)

Fig. 19-34. Some water-recreation vehicles use jets for steering control. (Kawasaki)

other events sponsor balloon races. See Fig. 19-36.

Blimps and *dirigibles* are lighter-than-air vehicles that are able to control both vertical and horizontal dimensions of flight, Fig. 19-37. Some types use rudder systems similar to those on boats. By manipulating the rudder, pilots control the flow of air. Airflow, in turn, influences direction of travel. Other types of direction control actually swivel components of the propulsion systems. Thrust in a different direction reorients the position of the craft. Propulsion fans driven by the engines swivel to swing the blimp in the desired direction.

Steering Airplanes

As we learned in an earlier chapter, airplanes are heavier-than-air vehicles capable of great speed and

Fig. 19-37. Goodyear blimps over Houston. Once under consideration as military reconnaissance vehicles, they are now mainly used for advertising purposes.   (The Goodyear Tire & Rubber Co.)

Fig. 19-35. Hot air balloons are often used for advertising because they attract attention with their bright colors.

controlling three degrees of freedom, Fig. 19-38. A system of movable surfaces on the airplane allows pilots to use the airflow around the plane for control. Fig. 19-39 names the various surfaces and locates them on the plane.

Basically, the elevators, flaps, and ailerons control the vertical dimension of flight. The ailerons and rudder control the lateral or sideways movement. Fig. 19-40 illustrates the various surface positions and their control functions. Pilots use these surfaces in combination with each other. Only in this way can they control the various maneuvers needed to direct a flying airplane.

Steering Helicopters

Helicopters are rotary-wing aircraft that can move in different directions with greater speed and agility than airplanes. They are more maneuver-

Fig. 19-36. Balloon racing is often an attraction at county fairs.

Fig. 19-38. Airplanes are capable of great speeds and control three degrees of freedom.
(U.S. Air Force)

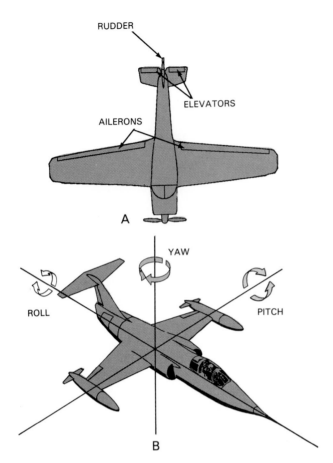

Fig. 19-39. A—The named parts control the flight of an airplane. B—Aircraft can change attitude on three planes. (Estes)

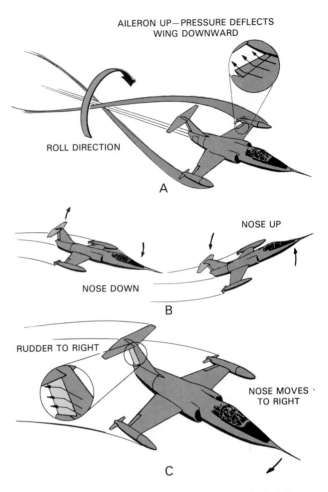

Fig. 19-40. Aircraft control surfaces and their functions. A—Use of ailerons. B—Use of elevators. C—Use of rudder. (Estes)

able. See Fig. 19-41. Various rotor functions have been discussed in previous chapters. Steering is also achieved by manipulating the rotor blades. We have seen how lift is achieved by changing the pitch of all the blades at once. Directional control is possible through *cyclical pitch*. This changes the pitch of the blades as they pass a certain point in their rotation.

If the pilot wishes to steer the helicopter to the left, she or he increases the pitch of the rotor blades as they swing past the right side of the vehicle. This increases lift on the right side and banks the helicopter so it moves to the left. Reversing the process moves the helicopter to the right. See Fig. 19-42. By controlling cyclical pitch, pilots determine the vehicle's direction of flight forward, backward, and laterally (to left or right).

SUMMARY

Control systems consist of the parts of a vehicle that control speed and direction. These systems are needed to run a transportation system practically

Fig. 19-41. Helicopters are more maneuverable than airplanes. They can hover as well as change direction almost instantly. (Bell Helicopter)

and safely. Speed is controlled in terms of acceleration and deceleration. Most vehicles are able to disconnect propulsion systems from drive systems

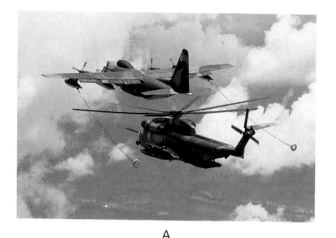

A

B

Fig. 19-42. Maneuverability of a helicopter is most apparent during a midair refueling. A—The helicopter approaching the tanker must nearly match the plane's speed. B—The refueling has commenced.   (USAF)

to allow a complete stopping without shutting down the engine.

Clutches and fluid couplings are used to transmit power from a source to the drive system. Transmission systems are used to convert power created by the engine to do more work (such as climb hills and move heavy loads). Most vehicles rely on forcing additional fuel into the system to accelerate.

Deceleration is brought about through various brake devices. Drum and disc brakes are activated hydraulically to create friction that slows the vehicle. Asbestos linings or pads are used on these devices to protect metal parts from heat and wear.

Steering is controlled by manipulating the way a vehicle comes in contact with its environment. Some land vehicles follow a guide structure and are not able to deviate from the path of the structure. Other land vehicles control the direction of wheel and track movements. Vehicles that operate in marine environments like boats, submarines, and hydrofoils use rudders to change their direction. Airplanes use a system of movable surfaces to control the flow of air over and around the vehicle. Air flowing over these surfaces changes the position of the plane and thereby, its direction of travel. Helicopters vary the pitch of the rotor blades to provide great agility in directional control.

KEY WORDS

All of the following words have been used in this chapter. Do you know their meaning?

Acceleration
Articulated
Blimps
Camber
Caster

Clutches
Control systems
Cyclical pitch
Deceleration
Degrees of freedom

Dirigibles
Disc brakes
Drive system
Drum brakes
Electromagnetic
  levitation
Hot air balloons

Hovercraft™
Hydraulic braking
  system
Power brakes
Rotor
Rudders
Transmission systems

TEST YOUR KNOWLEDGE

Write your answers on a separate sheet of paper. Do not write in this book.

Matching:

1. __ Control systems.
2. __ Acceleration.
3. __ Rudders.
4. __ Deceleration.
5. __ Clutches.

A. Movable surfaces used on vehicles in water and air to steer them from side to side.
B. Changing the speed of a vehicle so that it moves faster.
C. Changing the speed of a vehicle so that it moves slower.
D. Parts of vehicles that are used to change speed and direction.
E. Mechanical devices that are used to separate the power and drive systems.

Fill in the blank:

6. Transmission systems are used to _____, _____, or _____ the power coming from the engine.
7. The four basic systems for controlling the direction of wheeled vehicles are _____,

_____, _____, and _____.

8. Generally, _____-than-air vehicles have more directional control than _____-than-air vehicles.

9. Five movable surfaces on airplanes that allow directional control are _____, _____, _____, _____, and _____.

10. Two common types of brake devices are _____ brakes and _____ brakes.

Multiple choice:

11. Which of the following describes how many directions a vehicle is allowed to travel.
   A. Power systems.
   B. Degrees of freedom.
   C. Drive systems.
   D. Jet engines.

12. Most vehicles accelerate by forcing extra _____ into the propulsion system.
   A. People.
   B. Lubricant.
   C. Water.
   D. Fuel.

13. _____ is a carcinogenic material used to protect brakes from heat and wear.

   A. Nylon.
   B. Plastic.
   C. Asbestos.
   D. Argon.

14. Controlling _____ enables helicopter pilots to steer their vehicles.
   A. Rotor blades.
   B. Speed.
   C. Wind direction.
   D. Electricity.

ACTIVITIES

1. Demonstrate to the rest of the class the function of steering systems for airplanes. Use a wind tunnel or a fan to provide the airflow needed.

2. Examine the speed control mechanisms for a small gas engine. Research carburetion principles and prepare an illustrated paper or a five-minute talk on what you have learned.

3 Organize a competition to design the most effective braking mechanism to stop a mousetrap-powered model car.

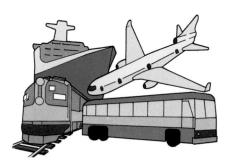

Chapter 20
SUSPENSION OF A VEHICLE

After studying this chapter, you will be able to:
☐ Explain the purpose of suspension systems in transportation technology.
☐ Describe the function, and construction of the main parts of an automobile suspension system.
☐ Explain how airplanes can fly.
☐ Describe the design of vehicles that operate in fluid environments.

The law of gravity dictates the need for some kind of system to support vehicles. Otherwise, the vehicles would crash to earth, sit there, and be unable to move. Air travel would be impossible with no system to keep aircraft airborne. Roads with their hard surfaces would serve no purpose. Friction would keep automobiles and trucks in one spot. Vehicles need suspension systems.

WHAT ARE SUSPENSION SYSTEMS?

Suspension systems are the parts of vehicles that support, or suspend the vehicle in its environment. Land vehicles are very different from air or marine vehicles. They travel on top of a hard, and uneven surface. Air and marine vehicles can fly, or float, in a fluid environment. Because of the nature of the mediums in which they operate, suspension system designs obviously need to be different.

Suspension systems also provide a method to smooth the ride for passengers and cargo. Automobiles travel on roads that may, or may not, be smooth. Because of the demand for comfortable rides, car manufacturers have developed systems that "soften the ride." Modern cars can travel over potholes, ruts, dips, and bumps with little discomfort to the passengers, Fig. 20-1.

Suspension systems for air and marine vehicles are generally not as complex as those for land vehicles. The basic designs that let these vehicles fly or float is their suspension system. Airplanes, however, do need a strong suspension system to ease their landings and support them when they are on the ground. There are special additions to these vehicles that add stability and comfort. These will be studied later in this chapter.

SUSPENSION SYSTEMS FOR LAND VEHICLES

Automobile technology is at the forefront of suspension system design. Systems for many land vehicles have used the basic designs used for car suspensions. Trucks use the same components but they are stronger and heavier duty. Even golf carts and tractors have borrowed components from car suspension technology. For this reason, we will focus on the suspension components of automobiles. Remember, as you look at vehicles that travel on land, you can see these same components in various forms on other vehicles.

Pneumatic Tires

Pneumatic (air-filled) *tires* are an important part of suspension systems. They provide the contact

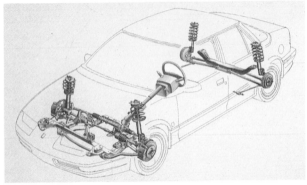

Fig. 20-1. Top. Suspension systems support a land vehicle above its pathway and smooth the ride. Bottom. Phantom view of the steering and suspension components of a passenger car. (Saturn Corp.)

points between the vehicle and the surface where it travels. Tires are fitted onto metal wheels that bolt to the axles, Fig. 20-2. Each modern tire can support 50 times its own weight when it is properly inflated. Ninety percent of the weight is held by air. The tire supports the other 10 percent. Keep in mind, however, that the tire must contain and withstand the pressure of the air.

Tires actually have two important functions.

- They provide a cushioning effect as the vehicle travels over bumps and ruts. The air inside the tire compresses and the sidewalls help to absorb the shock. Can you see how this fits the description of suspension as far as smoothing the ride?
- Tires also provide traction. This enables the car to "grip" the road surface for greater safety and good handling. Well-designed tires have tread designs that will push water away and let the tire surface contact and grip the firm road surface. The *contact patch* is the part of the tire that is actually touching the road as the tire spins. If much water gets between the contact patch and the road, the car will hydroplane. This is a term that means there is a film of water between the tire and the road surface. This is very dangerous because the driver does not have complete control anymore. That is why old, bald tires are not safe. Tires should be replaced as they become too worn.

A

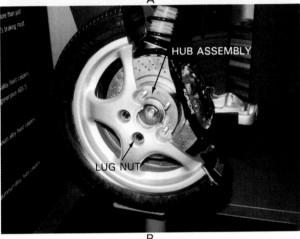

HUB ASSEMBLY

LUG NUT

B

Fig. 20-2. A—Air-filled tires are attached to a wheel called a rim. This assembly is then attached to the axle of land vehicles. (Greyhound) B—Lug nuts attach the wheel to the hub assembly.
(Goodyear Tire & Rubber Co.)

Tires are constructed of various rubber compounds and fabric. The fabric is usually a type of polyester, rayon, or nylon. It is then impregnated, or filled with rubber compounds. Fig. 20-3 shows the construction of a typical bias tire. Notice the many layers of fabric, called plies, that go into the tire. The cords of each ply are running in a different direction. This is called bias, meaning crisscrossed. Bias tires are strong, but their strength can be decreased if the bias between plies is off by only a few degrees.

Steel-belted radial tires are common today, Fig. 20-4. They include a fabric made of steel that is cut into wide strips. These strips are placed under the tread area. The plies on radial tires are placed

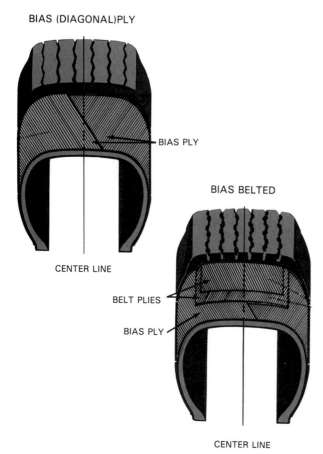

BIAS (DIAGONAL) PLY

BIAS PLY

CENTER LINE

BIAS BELTED

BELT PLIES

BIAS PLY

CENTER LINE

Fig. 20-3. Tires are carefully constructed to provide safety and longer service. Note arrangement of various plies on bias ply tires. (Goodyear Tire & Rubber Co.)

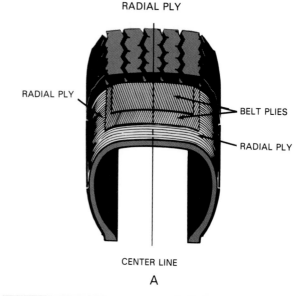

RADIAL PLY

RADIAL PLY

BELT PLIES

RADIAL PLY

CENTER LINE

A

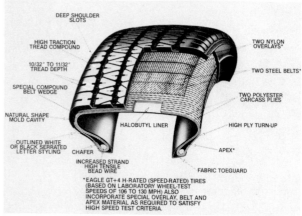

DEEP SHOULDER SLOTS

HIGH TRACTION TREAD COMPOUND

10/32" TO 11/32" TREAD DEPTH

SPECIAL COMPOUND BELT WEDGE

NATURAL SHAPE MOLD CAVITY

OUTLINED WHITE OR BLACK SERRATED LETTER STYLING

CHAFER

INCREASED STRAND HIGH TENSILE BEAD WIRE

TWO NYLON OVERLAYS*

TWO STEEL BELTS*

TWO POLYESTER CARCASS PLIES

HIGH PLY TURN-UP

HALOBUTYL LINER

APEX*

FABRIC TOEGUARD

*EAGLE GT+4 H-RATED (SPEED-RATED) TIRES (BASED ON LABORATORY WHEEL-TEST SPEEDS OF 106 TO 130 MPH) ALSO INCORPORATE SPECIAL OVERLAY, BELT AND APEX MATERIAL AS REQUIRED TO SATISFY HIGH SPEED TEST CRITERIA.

B

Fig. 20-4. Radial tire construction. Radial ply is made of steel strands. A—Note names of plies. B—Features of a specific all-season tire. (Goodyear Tire & Rubber Co.)

so that the cords run perpendicular (at right angles) to the centerline of the tread. Steel-belted radial tires provide better traction, longer tread life, and permit a softer ride than other tires.

At the sides of the tire, where it fits over the rim of the wheel, there are bead wires. These provide an anchor point that runs the whole diameter of the tire. The bead wires provide the tension that allows the tire to grip the lip on the wheel so that the tire is airtight and rigid. Tires cannot be allowed to slip on the wheels or they will lose air and be useless.

There is a thin rubber coating or liner on the inside of the tire. There is also a thick rubber exterior covering. The tread pattern is formed on the exterior of the tire. Tread patterns differ with the purpose of the tire, Fig. 20-5. There are all-season tread patterns, as well as winter, or summer treads. Some specially designed tires have a smooth tread. These are racing tires and are not used for street vehicles.

Each tire must be marked with its specifications. These include maximum load rating, size, maximum air pressure, type of tire, and materials used

in construction. Fig. 20-6 identifies some markings that need to be on tires.

Springs

You have probably seen all types of springs applied to many devices. *Springs* are devices that are able to temporarily store energy, then use the energy. The springs used on automobiles are relatively large and heavy duty; they need to support a heavy weight.

One type of automotive spring is called a coil spring. It is made by taking long steel rods and forming them around a cylinder into a helix shape, Fig. 20-7. The springs are then taken off the cylinder and heat treated. They then retain their shape and give the proper tension.

A

B

C

Fig. 20-5. Tire tread designs differ to serve different purposes. A—All season performance tire. This type is suited to combine the features of a performance tire and an all season tire. B—Highway tire is designed for smooth, quiet highway driving in all weather conditions. C—This radial tire is designed to provide traction under the most severe conditions on or off road. (Goodyear Tire & Rubber Co.)

Fig. 20-6. Molded into the sidewall of every tire is a wealth of information about the tire, such as its pressure rating and how it is to be used. (Goodyear Tire & Rubber Co.)

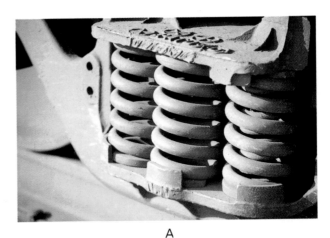

A

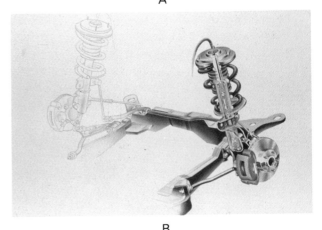

B

Fig. 20-7. A coil spring is used on vehicles to support the weight of the body. Springs like these are designed to be compressed. A—Railroad cars have heavy springs to support heavy loads. B—Front wheel spring arrangement for a passenger car. (Cadillac)

Coil springs are usually placed between the vehicle frame and the axle. Fig. 20-8 shows one arrangement where coil springs are used. When the wheel goes over a bump, the spring compresses and stores potential energy. As the wheel moves off the bump, the spring uses the energy to expand and push the wheel back onto the road. This way, the wheel and spring move over the bump, but the vehicle frame can keep moving in a straight line.

A type of automotive spring is the leaf spring, Fig. 20-9. It is made of a series of steel strips, each one shorter than the next. The leaves are held together by a bolt that runs through the centers of each strip. The longest one, on top, has ends that are formed into loops. Two square clips surround the leaf spring midway between the center and the ends. These prevent the leaves from rotating away from each other when stressed.

The leaf spring is attached to the vehicle at three places, Fig. 20-10. The front loop is attached to the vehicle frame, about two feet in front of the axle. The rear loop of the leaf spring is attached to a shackle which is connected to the frame. The shackle can swing forward or backward if the spring is heavily compressed or stretched. The leaf spring is usually attached to the axle by strong U-bolts around its middle. Thin rubber, or neoprene pads are sometimes placed in the leaf spring to reduce squeaks and friction.

As a wheel hits a rut or a bump, the leaf spring acts the same as a coil spring. It flexes up and

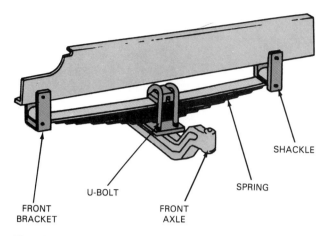

Fig. 20-10. Leaf springs are always attached to a vehicle frame in three locations.

down, storing potential energy. By returning to its original shape, the spring forces the axle up, or down, to force the wheel firmly onto the road surface. This lets the wheel go over the obstacle while the vehicle continues to travel in a straight line.

Torsion bars are another commonly used "spring" on modern land vehicles like trucks and automobiles. Torsion bars do not resemble normal springs; they look more like metal rods. Fig. 20-11 is an illustration of a torsion bar. One end is attached to the wheel assembly through a lever arm. The other end is attached to a cross member of the car frame. When the wheel hits a bump or rut, the lever arm will swing up or down. The torsion bar will resist this movement, and force the wheel assembly back to its normal position. Torsion bars are more stable than coil springs because they will not let the car sway from side to side as much.

Fig. 20-8. Springs are usually placed below the frame of the vehicle.

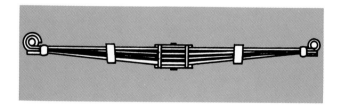

Fig. 20-9. A leaf spring is made up of tempered steel strips. The load of the vehicle is carried at its ends.

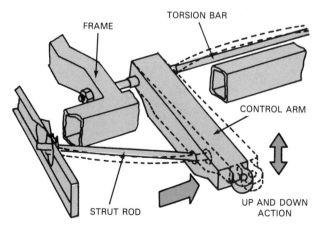

Fig. 20-11. Torsion bar suspension uses the tension or flex in a steel bar to support the load of a vehicle.

Springs are valuable parts of an automobile suspension system. They may, however, make the car feel like it is on a rough sea. When a spring compresses, then rebounds, it will spring past its normal position. As it rebounds, it will compress past its normal position again. This is called *spring oscillation*. This oscillation needs to be controlled so that the vehicle can have a stable, firm ride.

Shock Absorbers

Shock absorbers do not absorb a road's unevenness so it isn't transferred to the vehicle structure. This job is done quite well by the system of springs. The job of a *shock absorber* is to control spring oscillation. A more accurate description of these devices, as used by the British, is spring dampener.

Shock absorbers are connected between the car frame and the axle. There is one for each spring, usually one at each wheel. The most common type is filled with hydraulic fluid. When the spring compresses and tries to oscillate, the shock will resist this motion. This type of shock absorber was originally designed for use on aircraft. Hence, it is called an airplane type shock.

A shock absorber looks like two pipes, one fitting inside the other. Fig. 20-12 shows a typical telescoping shock absorber. One end is attached to a piston rod that moves inside the other pipe. The piston on the end of the rod is made so that it creates a seal between itself and the inside of the shock. On the piston, there is a two-way valve arrangement or simply ports (holes).

When the shock is compressed, hydraulic fluid in it is put under pressure too. The fluid is allow-ed to escape slowly through the valve or the ports at a fixed rate. That rate is determined by the valve opening or the size of the ports. As the shock is then stretched by the spring recoiling, hydraulic fluid moves through the valve arrangement in the opposite direction. The oscillation of the shock is slowed because fluid can only pass through the shock absorber piston at a fixed rate.

Some shock absorbers are made with a dome of air above the hydraulic fluid. If the load on the vehicle is going to be greater than normal, air can be compressed into this space. This will make the shock absorber more rigid. This helps keep the vehicle from overcompressing the springs.

Stabilizer Bars

A *stabilizer bar* or sway bar is a long steel rod that is mounted between the two front wheel assemblies, Fig. 20-13. It helps to keep the vehicle from leaning out too far when the vehicle is going around corners. When the centrifugal force caused by the turn causes the vehicle's body to dip on the outside and lift on the inside, the bar is twisted. The stiffness of the bar resists this twisting and helps to keep the car level. This makes for a more comfortable ride. It also makes the vehicle easier to control.

SUSPENSION SYSTEMS FOR AIRPLANES

So that airplanes can takeoff, land, and maneuver on the ground, they must have a suspension system that can support it. Usually, airplanes

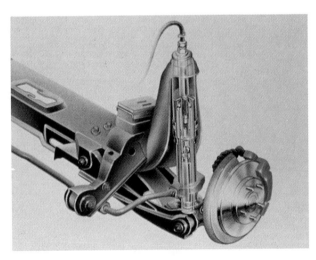

Fig. 20-12. Shock absorbers control the tendency of springs to bounce a vehicle up and down on bumpy roads. This cutaway shows the interior of a telescoping shock. (Cadillac)

Fig. 20-13. A stabilizer (arrow) keeps a vehicle from leaning over to the outside on tight turns. (Saturn Corp.)

have wheels. This part of the suspension system is called landing gear. Small aircraft usually have their landing gear arranged in one of two ways.

The first is the conventional arrangement as shown in Fig. 20-14. The single wheel is at the tail of the plane, and the two main wheels are under the cockpit. This was one of the first ways people put wheels on their planes. It has a disadvantage in the fact that the pilot has poor visibility when the plane is on the ground. This is because the fuselage of the plane tends to point upward when at rest. This also makes takeoffs more difficult.

The second arrangement is the tricycle-style landing gear. It can be seen in Fig. 20-15. The two main wheels are placed just behind the cockpit area. The single wheel is in the plane's nose, usually under the engine area. This arrangement keeps the plane more or less level when it is at rest. The pilot has an easier time seeing when he or she is maneuvering the plane on the ground.

Large commercial passenger planes, like the one in Fig. 20-16, use the tricycle-style landing gear. Instead of three wheels, they have multiple sets of wheels. This enables the suspension system to hold the weight of the aircraft on landings. You can imagine how heavy one of these vehicles must be.

Wheels are attached to the aircraft with struts. Struts are designed so that they absorb the shock

Fig. 20-14. This plane has conventional landing gear with two wheels forward and one at the tail.

Fig. 20-15. Tricycle landing gear keeps the plane more or less level when the plane is on the ground.

Fig. 20-16. Commercial jets are so huge that the landing gear has multiple sets of wheels. (United Airlines)

of the airplane touching the ground. They are made differently depending on the size of the vehicle they must support. Small planes can use one piece metal struts. Large planes use hydraulic shock absorbing devices similar to the ones used on automobile suspensions. Of course, the shock absorbers on large planes must be stronger than those used on cars.

Some airplanes are designed to land on water. Their suspension systems use pontoons instead of wheels. See Fig. 20-17. The pontoons are hollow cylinders so that they float. Some planes can land on solid ground or water. These use wheels that are attached to the insides of the pontoons. Planes used on snow and ice can be fitted with skis.

How Planes Fly

The components of airplanes that make them fly must be included in their suspension systems. They are "suspended" by air flowing over specially shaped wings. Even though the function of wings as part of the suspension system is not easy to understand, their purpose is just as important as wheels.

Lift is the upward force that an airplane's wings produce to keep it in the air. It is one of four forces that act on the plane in flight, Fig. 20-18. Lift acts

Fig. 20-17. Water-based planes use floats called pontoons in place of wheels on their landing gear.

Fig. 20-23. Large marine craft use displacement hulls. This means that there is enough additional buoyancy to carry large amounts of cargo. (Thunder Bay Harbor Commission)

Displacement hulls must be large enough to displace, or move, their own weight of water. For example, if you put a 450 lb. displacement hull in water, it would displace an equivalent (equal) weight of water. As the ship takes on more weight by loading passengers and cargo, it will "sink" in the water until it displaces that amount of added weight.

Fig. 20-24 shows a barge being loaded. Barges like this must be loaded evenly so that the weight is distributed evenly. This way the craft will remain stable in the water.

Fig. 20-24. A barge is a common example of a displacement hull. As the barge is loaded it sinks deeper into the water.

Pleasure boats are generally smaller craft that make use of very buoyant materials for their construction. These boats rely on the shapes of their hulls for various degrees of performance and stability. The five basic hull shapes are:
- Round hull.
- Flat hull.
- V-hull.
- Catamaran.
- Tri-hull.

Fig. 20-25 shows most of these hull shapes as used for small boats.

Round hull boats are the least stable of the group. They tend to roll in the water. Many older boats have this hull shape.

Flat hull boats are generally more stable because of the surface area that comes in contact with the water. Their stability can be compared to a book resting on a table. They do not roll easily. Many small utility, and fishing boats take advantage of this design.

The V-hull design is similar to the round hull, except its undersides are flatter. Because of this, it is generally more stable than the round hull design.

V-hull characteristics can be found in many boats. The pointed bow (front) of boats leads to

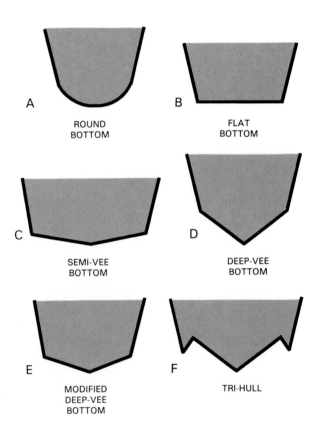

Fig. 20-25. Hull designs for pleasure or fishing boats vary.

a partial V-shape in many hulls.

Catamarans and tri-hulls are the most stable type of boat hull. Catamarans essentially have two hulls in the water. They are placed far apart so the boat is difficult to roll. Tri-hulls are made so that they seem to have three hulls in the water. They are side-by-side to increase stability.

Submarines

Submarines are vehicles that can operate at many depths under the surface of the water. They have very specialized suspension systems. Basically, they can increase or decrease their buoyancy by controlling the amount of air in flotation tanks. Once a submarine is under water, it uses propellers, wings, and rudders to maneuver.

Like all marine vehicles (and aircraft), submarines have a symmetrical design. This way the forces acting on one side of the vehicle will be the same as the forces acting on the other side. This adds to both stability and ease of control.

Hydrofoils

Hydrofoils are marine vehicles that use airfoil-shaped devices to hold them up in the water. The main hulls of these vehicles rise out of the water when the vehicle is in operation.

Hydrofoil action is similar to an airfoil's action. The basic difference in a hydrofoil is that the fluid environment is water, not air. The foil creates a pressure difference between the top and bottom of the wing. When the boat is in motion, a low pressure area is created above the wing, and a high pressure area below. As the high-pressure area tries to move toward the low, it forces the wing upward in the water. The wings are attached to the vehicle with long struts, so that they push the main hull of the vehicle out of the water.

There are basically two different configurations of hydrofoil wings. They are illustrated in Fig. 20-26. The surface-piercing, V-foil type is a very stable design. It has the characteristic of self-stabilizing. If the vehicle banks to the right or left, more lift will automatically be created on that side. That is because whichever side dips automatically has more surface area in the water. More wing surface in the fluid environment means more lift.

Horizontal foils have straight wings mounted onto struts, like the surface-piercing foils. Horizontal foils are always totally submerged. Lift is controlled by the use of holes located on the top surface of the wing. When the holes are opened, lift is reduced and the craft rides low in the water. As the

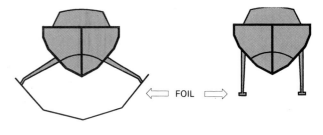

V-FOIL   FULLY SUBMERGED FOIL

Fig. 20-26. There are two basic hydrofoil designs. The surface-piercing or V-foil is very stable though not suited for rough water. The fully submerged or horizontal foil never break the surface of the water but ride below it. This provides smooth sailing in rough waters.

holes are closed, more surface area is created on the top of the wing. Again, more surface area means more lift. The vehicle will then rise up in the water. Controlling the surface area on horizontal wings produces a smoother ride in rough water.

Some hydrofoils control lift by pivoting the wings up and down on their struts. This increases or decreases the angle of attack, and directly affects lift. Recent developments for hydrofoils include sonar-type devices that monitor the craft in relation to water conditions. The vehicle basically reads the oncoming waves, and automatically adjusts lift to avoid them.

Air Cushion Vehicles

Air cushion vehicles, sometimes known as *Hovercraft*®, are hailed as a revolutionary idea in transportation, Fig. 20-27. They are designed to ride on a cushion of air the vehicle generates. This type of suspension system allows travel over land or water. Flexible skirts at the bottom of the vehi-

Fig. 20-27. Air cushion vehicles are equally ''at home'' on land or water.   (U.S. Navy)

cle let it pass over obstacles without jarring the vehicle.

Air cushion vehicles generate the cushion of air with powerful fans. The fans draw air from the top or sides of the vehicle and force it out the bottom. Two types of Hovercraft® configurations are the plenum chamber and the annular jet.

The plenum chamber is the simplest, Fig. 20-28. Air is essentially pumped straight through the craft to produce lift. The annular jet configuration directs the air so that it comes from the sides of the vehicle's bottom. The air is directed inwards. The cushion of air created by the annular jet is stronger than that of the plenum chamber. It is also created with less energy.

Antirolling Devices

Stability is an important aspect of suspension systems. Vehicles must be able to remain upright while in operation. Safety of passengers and cargo is compromised by unstable vehicles.

Ships are subjected to large waves on the ocean. These waves can cause the ship to roll, leading to an uncomfortable ride. It may even cause the ship to capsize (roll over). There are several methods of stabilizing ships and boats so that they do not roll. *Bilge keels* are extensions that protrude downward from the centerline of a boat. You may have seen these on sailboats, Fig. 20-29. The keel increases the amount of surface area below the water sur-

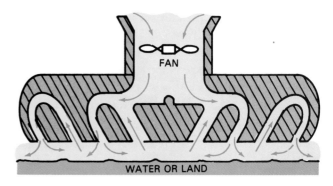

Fig. 20-28. A plenum chamber type air cushion vehicle. A fan pumps air down through the craft to provide the cushion that floats the vehicle above the surface of the water or ground.

face. If the boat starts to lean, the keel pushes against the water in the opposite direction. This makes the boat hard, if not impossible, to tip over.

Antirolling, or passive stabilizer tanks are another type of antirolling device. These are U-shaped tanks, partially filled with water, that are located inside the hull of the ship. As the ship rolls to one side, the water in the tank will flow to the low side. This action causes the ship to roll back in the opposite direction, righting itself.

Activated fin stabilizers are another commonly used antirolling device. These are fins that are located on the sides of the ship, below the waterline. They may be permanently attached, or retractable. Fin stabilizers basically act the same as bilge keels.

Fig. 20-29. Antiroll features can be designed into the hull of a boat. The deep hull of a sailboat acts like a stabilizer.

When the ship rolls to one side, the increased surface area offers resistance to keep the ship upright. Retractable fin stabilizers are activated by sensitive gyroscopes.

SUMMARY

Suspension systems are the parts of vehicles that support or suspend the vehicle in its environment. They also make it possible to maintain a smooth, and stable ride. Suspension systems for land transportation vehicles include springs, shock absorbers, and pneumatic tires. The two common types of springs are the coil and leaf springs. Their action is regulated by the shock absorbers.

Vehicles that operate in fluid environments are also supported by suspension systems. Airplanes are supported in the air by the shape of their wings. This shape is called an airfoil. Lighter-than-air vehicles use a gas that is lighter than the ambient air to keep them aloft. Marine vehicles are designed to stay afloat either through special materials or displacement hulls.

There are some suspension components that aid these vehicles when on land, or in special cases. When airplanes take off, land, or maneuver on the ground, they need special land-based suspension systems. Pneumatic tires, struts, and shock absorbers are the devices that usually fill this need.

Hydrofoils use wings that create lift to suspend the main hull of the vehicle out of the water. Air cushion vehicles create a pocket of air that keeps them from touching land or water when they are in operation.

Antirolling devices are parts of suspension systems that help keep vehicles upright when they are in operation. These are especially important in the case of ocean-going ships and boats.

KEY WORDS

All of the following words have been used in this chapter. Do you know their meaning?

Air cushion vehicle	Hydrofoils
Airfoil	Lift
Ambient air	Pneumatic tires
Bernoulli effect	Shock absorber
Bilge keels	Spring oscillation
Buoyancy	Springs
Contact patch	Stabilizer bar
Drag	Submarines
Gravity	Suspension systems
Hovercraft®	Thrust

TEST YOUR KNOWLEDGE

Write your answers on a separate sheet of paper. Do not write in this book.

Fill in the blank:
1. Loss of control because water gets between a tire and road surface is called _____.
2. Land vehicle suspension systems have used the basic designs from _____ technology.
3. Shock absorbers are normally filled with _____.
4. _____ tires are filled with air.
5. The rear loops on leaf springs are attached to the car frame with a _____.

Matching:
6. __ Stabilizer bar.
7. __ Springs.
8. __ Hydrofoil.
9. __ Dislacement.
10. __ Airfoil.
11. __ Bias.
12. __ Antirolling devices.
13. __ Shock absorbers.
14. __ Landing gear.
15. __ Lift.
16. __ Buoyancy.

A. Criss-crossed.
B. Absorb road shocks.
C. Reduce spring oscillation.
D. Keeps vehicle from leaning while cornering.
E. Suspension for planes on the ground.
F. Shape of airplane wing.
G. Upward force created by airplanes.
H. Tendency for objects to float or rise in a fluid environment.
I. Type of hull used on barges.
J. Creates lift under water.
K. Keeps vehicles upright and stable while in operation.

Short answer:
17. What is the suspension system for an air-cushion vehicle?
18. Sketch and describe the construction of a steel-belted radial tire.
19. Sketch a coil spring and a leaf spring.
20. How is an air shock different from a regular shock absorber?
21. Describe how an airplane can stay in the air.

ACTIVITIES

1. Build various wing shapes and test them, if possible, in a wind tunnel or behind a fan for lift.

2. Build a working model of a hot air balloon and demonstrate it to your class.
3. Design and build a working model of an air cushion vehicle.

4. Help organize and then take part in a competition to build a boat hull design to carry the most weight without sinking. (Limits must be placed on the dimensions but not on the construction or construction materials.)

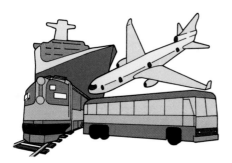

Chapter 21
STRUCTURE OF A VEHICLE

After studying this chapter, you will be able to:
☐ Explain the purpose of structural systems in transportation technology.
☐ Describe structural systems for various types of vehicles.
☐ List materials used in vehicle structures and explain why they are used.
☐ List and describe structural components of various types of vehicles.

What do you think of when you hear the word structure? One meaning of the word is something that is built to contain a load such as cargo or people. Every vehicle used in transportation must have structure to be at all useful.

This chapter will focus on the structural systems of all types of vehicles. As we have progressed through the study of transportation technology, we have seen many vehicular systems. Your knowledge of these will be drawn upon as you look at their relationships with structural systems.

WHAT ARE STRUCTURAL SYSTEMS?

Structural systems are the parts of vehicles that hold other vehicular systems and the loads they will carry. In most cases, vehicular structures need to be strong and rigid. They provide mounting places for propulsion, control, suspension and some guidance systems. Sometimes, structural members need to be flexible but just as strong as rigid ones.

You will see examples of rigid and flexible structures as you read on.

Vehicular structures also provide an enclosure for passengers and cargo. The enclosure provides protection from the environment. This includes rain, hail, mud, and extremes of heat or cold.

Structures also provide protection from hazards that come about as a result of transportation in society. There is always a danger of accidents. Structural systems are designed to take passenger safety into account. Thorough structural testing is done on most vehicles to improve passenger safety. Fig. 21-1 shows one type of structural testing.

Structures usually determine the shape of the vehicle. Car bodies are a good example. You are aware of the many styles and shapes that automobiles have. Some are plain and basic shapes. Others are flashy, sporty, and even exotic-looking. No matter what their styling, a function of all cars is to protect their occupants.

Structural Systems for Automobiles

The main parts of an automobile structure are the *body* and *chassis* (frame). The two have conventionally been made separately, then joined with bolts. Rubber blocks (spacers) are usually inserted between the body and frame to reduce vibrations from the engine and the road surface.

Unibody construction is very common on many automobiles today, Fig. 21-2. It is also called integral frame or unit body construction. This type of structure combines the body and frame in one

Fig. 21-1. Automobile manufacturers crash test new vehicles to evaluate their ability to protect passengers in an accident. (General Motors Corp.)

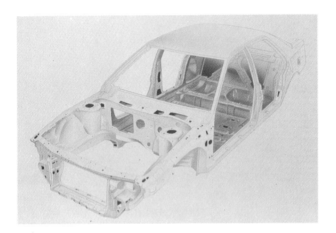

Fig. 21-2. In unibody construction, the frame is combined with the body. (Cadillac)

Fig. 21-3. Often, automobile bodies are recognized by the number of doors they have. (Ford Motor Co.)

unit. Suspension parts may be attached directly to the unibody. Sometimes, a partial frame may be attached. Partial frames are made to carry the weight of the propulsion system. They also withstand the stress put on the suspension system.

Unibody construction is almost universal for all subcompact, compact, and midsize automobiles. Manufacturers, however, have kept the conventional frame for many larger cars. The conventional style is better at reducing road noise.

Automobile Bodies

Automobile bodies may be placed in classes by the number of doors, or the type of roof. Two-door and four-door cars are clearly different, and easily recognized, Fig. 21-3. The roofs of many automobiles are solid sheet metal. Usually, these are supported by six columns, three on each side. This arrangement provides relative safety if the vehicle should roll over. One method of roof support eliminated the middle column on each side. The roof was supported only at each corner. This

style improved visibility, but the roof crushed easily in roll-over accidents. Many modern cars have gone back to the six-support system for safety. Designers pay special attention to placement and shape of the middle column to improve visibility.

Convertibles are automobiles that have a removable roof. The tops may be made of either fabric, or steel. Fabric tops fold down behind the passenger compartment for storage. Convertibles with metal roofs have special latches that secure them onto the body. These cars are popular, but they also have obvious safety disadvantages. Can you name any? How about very little protection in a rollover accident?

Most car bodies are made of sheet steel. Many times, special additives help the steel withstand manufacturing processes. Body parts are usually pressed, or stamped into shape with large hydraulic presses. Fig. 21-4 shows an automotive assembly line. The body panels have been shaped by stamping.

Some designers and manufacturers are using fiberglass reinforced plastic for body parts. See Fig. 21-5. Being lighter, these cars have higher fuel efficiency.

The manufacture of body parts from plastic is relatively easy. One drawback, however, is that the plastic does not withstand impact as well as steel. Designers must keep this in mind when designing the total automobile. They do not want to reduce the level of safety for buyers of their cars.

Aluminum alloys, stainless steel, and other alloys have also been used for automobile bodies. Each has its own advantages and disadvantages. Modern automobiles are largely dependent on the use of steel for the construction of their bodies.

Fig. 21-4. Steels used in stamping of auto body parts often have special properties to withstand the stress of manufacture. (SI Handling)

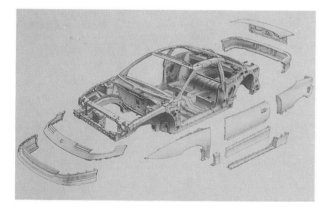

Fig. 21-5. Plastic panels for automobile bodies resist denting and will not rust like metal panels. (Saturn Corp.)

Automobile Frames

Automobile chassis are the main "skeletons" of the vehicles. They are made to support, and hold together, the total vehicle. As was explained earlier, frames may be separate from or an integral (cannot be separated) part of a unibody construction.

Conventional automotive frames are made of steel. The metal sheets are pressed or rolled into a box or channel shape. The frame usually consists of two long pieces that run the length of the car. These are joined by steel cross members. The parts are usually welded, but they may also be cold riveted. Either way, the frame members must be securely joined so that they provide a rigid structure.

Structural Systems for Trucks

Highway cargo transportation requires the use of special vehicles. Trucks are the vehicles of the trade. There are many types. The basic vehicular systems are the same for many trucks. There are different designs, however, to suit the type of cargo the truck will be hauling. Fig. 21-6 shows various types of truck bodies. Single-unit trucks have one-piece structures. They are relatively short so they can maneuver easily in tight places.

Tractor-trailers are the large two-piece vehicles you see on highways, Fig. 21-7. The tractor is the workhorse with a propulsion system capable of producing a great amount of horsepower. These vehicles usually have more than 12 speeds in their transmissions. This enables them to start out while pulling heavy loads, shifting up to a more efficient gear when hauling on the open road and over modern expressways.

Trailers are made in various shapes and sizes. Depending on the type of cargo, bulk or break-bulk, trailers will take on many different appearances. (Bulk cargo is loose material like grain or oil. Break-bulk cargo is single unit or cartons of freight.) Fig. 21-8 shows some of the more common types of trailers. More than one trailer may be attached to one tractor. You may have seen these vehicles that resemble trains traveling down a highway, Fig. 21-9.

Structural Systems For Rail Vehicles

Rail vehicles have taken on many shapes, according to their purpose. Ones that are used for passengers are obviously different than those used for cargo. Basically, all rail vehicles use trucks, also

Fig. 21-6. Truck designs vary according to specific types of cargo they will haul.

A

B

Fig. 21-7. A—A typical tractor-trailer "rig." Such vehicles are normally used to haul freight long distances. B—The tractor is the "workhorse" of a tractor-trailer combination.

Fig. 21-8. These trailers represent different types of cargo haulers found on the highways. (Fruehauf Trailer Operations)

Fig. 21-9. Some tractors are seen on expressways pulling more than one trailer. (UPS)

called bogies, that hold the axles. The trucks can swivel. They also have springs to act as a suspension system. Most cars have four axles, two on each truck.

The basic framework or structure of all rail cars is steel. Most passenger cars are covered with aluminum alloy to save weight. Some passenger trains use a fiberglass reinforced plastic body. Rail car builders are starting to use this material more because of its manufacturing ease and good appearance.

Passenger trains have a variety of cars with flexible coverings between them. Fig. 21-10 shows a close-up of a typical passenger train. The cover-

Fig. 21-10. Top. Passenger trains are designed to carry people in comfort. Bottom. Accordian-type protective shields between cars allow passengers to move between cars.

ings between cars permit passenger movement between the cars. At the same time, they offer protection from the environment.

Passenger rail cars average about 85 feet in length and are fitted with many luxuries. Coach cars are set up for comfortable passenger travel with rows of upholstered, adjustable seats, Fig. 21-11. Windows surround these cars so passengers may have full view of the countryside. Sleeping cars are divided into private berths or bedrooms. Windows have shades to make sleeping easier and more comfortable. Dining cars have tables set for a comfortable, and sometimes luxurious, dining. Other cars are set up as coffee shops, or lunch counters.

Cargo rail cars are designed to be functional, not comfortable. They are usually constructed of steel for strength and durability. The structure of cargo haulers is varied to suit the type of cargo they will be hauling. They are designed to carry weights from 50 to 150 tons. Fig. 21-12 represents some of the various cars used to carry rail freight.

The four basic types of cars are the open-top gondola car, box car, flatcar, and tank car. Variations include refrigeration units and special designs for material handling. For example, the structure (boxes) of some gondola cars can be tipped so that the contents may be dumped. Tank cars may be fitted with pumps and boxcars may have extra-large doors so forklifts can move easily in and out. Special rail cars, called auto conveyors, may have two or three levels. Sheet metal coverings protect the autos.

Designers have found a few advantages to creating special rail cars. One is that when a car is designed for a particular product, it can be made so the product can be stacked on the car more efficiently. This allows each car to carry more. It also

Fig. 21-11. Interior of a modern, high-speed passenger train provides a comfortable ride for commuters and travelers. (HSST—Nevada Corp.)

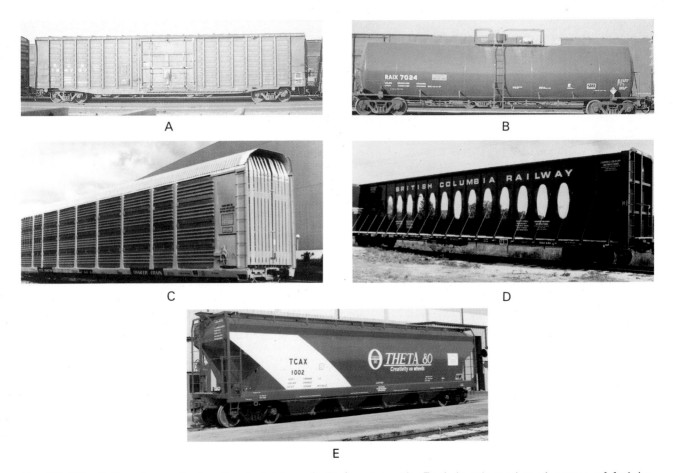

Fig. 21-12. Railroad cars for hauling freight are built for strength. Each is adapted to the type of freight it will haul. A—A boxcar has a roof and sliding doors that protect freight from the weather. B—Tank cars haul only liquids. C—An automobile rack car has several levels so cars can be "stacked" inside. (Thrall Car Mfg. Co.) D—Center beam flat car carries lumber. E—Covered hopper car is designed to haul and protect grain. (Thrall Car Mfg. Co.)

reduces the need for special dunnage. *Dunnage* includes the straps, blocks, and special rigging needed to securely fasten freight to a vehicle.

Structural Systems For Lighter-Than-Air-Vehicles

Lighter-than-air vehicles, as we have seen, are designed to displace a large amount of air. Their structures need to be large; they do not have to be rigid, however. Usually some sort of strong, lightweight fabric is used to hold the light gas that makes them buoyant.

Blimps may have either nonrigid, or semirigid construction. The pressure exerted by the gas maintains the shape of the vehicle. The cars, or gondolas, are attached by cables that run through the fabric structure. Propulsion systems are usually contained within the car.

Rigid airships, sometimes referred to as Zeppelins, have a stiff framework that serves as a hull.

They were named after Count Ferdinand von Zeppelin, a German general and aeronautical designer. Mounting brackets for the propulsion systems were attached to the hull structure. Large, hotel-like gondolas were also part of the rigid superstructure. These airships were popular until the fiery destruction of the Hindenberg at Lakehurst, New Jersey. Refer to Fig. 21-13.

Hot-air balloons are similar to blimps. Their shape is held by the pressure of the hot air they contain. Balloons are made of rip-stop nylon, similar to the sails on sailboats. Steel cables running through the fabric are attached to the wicker basket which holds the fuel and the occupants. Fig. 21-14 shows a typical hot-air balloon basket. It is made of wicker. Tough and lightweight, this material tends to absorb well the shock of landings.

The envelope (the name given to the air bag) is first filled with air by an inflator fan. This gives the balloon its initial shape while it is still on the

Fig. 21-13. The German airship Hindenburg burned while landing at Lakehurst, New Jersey, in 1937. The accident killed more than 30 passengers and spelled the end of airships as passenger carriers. (Smithsonian Institute)

Fig. 21-14. Typically, hot-air balloon baskets are made of wicker, which is lightweight and shock-resistant.

ground. When the pilot is ready and has done a safety check of all the vehicle's systems, she or he heats up the air inside the envelope with large propane-fueled burners. As the air heats, the

balloon begins to rise and stands straight up. After a few more safety checks and more heat, the balloon is ready to ascend.

Structural Systems of Airplanes

When powered flight first became a reality, airplane structures were made of wood. They had wire and cables for support and bracing. The wooden structures were covered with fabric that gave the vehicle a smooth skin. This was the surface that enabled airflow to generate lift.

Modern aircraft make use of strong metal alloys that resist corrosion. Metals frequently used include aluminum, stainless steel, magnesium, and titanium. The materials are formed into sheets, or extruded into tubes and other special shapes.

Early aircraft had a truss-type construction. (A truss is a rigid, open framework of interconnecting pieces.) These aircraft had little room inside for passengers or cargo. The structures consisted of pieces of wood or steel that ran the length of the plane. These were called *longerons*. The longerons were attached by cross members called webs. The resulting truss structure was very strong and rigid but filled the interior with braces and wires that cut down on usable space.

Modern aircraft make use of monocoque, or semimonocoque construction. Monocoque means "one shell." This results in a hollow structure with plenty of room for passengers, cargo, and equipment, Fig. 21-15. Tail and front sections, where added strength is beneficial, make use of truss construction.

Fig. 21-15. Monocoque construction allows spacious unobstructed cargo areas in modern aircraft cabins. (U.S. Air Force)

Smooth, aerodynamic shapes are also possible with monocoque construction. Instead of structural members that run the length of the plane, monocoque construction relies on a series of ringlike ribs. These form the skeleton of the structure. They are attached to the strong metal outside covering of the plane.

Semimonocoque aircraft structures make use of **bulkheads,** stringers, and formers to give them greater strength. Some modern aircraft make use of a combination of structural types.

The main body of the plane is called the *fuselage.* This is where passengers sit, and where cargo is held. Ahead of the fuselage is the cockpit. This is where the pilots and flight crew control and navigate the plane. There are doors at the front, rear, and sometimes, middle sections of the fuselage. These doors permit ready entry and exit from the vehicle.

The tail section of the plane is called the *empennage.* It is the part that contains many of the vital control surfaces that were talked about in Chapter 19. The empennage consists of a tapered continuation of the fuselage to maintain an aerodynamic shape. Attached to this are the horizontal and vertical stabilizers. The rudder is attached to the vertical stabilizer, and the elevators are attached to the horizontal stabilizer.

The wings are an extremely important structural part of the aircraft. Essentially, the wings must support the weight of the vehicle when it is in flight. At the same time, they must withstand the forces acting on the craft during flight. The wings usually contain the plane's fuel tanks. Many times propulsion systems are mounted on them also. These added stresses require a very strong wing structure.

The main structural members are two aluminum alloy spars. These run the length of the wing, starting at the fuselage. The airfoil shape is made by adding strong, lightweight ribs. These are spaced at regular intervals between the fuselage and the tip of the wing. The ribs are braced with cross members to give the structure strength. This framework of spars, ribs, and braces is covered with thin, lightweight sheets of aluminum alloy. This forms the skin, and provides the smooth aerodynamic shape essential for flight. The skin is also essential to the strength of the wing structure.

Wings must be securely attached to the fuselage. Usually, wings are cantilevered out from the plane. (In cantilevering, a structural member is only supported at one end.) No external bracing is needed. Fig. 21-16 is a CAD drawing showing the wing and fuselage construction of a small plane. Note the

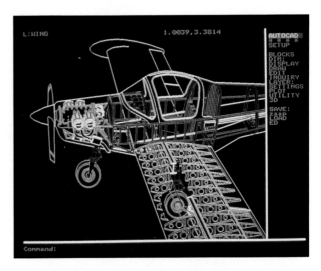

Fig. 21-16. The CAD drawing shows a semimonocoque fuselage construction. (Autodesk, Inc.)

rib construction in the wing.

On small planes, however, external bracing is needed when the wings are attached to the top of the fuselage. External bracing gives much structural support, but decreases the plane's efficiency. Braces tend to increase the drag produced by the vehicle. Remember that drag is the force that resists forward movement. The more drag a plane has, the more fuel it consumes suppling extra horsepower to maintain air speed.

Airplane wings have taken many shapes and forms. This is the result of designers trying to improve flight characteristics of aircraft. Fig. 21-17 illustrates some common wing shapes.

Structural Systems For Helicopters

Helicopter structures follow designs that are similar to airplanes. Usually, a combination of truss and semimonocoque construction methods are employed. The two main sections of the helicopter are the tail section and the cabin. The cabin may be compared to the fuselage of an airplane. It is where the passengers, pilot, and cargo are located. The fuel and propulsion systems are also part of a helicopter cabin. Fig. 21-18 illustrates typical helicopter cabin construction.

The tail section of a helicopter is usually of the truss type. It needs to be rigid; however, it usually does not need to support cargo or passengers. Attached to the rear of the tail section are a stabilizer, tail rotor, and the tail cone housing. Mounted on the sides of the tail section are trim stabilizers. These are small wings that help the pilot maintain a stable flight.

A

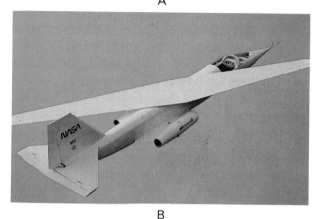

B

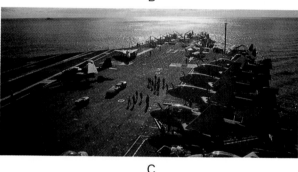

C

Fig. 21-17. Different wing shapes. A—This experimental aircraft, known as the X-29, has a forward swept wing. (NASA) B—A pivot-wing aircraft. C—Folding-wing aircraft on the flight deck of an aircraft carrier. (U.S. Navy)

Structural Systems For Marine Vehicles

Many types of materials are used for the construction of marine vessels. These include wood, fiberglass, and lightweight metals. Traditionally, wood was used. Wood has natural buoyancy, is easy to work, and readily available.

Typical wooden boat construction requires a set of ribs built up around a keel. The keel is a frame member that runs the length of the boat on its centerline. Attached to this skeleton is wooden planking. The planking is cut and formed so that

Fig. 21-28. Cabins of helicopters are not unlike airplane cabins. (Bell Helicopter Textron, Inc.)

it follows the contours of the skeleton.

Modern boat technology makes wide use of fiberglass reinforced plastic, aluminum, and other lightweight alloys. Pleasure crafts of all sizes are made of these materials. As the size of the boat increases, the preferred structural materials become the metal alloys.

Small, fiberglass boats usually do not need to be built around a central structure. Manufacturing processes allow a relatively strong shell to be made in a mold, Fig. 21-19. Attached to this shell are the propulsion and control systems. Other features that add to comfort and pleasure are also built onto these structures. Fig. 21-20 shows a number of fiberglass-constructed boats built for racing.

Ocean-going ships are made of metal and metal alloys. The main structural hull, as well as supporting bulkheads, are steel. Other structures on the vessels, like the crew's living areas, passenger areas, and control room areas may be constructed of a lighter material. Aluminum alloys and other similar materials are often used in these areas.

Shipbuilders must follow a rigid set of rules and regulations for construction of their vessels. Almost every shipbuilding country has its own *classification society*. These societies set and enforce the construction standards. A prominent classification society is Lloyd's Register of Shipping in the United Kingdom. The American Bureau of Shipping is another large classification society. These organiza-

Structure of a Vehicle 241

Fig. 21-24. Saturn V as it left its launch pad. It consisted of several stages, each having its own propulsion unit. (NASA)

Fig. 21-25. Space shuttle on take-off. It consists of two solid rocket boosters, a large external tank, and the shuttle orbiter. (NASA)

tion of this vehicle is distinctive, Fig. 21-25. It consists of two *solid rocket boosters (SRBs),* a large external tank, and the shuttle orbiter itself. The SRBs are the largest solid-fuel rocket engines ever developed. They are also the first ones to be used on any manned space vehicle. The boosters are constructed of a series of hardened steel rings. They are precisely machined to fit into adjoining rings. The booster sections are attached with high strength steel pins. Resulting joints are sealed with rubberlike O-rings. The joints are then covered with a fiberglass tape to make a smooth, aerodynamic shape. The tape provides no structural strength.

The large external tank is the largest part of the launch vehicle. It holds the liquid fuel to be used by the shuttle's main engines. There are three parts to the external tank. The top section is the liquid oxygen tank. The top of this tank is tapered to a point to produce an aerodynamic shape. The bottom section is the liquid hydrogen tank. It is the larger of the two tanks. It also holds the mounting brackets for the SRBs and the shuttle orbiter. The two tanks are joined by a collar. This is the third part of the external tank structure.

Because of its design, the shuttle orbiter makes use of the construction techniques found in the aircraft industry. Main structural components are made of aluminum alloys covered with special insulation. The major components are:

• The fuselage, which is constructed in different sections and joined with rivets and bolts.

• The crew compartment.
• The vertical stabilizer.

The front of the craft is composed of an upper and lower fuselage section. The heavily protected crew compartment is sandwiched between these two sections. Joined to these is the mid-fuselage section, which holds the cargo bay. After that is the aft fuselage section which holds the shuttle's propulsion systems. The vertical stabilizer and body flap are attached to the aft fuselage section. The body flap is designed to deflect heat away from the vehicle and to act as a stabilizer when the craft operates in our atmosphere.

SUMMARY

Structural systems are the parts of vehicles that provide the framework that holds other systems. They also protect passengers and cargo. Automobile and truck structures consist of chassis and bodies. The many types of autos and trucks you see on the roads demonstrate the many shapes vehicular structures can have.

Lighter-than-air vehicles usually have flexible structures. The pressure exerted by their internal gases keeps the vehicle's shape. Heavier-than-air vehicles use either truss, monocoque, or semimonocoque construction.

Marine vehicles have been traditionally made of wood. Modern marine vehicles make wide use of fiberglass-reinforced plastic, and metal. Classification societies are set up to insure that ocean-going vessels are built well.

Space vehicles use construction techniques that are similar to airplanes. The designs vary according to the type and purpose of the vehicle. The major differences are in the types of materials used, and the configuration of the propulsion systems.

KEY WORDS

All of the following words have been used in this chapter. Do you know their meaning?

Body	Empennage
Bulkhead	Fuselage
Chassis	Longerons
Classification society	Solid rocket boosters
Conning tower	(SRBs)
Convertibles	Staging
Dunnage	Unibody construction

TEST YOUR KNOWLEDGE

Write your answers on a separate sheet of paper. Do not write in this book.

Fill in the blank:

1. The main parts of automobile structures are _____ and _____.
2. Some car builders use _____ body parts to make their cars lighter.
3. Modern aircraft use metal alloys that resist _____.
4. Shipbuilding countries set up _____ to insure quality ship construction.
5. Three types of rail cargo vehicles are _____, _____, and _____.

Matching:

6. __ Unibody.
7. __ Wood.
8. __ Convertible structures.
9. __ Gondola.
10. __ Monocoque.
11. __ Fuselage.
12. __ Double hull.
13. __ SRB.
14. __ Truss.
15. __ Aluminum.

A. Car with removable roof.
B. Metal alloy used in many vehicle structures.
C. Type of structure that combines chassis and body.
D. One shell.
E. Material traditionally used for boats.
F. Passenger compartment on blimps.
G. Main part of aircraft structure.
H. Solid rocket booster.
I. Construction method used on ships and submarines.
J. Construction method used on older airplanes.

Short answer:

16. List and describe three types of trucks.
17. How is a hot-air balloon launched?
18. What are the differences between truss, monocoque, and semimonocoque airplane structures?
19. Give two reasons why space vehicles need to use heat-resistant materials on their surfaces.
20. Give two reasons why vehicle manufacturers make use of fiberglass-reinforced plastic.

ACTIVITIES

1. Research your library or resource center for information on loads and bracing systems. Relate this information to the structure of vehicles. Then build a model and prepare a report on the bracing system you researched. Include sketches or CAD drawings to illustrate your report.
2. Design, build, and test simple frames to determine the rigidity given the frames by various methods of bracing. Develop a chart and record your test result for each design.
3. Use a wind tunnel to demonstrate aerodynamic qualities of vehicular structures, using various model vehicles such as automobiles, trucks, aircraft, and spacecraft.
4. Study various fastening techniques (rivets, welds, and screws, for example) and give examples of where these can be used on a variety of vehicles.

Transportation support systems include various structures such as bridges, railroad beds, roads, and tunnels for land transportation. Water transport requires locks, and space transportation needs launching pads, among other structures.   (NASA, and Norfolk Southern Corp.)

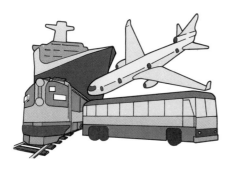

Chapter 22
SUPPORT OF A VEHICULAR SYSTEM

After studying this chapter, you will be able to:
- [ ] Explain the need for support systems in transportation technology.
- [ ] List the types of support systems and facilities.
- [ ] Describe types of construction related to transportation technology.
- [ ] Describe passenger and cargo facilities.
- [ ] Explain the importance and types of maintenance.

Most of the preceding chapters have dealt with various systems. Among those you have studied are energy systems, power systems, power transmission systems, and systems that are a part of the vehicles themselves. There is one other system that is not part of the vehicle. It is a group of structures known as support systems.

WHAT ARE SUPPORT SYSTEMS?

Support systems are essential for the operation of any vehicle. Support systems consist of all the external (meaning outside the vehicle) operations and facilities needed to maintain transportation systems. The systems include maintenance, passenger and cargo handling, life support, vehicle support, and guideways. Most support systems are not a part of the actual vehicle. Even so, they are an important link in transportation technology.

One of the more obvious support systems for land vehicles is the road and highway network. Without this system of paved, or hard-surfaced

roads, vehicle travel would be uncomfortable and unsafe. Vehicles would not be able to travel at the speeds that they do today.

For rail vehicles, the same can be said of the system of railbeds and tracks that connect various communities throughout the country. Obviously, this transportation system would be useless without railroads.

Air transportation industries rely on airports. This makes runways and terminal buildings important support systems.

Overseas and inland shipping companies need harbor and port facilities so that they can make the transition from water to land. Can you imagine trying to run a shipping industry if you did not have access to any harbor facilities? You would have no way to receive or deliver cargo or passengers.

SUPPORT SYSTEMS FOR LAND VEHICLES

Support systems can be divided into five categories, or types of physical facilities. They are:
- Related construction - The structures on which vehicles travel.
- Passenger facilities - The buildings and facilities that provide comfort and services to passengers.
- Cargo facilities - The buildings and facilities that provide loading, unloading, and storage for various types of cargo.
- Vehicle maintenance - Those facilities designed to maintain and repair vehicular systems.
- Other support systems - Any other system that

is needed for safe transportation, such as: life support/rescue operations, communications systems, or regulatory agencies.

Roads and Highways

Roads and highways are constructed structures which should be included in the study of transportation technology. There is a common link between the two. One is essential to the other. Improved construction designs and techniques can benefit both construction and transportation technology.

Roads and highways begin with the clearing of land to make way for a *roadbed*. This is the foundation that supports the surface and the vehicles. Once the route is chosen, surveyed and staked, hills and valleys are "moved" to level the roadbed. Construction workers on road-building equipment make cuts and fills. *Cuts* remove excess earth from hills. This earth is usually moved to low spots, or valleys along the route where fills are needed. *Fills* are the addition of material such as rock and soil to build up low-lying areas. By cutting and filling, construction engineers form a relatively level roadbed that will provide a safe and comfortable path for vehicle travel.

The soil in the roadbed is then compacted, and covered with a gravel, or stone subbase. This provides a strong foundation for the road surface. The road surface is usually made of asphalt or concrete. These materials make a hard, durable driving surface. Often the road receives a surface texture that gives vehicles extra traction, especially in wet weather.

Once the road is built, shoulders are made along its sides to provide emergency and stopping lanes. Then guidance systems in the form of road signs, traffic lights, and highway markers are placed. All this leads to a finished support system essential for car and truck travel.

The United States has an excellent system of interstate highways whose development began in the 1950s. Their surfaces are smooth and wide. Many of them have four lanes, two in each direction, to promote safety and speed. The highways connect cities, usually with the shortest route possible.

Traffic planners have a major role in the design of highway and road networks. They have come up with many ways to make these systems safer and more efficient. Beltways are constructed around larger cities so that all traffic does not have to go through the center of town, Fig. 22-1.

Cloverleafs are used where two highways intersect, Fig. 22-2. They have been so named because

Fig. 22-1. This map shows the beltway around Boston, Mass. (Rand McNally)

Fig. 22-2. Cloverleaf interchanges connect major highways. (Federal Highway Administration)

the ramps that connect the highways are looped and look somewhat like the leaves of a clover plant. One highway actually goes over the other on a bridge, or overpass. At the ends of the ramps are acceleration or deceleration lanes that run along the edge of the highway. They make it possible to leave and enter each highway while maintaining a safe rate of speed.

Traffic planners have improved on the cloverleaf design by extending the lanes where vehicles enter and exit the main highways. Where an "on" ramp and an "off" ramp are close to each other, highway engineers have added extra safety lanes that are separate from the main highway. This provides a safer area for drivers to enter and exit the highway.

Railroads

Railroad construction has some similarities to the construction of highways. First, the route is planned; then the land is obtained. Because locomotives are made to pull heavy loads and ride on smooth iron wheels, they cannot climb hills like highway vehicles can. For this reason, cuts and fills must be made accurately. There can be no steep grades (hills) anywhere on the line. There can be no sharp turns on a railbed either. Trains are not designed to make sharp turns. The tracks must be laid so that there are gradual, large-radius turns, Fig. 22-3.

After the land is cleared and the soil compacted by earth-moving equipment, the railbed is put down. This is made up of several layers of stone designed to spread the weight of the trains evenly over the compacted surface. The first is a layer of crushed stone called the *subballast*. Then, a thick layer of *ballast* is added. It is composed of larger stones. The crossties, usually made of wood, are then laid on top of the ballast. Their purpose is to secure the rails that are later fastened to them. More ballast is added to fill the spaces between and around the ties. The ballast holds them in place.

Rail construction crews, in the next step, lay the track on top of the ties. A track consists of two parallel rails. The wheels of a train ride on the rails. The distance between them must be kept at a constant width (gauge). This keeps the train from derailing (jumping off the track). The standard gauge for railroads in North America is 4 ft. 8 1/2 in. *Rails* are long pieces of steel that have an I-shaped cross section, Fig. 22-4. There are joints between each section of rail. Modern railroad construction techniques use continuous rails instead of jointed ones. Long sections of rail are welded together so that the ride is smoother and quieter.

Bridges

Bridges are those all-important structures that span waterways, ravines and other barriers. Bridges have been around for a long time. They have undergone many changes to make them easier, safer, and more efficient to build.

The beam bridge is the oldest type. They are currently made of steel and concrete. Beam bridges are commonly seen connecting short spans in cloverleaf interchanges, or overpasses, Fig. 22-5. A variation of beam bridges are the truss bridges. These often were used as railroad bridges.

Arch bridges are commonly seen connecting longer spans over rivers. The road deck may either be built on top of the arch, or suspended from the

Fig. 22-3. Rail lines must have gentle curves and grades. (Norfolk Southern Corp.)

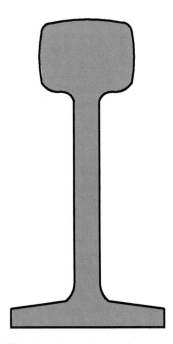

Fig. 22-4. This drawing shows the cross section of a rail.

Fig. 22-5. This highway overpass is a beam bridge.

Fig. 22-7. This is a cantilever bridge.

arch. Fig. 22-6 shows some basic arch bridge designs.

Cantilever bridges, Fig. 22-7, are noted for their strength. They are able to span longer lengths than beam and arch bridges. Because of their strength and spanning ability, they are often used as railroad bridges over large rivers. These bridges are basically made of two first-class levers (see-saws). Their ends are secured firmly to the ground so that the middle will not fail when heavily loaded. The large concrete and steel supports provide the fulcrum for each lever.

Of all the bridge designs, suspension bridges are capable of spanning the longest distances, Fig. 22-8. The Golden Gate bridge in California is a suspension bridge. The road deck is suspended with smaller cables from strong main cables that run from one end of the bridge to the other. These cables are anchored firmly to the ground at both ends. Two towers provide support for the main cables. The height of the towers is directly related to the length of the bridge. Taller towers are needed as the span increases.

Tunnels

Where road builders have encountered mountains, they have borrowed from mining technology. Tunnels are dug or bored so that straight, level paths can be maintained for vehicle travel. Tunnels are often more cost efficient than building roads over or around mountains. Fig. 22-9 shows a tunnel digging machine. It can bore through soil and soft rock with ease. The largest tunnel-boring machines (TBMs) are 9 1/2 yd. (about 9 m) high and about the length of two football fields. Operators control them with the aid of computers and television monitors.

Tunnels are also used under bays and other bodies of water. Instead of digging the tunnel underwater, prefabricated tubes are often sunk in

Fig. 22-6. These photos show two kinds of arch bridge. The bridge on the left has the roadway on top of the arches. The photo on the right shows an arch bridge with a suspended roadway. Also note the truss bridge in the background, and the suspension bridge in the foreground.

Fig. 22-8. Suspension bridges (foreground) can span long distances. This photo shows a suspension bridge built for a rapid transit system in Vancouver, British Columbia.   (BC Transit)

Fig. 22-9. Tunnel boring machines can burrow through soil and rock with ease. The teeth on the cutting head are tungsten carbide capable of cutting through marl at 1000 meters (about 1100 yards) a month.   (British Information Services)

the water. Once the tubes are anchored and connected, they are pumped out, and ready for completion. This type of tunnel technology is now commonly used.

The Chesapeake Bay Bridge Tunnel is an ambitious project that was undertaken on the east coast of the United States. It is a series of bridges and tunnels that allows vehicles to drive from Maryland to Virginia, over and under the Chesapeake Bay. The bridges consist of a series of beam bridges. The tunnels were constructed using the sunken tube method.

The Eurotunnel which links Great Britain with the European continent was lined with curved segments of reinforced concrete behind the tunnel-boring machine. Cement grout was used to seal and strengthen the joints between the segments.

Passenger Facilities

Transportation companies that move passengers need special buildings and spaces for travelers. Bus stations, airport terminals, and train stations provide comfort and services for people who are traveling. Here, passengers can buy tickets and wait in sheltered areas. Many times, goods and services are offered, as well. Passengers can eat, shop, have their shoes shined, or read a newspaper while waiting for their rides. Planners of passenger terminals consider the special needs of handicapped people. These facilities must be built so everyone can use them.

Safety must be built into structures. Waiting platforms are special areas where passengers can stand before boarding their vehicle, Fig. 22-10. Here there is no danger of being in the path of vehicles that are arriving or leaving. Usually, these areas are out of the way of regular traffic flow. They are located so that the vehicles can enter and exit easily.

Many successful businesses have been founded on providing service to motorists. As car transportation grew in popularity, people were able to travel farther from home. Families and businesspeople began to take road trips that lasted several days. This led to the start of motels. Motels are given their name because they were first referred to as motor hotels. Besides a place to sleep, motels of-

Fig. 22-10. The passengers waiting for this train are not in the way of other vehicles.   (Amtrak)

fer travelers other services. Relaxation by a pool, or in front of a television, awaits weary travelers. Today, you can probably name a number of major motel chains. Your list might include Howard Johnson, Holiday Inn, and Red Roof Inn.

Rest stops are another type of transportation support system. many states build structures along their major highways so that travelers can stop and rest. These may include parklike surroundings for comfortable walks. Picnic tables are often placed so that meals can be eaten in quiet, peaceful surroundings. Restrooms and information centers are also part of highway rest stops.

Truck stops are a type of physical facility for over-the-road cargo haulers, Fig. 22-11. These facilities offer services for both vehicle and operator. These include fuel and maintenance services, restaurants, and motels. Some even have special truck washing services. Imagine what that must mean to truckers who spend days at a time on the road—places to refuel their trucks and themselves!

Cargo Facilities

When you realize that everything in your house, including the materials that it is made of, was carried on a truck, you have an idea of the scope of cargo that is hauled over the road. It should be no surprise then that trucking companies need special cargo facilities. Cargo terminals are not as comfortable as passenger terminals. Cargo facilities do, however, have well-designed spaces for storage and movement of freight. Some sections may even be refrigerated for perishables such as meats, fruits, and vegetables.

Depending on the type of vehicles they are made to serve, cargo facilities have different designs. For cargo arriving on trucks, loading docks are built next to large paved areas. Trucks can back up to the loading docks. The docks are built at a height that permits forklifts easy access into the trucks.

Cargo terminals that handle rail freight must be built near rail lines. Trains must be able to pull up next to the platforms. These facilities also must have loading docks that are elevated so that forklifts can easily move on and off the rail cars. Some rail cargo facilities have pits located in the ground between the tracks. Cars are positioned over the pits. Bulk (loose) cargo can be dumped from the bottoms of the cars. Conveyors carry the cargo out of the pit and move it into storage tanks or bins.

Pipeline transportation systems require special cargo handling facilities. In fact, the pipeline itself is a physical facility. It is constructed and remains in one spot where it is built. Pipelines require pumping stations every few miles. Pumps and compressors move material through the line. Large storage tanks are additional support facilities for pipeline transportation systems.

Facilities for Vehicle Maintenance

Proper maintenance helps vehicles last longer while giving better service. Many people enjoy working on their own cars. Private car owners can perform regular maintenance themselves, Fig. 22-12. However, for convenience some owners take their vehicles to commercial service facilities. Fast oil changes, "lube jobs," and tuneups are available so that car owners can maintain their vehicles without doing the work themselves. Fig. 22-13 shows some businesses set up for quick maintenance.

Fig. 22-11. Truck stops provide food and fuel to all kinds of travelers.

Fig. 22-12. Vehicle owners can perform their own maintenance.

Fig. 22-13. Many businesses perform maintenance on automobiles.

There are other types of maintenance that occasionally must be performed on automobiles. Engines are mechanical devices that are prone to wear and breakdowns. Other vehicular systems, like the electrical, fluid, or mechanical system could fail at any time. No matter how well a vehicle is designed, there are always things that can go wrong. When a car does not work properly, the problem must be found and fixed.

Early car engines could be fixed by almost anybody with a wrench and a screwdriver. However, modern auto engines are complex pieces of machinery. It takes special training and equipment to diagnose and repair problems. Mechanics are people that have that training and they work on other people's vehicles. They are employed by large businesses and small shops all over the country. They are capable of servicing every part of an automobile. Mechanics and their repair businesses provide a very important support service for transportation technology, Fig. 22-14.

Passenger bus services hire mechanics to service their vehicles. See Fig. 22-15. Bus companies usually own and operate their own maintenance facilities. There they can concentrate on keeping every part of their vehicles in top condition. Cleaning crews also wash the buses inside and out. All of this is aimed at providing safe, comfortable service for paying passengers.

For large vehicles, like trains, special support facilities need to be set up. Mechanics are able to work on the locomotives, but sometimes other parts of trains break down. When this happens, cranes are needed to lift the heavy vehicles so that they can be worked on.

When metal train wheels become worn, they often need to be reground. Special grinders built into the tracks at maintenance areas do this. They

Fig. 22-14. Repairing modern vehicles requires special training and equipment.

Fig. 22-15. Bus lines hire mechanics to service and repair their fleet of buses. (B.C. Transport)

regrind the small angle on train wheels so that they can go around curves easily. They also true the wheels so that they ride smoothly on the rails. All this can be done without lifting the rail car off its tracks.

Pipeline maintenance is minimal once the line is built. Line pressure is checked at pumping stations to determine if there are any leaks. Maintenance crews also survey the pipeline from helicopters. If they see any discoloration of the line, or dying foliage, they know that there is a leak. Crews are then dispatched to repair the pipeline. Occasionally, pumps and compressors must be repaired. People who do this work are considered part of the support system for pipeline transportation.

SUPPORT SYSTEMS FOR MARINE TRANSPORTATION

Because of the size of marine vehicles, support systems are usually built on a large scale. Among the needed facilities are docks, warehouses, and other structures known as "harbor" and "port" facilities. Other important support facilities are locks for moving marine vehicles to bodies of water at different levels. Repair facilities are large-scale structures called dry docks.

Harbor and Port Facilities

In Chapter 15, you learned that a harbor is a place along the coast where water is deep enough for ships to travel close to shore. Port facilities are built in ocean harbors, on lakes, and in rivers. These facilities are places where passengers and cargo make their transition from land transportation to water transportation.

As with land transportation, port facilities for passengers are different from facilities for cargo. Passenger terminals are very comfortable, and provide essentially the same services as bus and train stations. Tickets may be purchased, and restaurants are available for dining. A wide variety of shops is usually available for passengers who want to buy souvenirs and pass time. As with other types of passenger terminals, port facilities are made to be accessible for handicapped people. Elevators, ramps, and oversize doors are included for people in wheelchairs.

These facilities also house support services for the ships themselves. Fresh water, and food must be delivered to the ship. Baggage must be loaded and unloaded, and the ship may have to be refueled. All this is done at the port facility.

Cargo terminals are designed for efficient material handling, rather than passenger movement. The dock areas lead to large warehouses. Ships are unloaded with cranes, conveyors, and pumps, Fig. 22-16. Forklifts, and trucks move about on the docks to receive the incoming cargo. They either carry the cargo to a warehouse for temporary storage, or haul the cargo to a final destination. Many times rail lines are built next to the docks. This makes it possible to directly load cargo from ships to rail vehicles. Fig. 22-17 shows several typical cargo terminals.

Locks

Chapter 15 also introduced *locks*. These are physical facilities that are crucial for shipping on inland waterways, Fig. 22-18. Locks are built where there is a difference in the heights of two bodies of water. Usually there is dry land between the bodies of water. Sometimes, nature makes up for the difference in height with waterfalls. Since ships cannot travel over waterfalls or across land, locks must be built.

Fig. 22-19 illustrates the operation of a typical lock. It is basically a chamber that is located between the two bodies of water. Locks can be opened and closed at both ends so that they are watertight. The water level in the lock is raised or lowered with valves so that it is at the level of a ship approaching it. When the water levels are equal, doors are opened so that the ship can enter the lock. The doors close behind the ship to form a tight seal.

A lock acts like a huge hydraulic elevator. When the ship is raised or lowered to the height of the other body of water, doors are opened, and the ship is free to sail out of the new lock.

Fig. 22-16. Conveyors and cranes are used to remove cargo from ships and barges. (Jeffboat Shipyard)

Fig. 22-17. These photos show different types of cargo terminals. Containers, bulk cargo, and grain terminals are shown. (Port of Long Beach, Detroit Marine Terminal, Port of Thunder Bay)

Fig. 22-18. Locks make inland shipping possible. This series of locks are on the Panama Canal. Note the container ship in the foreground.

Marine Vehicle Maintenance

Special facilities are needed for marine vehicle maintenance, especially large cargo and passenger vessels. Smaller, pleasure crafts can find a wide array of support services at marinas. Marinas are set up in protected areas in harbors, lakes, and rivers. There, owners can dock their pleasure craft and enjoy a restaurant meal. They can also have maintenance services performed on their boats, because most marinas have boat mechanics on hand. Boats can also be refueled at marina facilities.

Large ocean-going vessels need to be brought into a dry dock if they need repairs. A *dry dock* is a facility where the ship can be held, and water pumped away from it. Dry docks make it easy to take ships "out" of the water without actually lifting them, Fig. 22-20.

Large, overhead cranes are suspended over dry docks. They are used to lift heavy structural steel pieces into place. Propulsion systems and other heavy equipment are also moved with the cranes. When repairs are complete, water is then pumped back into the dry dock. The ship can then sail out of the facility under its own power, or be guided by tugboats.

SUPPORT SYSTEMS FOR AIR TRANSPORTATION

Airports are facilities that house all of the major support systems for air transportation. If you have ever flown, you know that they are busy

OPERATION OF A LOCK

The purpose of a lock is to raise or lower ships. The reason for a lock is to bypass rapids in a river and/or to overcome changes in water surface levels. A lock functions on the basic principle that "water seeks its own level". Therefore, a lock does not need pumps to operate! Water is moved by gravity from the high water side to the low water side.

The basic feature of a lock structure is an enclosed area called the chamber. This chamber of concrete walls has watertight gates at each end and valves which admit or release water.

The process of raising or lowering a ship in the chamber is called a lockage.

HOW A SHIP IS LOWERED

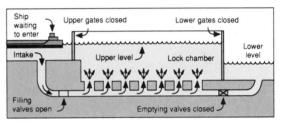

With both the lower and upper gates closed and the emptying valves closed, the chamber is brought to the upper level by opening the filling valves. This allows the water to flow from the intake into the chamber. Once the chamber is filled, the upper gates are opened and the ship enters.

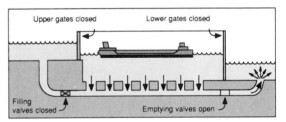

After the ship is in the chamber, the upper gates and the filling valves are closed. The emptying valves are then opened to allow water to flow out of the lock chamber to the lower level. As the water leaves the chamber, the ship is lowered.

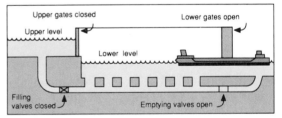

When the water in the chamber reaches the lower level, the ship is fully lowered. The lower gates are opened, and the ship leaves.

After this, the lock is ready for an upbound ship to be raised, or the lock may be filled to lower another downbound ship.

Fig. 22-19. These drawings show how a lock works.

places. One part is a communication center. Its main activity is to keep track of all planes coming into or leaving the airport. Controllers work in the control tower and use radar screens to keep track of all the planes. They are in voice contact with

A   B

Fig. 22-20. A—A ship is entering a floating dry dock. B—This ship is in a land-based dry dock and repairs are underway.

the pilots of the aircraft. Another important activity is ground support. This involves the people who guide the aircraft to the gates, service the planes, and handle baggage. Inside the terminal building are people who sell tickets and check in air passengers. Another important activity is cargo handling.

All types of support systems are represented at airports. Similar to other types of ports, airports are where passengers and cargo make the transition from land to air transportation.

Runways

In order to take off and land, airplanes need lengthy runways, Fig. 22-21. *Runways* are flat, straight paths that are specially lit and marked to aid pilots. Small airports use a single runway. As air traffic increases, other runways are usually added parallel to the first. Many airports have runways in different directions because of changeable wind patterns in the area. Airplanes usually take off and land headed into the wind. With a variety of runways, airports can always provide a relatively safe landing area.

Runways are constructed like roads. Heavy construction equipment operators clear the land, level, and compact it. After a stone base is put down, a hard surface is applied. Either asphalt or concrete is used.

Special markings are added to guide pilots of approaching and landing aircraft. Many runways are

Fig. 22-21. Aircraft need runways to land and take off.   (United Airlines)

fitted with recessed lights in the center of the runway to help at night or when weather creates poor visibility. A series of lights is also placed in a row along the sides of the runways. These help the pilot determine the runway width. Lights at the end of the runway blink in a sequence that indicates the direction of travel.

Airport Terminals

Two types of terminals are commonly found at airports. They are passenger and cargo terminals. These facilities are often very large at airports in major cities. Most airport designs incorporate their facilities in the land side-air side layout, Fig. 22-22. Here, passengers and cargo approach the airport from one side, and air traffic operates on the other.

Fig. 22-22. This photograph shows O'Hare International Airport in Chicago. The land side is toward the bottom, allowing access by car, bus, and rapid transit. The air side is toward the top allowing access by aircraft. (United Airlines)

This layout permits smooth traffic flow for both land and air vehicles.

Airport buildings are usually located in the center of the layout. These are the terminals and other support service facilities. Airport fire and rescue stations, however, are usually located away from the congested central area of the airport.

Airport passenger terminals have all the services of other transportation terminals. Ticket counters, restaurants, lounges, shops, and comfortable waiting areas are available for passenger use. Separate baggage areas are in the terminal so passengers can pick up their luggage on their way to securing land transport, Fig. 22-23. Airport terminals are also built to be accessible to handicapped people.

Cargo terminals at airports are usually separate from passenger terminals. Cargo planes are directed straight to them once they land. Unlike other cargo facilities, most air freight terminals are set up to sort packages. Cargo is generally not stored in these terminals.

Fig. 22-23. This baggage handling system allows passengers to retrieve their baggage in the safety of the terminal building. (United Airlines)

Aircraft Maintenance

It is extremely important that aircraft be well maintained. When something goes wrong, a pilot cannot just pull over and call for a tow! Proper and thorough maintenance on the ground can save lives, as well as cargo and vehicles. Fig. 22-24.

Inspections are a part of aircraft maintenance. The Federal Aviation Administration (FAA) requires thorough inspections on a regular basis. Because of the increasing number of accidents among aging aircraft, the FAA has increased the

Fig. 22-24. Careful maintenance is essential for safe air travel.
(United Airlines, America West Airlines)

number of inspections. For example, the inspection of engine mounting bolts for certain aircraft were only required after every 600 flights. Because of recent failures, the inspections are now required after every 300 flights. The FAA determines and enforces the inspections for all types of aircraft, commercial and private.

Various types of inspections are carried out on aircraft. They are used to find faults that may cause engine problems, landing gear problems, electronic or structural problems. Because the cabins must be pressurized to fly at higher altitudes, structural stress is great. Every time the vehicle takes off and gains altitude the fuselage expands or gets larger. When the vehicle descends to land, the fuselage contracts (gets smaller) because of atmospheric pressure changes. This flexing is not great by any means, but it causes metal fatigue after a while. Metal fatigue results in the weakening of the material until it is prone to breaking. Should the metal fuselage break, air disasters can easily happen.

The various inspections that airplane support crews undertake range from visual inspections to highly complex electronic inspections. Inspectors were once able to find cracks in the fuselage by locating small brown stains on the airplane. The stains are caused by tobacco smoke-filled air leaking from the fuselage. Now that smoking is not allowed on most flights, more advanced methods are being used. Bright lights and cleaning solutions help inspectors see small cracks.

X-ray techniques have been developed to study internal components of aircraft. The X rays can produce images of very complex parts. The problem is that the pictures are hard to read and interpret. Misread X rays have led to crashes.

Another type of inspection uses eddy currents. A magnetic field produces a small electrical current in a piece of metal. Any cracks will disturb the flow of current. These can be monitored on a meter or a screen. Cracks that are invisible to the naked eye can be detected in metal up to 5/8 in. (16 mm) thick. This type of inspection is very slow, and expensive magnetic probes must be used. Different probes are used on different parts of an aircraft.

Besides the conscious and rigorous inspections, normal vehicle maintenance must be performed on aircraft. The same types of things you would do for any other vehicle, you would do for an airplane. This only makes sense because you know that vehicles can last a lot longer with proper maintenance.

SUPPORT FOR SPACE TRANSPORTATION

As you are well aware, space transportation is very specialized and experimental. Governments of various countries support their space exploration efforts by supplying money for research and development. In the United States, the National Aeronautics and Space Administration (NASA) is the agency set up to conduct work in this area. NASA extends its arms into all areas of aviation and space travel. It is the prime support system of space transportation.

Other industries throughout the nation work for NASA, Fig. 22-25. There are private research, testing, and manufacturing facilities that do work for NASA. These operations, as well as NASA's own facilities like Cape Canaveral in Florida, comprise the support facilities for space travel. All of the types of support take place at these facilities.

Fig. 22-25. Companies that do work for NASA are called subcontractors. The booster rocket in this photo was built by such a company.   (NASA)

SUMMARY

While support systems are generally not parts of vehicles, they are essential to transportation systems. Five types of support systems are: related construction, passenger and cargo facilities, vehicle maintenance, and other support systems. As you can see, there are many ways vehicle systems need to be supported.

Related construction includes bridges, highways, railroads, tunnels, locks, runways, and all types of passenger and cargo terminals. Passenger and cargo facilities are also important in many other aspects of transportation support. They house communications centers, waiting areas, storage areas, people and cargo moving equipment. The facilities are designed to meet the needs of the general public, including handicapped people.

Vehicle inspection and maintenance are important support services. Proper care of any vehicle will make it last longer. This is true for every vehicle, from bicycles to space shuttles. Businesses are set up to help the private citizen maintain their vehicles. Transportation companies and space exploration agencies provide maintenance using trained workers.

KEY WORDS

All of the following words have been used in this chapter. Do you know their meaning?

Ballast	Locks
Bridges	Rails
Cuts	Roadbed
Dry dock	Runways
Fills	Subballast

TEST YOUR KNOWLEDGE

Write your answers on a separate sheet of paper. Do not write in this book.

Fill in the blank:

1. The five types of support systems are: _____, _____, _____, _____, and _____.
2. _____ span waterways and ravines so that vehicles travel safely and easily.
3. Proper _____ insures that vehicles last a long time.
4. _____ are hydraulic elevators for ships.
5. _____ is the government agency set up for the research and development of space travel.

Matching:

6. __ Cloverleaf.
7. __ Ballast.
8. __ Suspension bridge.
9. __ Motel.
10. __ Mechanic.
11. __ Beam bridge.
12. __ Tunnel.
13. __ Port.
14. __ Dry dock.
15. __ Airports.

A. Road structures that connect main highways.
B. Oldest type of bridge.
C. Used on railroads to spread the weight of trains.
D. Place where ships are removed from water for maintenance and repair.
E. Support facility built in harbors.
F. Longest type of bridge.
G. Person who is trained to maintain vehicles.
H. Support centers for air transportation.
I. Holes cut through mountains for vehicle travel.
J. Motor hotel.

Short answer:

16. Why are transportation systems essential?
17. Explain how locks work.
18. What types of things are found in passenger terminals?
19. How are cargo terminals different from passenger terminals?
20. Describe two types of structural inspections for aircraft.

ACTIVITIES

1. Break up the class into teams of four. The task: in 15 minutes, write down on a sheet of paper all of the support systems you can recall for any mode of transportation. Divide the list into two columns, one listing support systems that are structures, the other listing support systems that are services. Afterwards, compare lists among the teams and discuss them.
2. All technology systems are interrelated and support one another. Using the list of support systems developed in the first activity, list after each one the technological system to which you think it belongs: Production (constructing and manufacturing); Communications (delivering information over distance); Bio-related Manufacturing (using biological processes to produce products).
3. With your instructor's help, set up a demonstration to cover proper service techniques for a small gas engine.
4. Secure an automotive tool catalog and develop a list of tools you think would be needed by a mechanic going to work in a garage for a dealership. If possible, obtain a list of auto technician's tools from a garage's service manager. Add up the cost and report to the class.

One of the largest support systems for water transport ever attempted was the construction of the Panama Canal. This photo was taken during construction of one of the locks in 1913.   (Panama Canal Commission)

Section VI
TRANSPORTATION AND SOCIETY

Chapter 23
TRANSPORTATION AND THE FUTURE

After studying this chapter, you will be able to:
☐ List the goals for future transportation systems.
☐ State the reasons for the need of these goals.
☐ Describe changes that are needed in current transportation facilities.
☐ List and describe some vehicles and facilities that will probably be used in the future.
☐ Describe some applications computer systems will have in future transportation systems.

If you were to ask your parents and grandparents about the technological changes they have seen in their lifetime, you will hear many stories. Automobiles went from being a replacement of horse drawn vehicles to becoming a major force in changing people's life-styles. Airplanes have made tremendous advances in design since the first flying machine. In their day, space travel was only for dreamers and science fiction writers. Today, we hardly give it a thought when we see another manned space mission on our television sets.

When you consider that all this has occurred within the last 100 years, it seems incredible. There has been an explosion of innovative ideas that have helped to shape transportation technology. New and improved transportation vehicles and systems continue to affect the way we live, work, and take our recreation. What was new and exciting even 10 years ago seems commonplace now. The question is, will this trend change and invention stop?

The simple answer to these questions is: trends of the past will continue and inventions will continue to come from creative people. Transportation technology will continue to evolve. Improvements will be made to existing systems. New systems will emerge.

THE FUTURE OF TRANSPORTATION TECHNOLOGY

Future transportation technology will focus on three general goals:
• Improvements in safety.
• Greater energy efficiency.
• Reduction of damage to the environment.

Safety is naturally an important factor for the traveling consumer. Who would want to pay for a ride in a vehicle that is known to be unsafe? Surely, there are risks in everything, but people feel more secure when risks are reduced. Safety is stressed in commercial transportation. The travel industry wants passengers to return again and again to use its services. Therefore, they try to provide the safest, most comfortable transportation possible.

Private vehicle owners also know the need for safe transportation. We are all aware of the number of traffic accidents that occur every year. Changes are being made so that travel will be safer for the private car owner. You have probably seen ads claiming improved vehicle safety. These are meant to attract safety-conscious buyers. The use of seat belts is required in many states. Tougher laws revoke driver's licenses and give jail time for driving while under the influence of drugs or alcohol. There is obvious concern for improved traffic safety. This concern will undoubtedly continue.

We also need to increase energy efficiency in transportation. This will conserve the earth's limited supply of fossil fuels. Petroleum companies are expanding their technology and resources to produce an enormous volume of fuel and lubricants. However, we know that these sources of supply cannot last. There is a need to reduce our dependence on this precious, limited resource. To do this, we must continue to make changes in existing transportation systems. Fuel efficient cars are already on the market. Drivers have accepted them as never before. However, congested streets and highways have commuters asking if there isn't an easier, cheaper way to travel. The result? Public transportation is making a comeback. We can only imagine what travel in cities will be like in the future. Will most private auto travel be banned? It could happen. Then high-speed public ground transport would be even more important to us.

Vehicle designers will continue to experiment with new types of energy-efficient propulsion systems. Though still using petroleum fuels, new engines are more efficient than just a few years ago. Some experimental propulsion systems can store energy in a large flywheel or a fluid system. The stored energy can then be used for propulsion, saving fuel. Other experimental designs use alternate fuels such as alcohol or hydrogen. Electric-powered cars are already with us, Fig. 23-1. Alcohol- and hydrogen-powered vehicles will reduce pollution and the demand for petroleum-based fuels.

We also need to preserve our fragile environment from the side effects of transportation technology. We are now aware of the harm we have done by sending pollutants into the atmosphere, Fig. 23-2. Smog envelopes major cities; it is blamed mainly on traffic. Waterways have been polluted, mainly by manufacturing industries, but also by the vehicles that travel them. New fuel and exhaust systems on combustion engines have reduced the pollution they create. At the same time, they have

A

B

Fig. 23-2. A—Vehicle exhausts add pollutants such as hydrocarbons, carbon monoxide, nitrogen oxides and soot to the atmosphere. B—All major cities experience high levels of air pollution.

improved fuel economy. Some states have made emissions testing a must for all vehicles. Do you agree that this is a step toward reducing air pollution? Trends like these will likely continue.

Keeping these facts in mind, we should now look at the possibilities for more change in transportation. Improvements to existing systems will be pro-

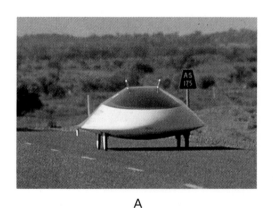

A

B

Fig. 23-1. Major attention is focused on development of electric vehicles. A—The Sunraycer, winner of international competitions, runs on electricity generated by photovoltaic cells. (GM/Hughes Electronics) B—Prototype of an electric-powered vehicle. (GM)

posed; futuristic transportation ventures will be explored. Remember, planners and designers will be limited only by their imaginations. You might well be part of the effort!

CURRENT AND FUTURE FACILITIES

We already have complex transportation systems. These range from a complete network of highways to numerous airports and terminals. All of these facilities are useful to varying degrees. Some, heavily used when first completed, were abandoned as transportation technology advanced. Other systems were underdesigned. Designers could not accurately predict the volume of traffic they would have to handle. Future transportation technology will likely retain these existing facilities; it will have to improve upon them, however.

FUTURE HIGHWAY FACILITIES

Highway travel will continue to be important. However, many highways need repair, Fig. 23-3. The traffic on them has increased dramatically. The combined weight of vehicles, as well as the effects of weather, have led to the deterioration (falling apart) of roads and bridges. States have set aside billions of dollars for rebuilding and new construction. The new highways will be designed to handle more traffic. They will also be safer.

Planned improvements to the automobile may also dictate highway improvements. *Electronic guidance systems* have been proposed that would require the burying of electric cables in the road surface. These cable systems would automatically control vehicles. At the same time they could provide information about the best routes and the travel conditions ahead. Traffic control systems are being proposed in metropolitan areas that would reduce traffic congestion. These systems would employ sensors in the road surface and cameras to collect information. The information would then be input to a computer system. The computers could use the information to determine the best routes for drivers. Lighted highway signs, also controlled by the computer system, would then signal this information to drivers.

WATER TRANSPORTATION FACILITIES

Watercraft haul an enormous amount of cargo on our system of inland waterways. These waterways, like our roadways, need updating.

Some inland waterways use locks, Fig. 23-4, to aid shipping. Many of these were built in the early or mid 1900s. Weather has caused damage, and larger ships need bigger locks.

Freight terminals along these waterways are often old and obsolete. They also need to be updated to answer today's needs.

As these cargo terminals are modernized, they will need computer and robotic systems. *Computer inventory systems* are automatic methods of keeping track of materials and products. Robotic

Fig. 23-3. States have been hard pressed to keep roads updated to handle traffic growth. (Caterpillar Inc.)

Fig. 23-4. A lock on the Mississippi at Dubuque, Iowa. Inland waterways have many of these to allow river transportation of cargo. Larger craft and barges are making many of these locks obsolete. (U.S. Army Corps of Engineers, Rock Island District)

systems are being developed that can unload and store cargo under computer control. The robotic systems will be able to understand directions given by the computer system. They will then follow the instructions without human control.

Many port facilities for passenger transportation are little used because of the decline in ship travel. However, passengers are being won back by water transportation companies. Future port facilities will most likely be adapted to handle both passengers and cargo.

FUTURE AIRPORT FACILITIES

When airports were first constructed, who would have suspected that air travel would become so popular? Airports soon became outdated in spite of frequent improvements. Electronic guidance equipment, as well as larger passenger and cargo terminals had to be built. As aircraft became larger, longer runways had to be constructed for safe landings and takeoffs.

Modern airports are a complex, organized system of people handling, Fig. 23-5. Some facilities became so large that planners began adding people movers. These moving sidewalks carry people between the main terminal and the loading gates.

Airport operators are having to cope with space limitations and public reaction when they prepare for expansion. Cities have grown up around them. Thus, there is little land available for extension of runways. Then too, citizens complain about in-

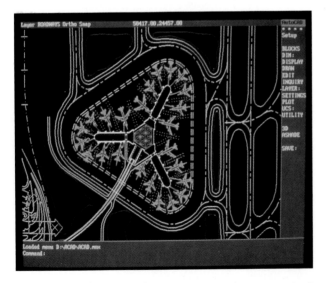

Fig. 23-5. This is a CAD (computer-aided drawing) representation of the Orlando, Florida airport terminal. (Autodesk, Inc.)

creases in airport traffic and the noise that comes with it.

One solution may be the creation of large, artificial islands. These structures would float just offshore. Large aircraft could take off and land without disturbing urban dwellers. Smaller shuttles, helicopters, or high-speed surface transport would then take passengers to their final destination.

FUTURE OF RAIL TRANSPORTATION

The future of rail transportation promises to be interesting. With new, high-speed trains and a return to public transportation, rail travel will be a growing industry. New equipment and facilities are coming. Trains that travel at high speeds need a smooth, level track with no sharp curves. Railroad tracks and beds need to be updated and improved. Where this is not possible, new rail lines will have to be built. As magnetic levitation vehicles rise in popularity, new types of guideways will be seen stretching through the countryside. Some experts believe that new guideways could follow the median strip between highways. This would hold down construction costs.

One futuristic rail system that has been proposed is the tube train. It would travel at high speed through tunnels stretching from coast to coast. Futurists envision travel at many times the speed of sound with minimal damage to the environment. The tubes would have a partial vacuum so that there would be little air resistance as the vehicles pass through the tubes.

FUTURE SPACE FACILITIES

In our short history of space flight, we have witnessed many technological marvels. We have landed astronauts on the moon and sent spacecraft to other planets and beyond. Surely, future space travel and exploration promise to be vast and interesting.

Proposed projects include the construction of a space station where people will live and work. See Fig. 23-6. Designs are already being considered. One proposal has the structure being assembled from several pressurized modules. Assembled modules would be carried into space by a shuttle. The station would be small with the separate units combined to make a livable habitat. As the project grows, more units could be added. The sta-

A
B

Fig. 23-6. Future plans for the U.S. space program call for a space station. A—An artist's rendering of a space station. A space shuttle is shown docked at the station. B—The interior of a space colony "wheel." (NASA)

tion would have its own earthlike environment so workers could live as if on earth.

The proposed modules would provide astronaut-workers with all the necessities for living. Facilities would include a solar-powered communications center, living areas, laboratory areas, and a docking facility. The dock would be used to receive regular shipments of food, supplies, equipment and other needs.

People will be able to learn an incredible amount while working in a weightless environment for extended periods of time. New manufacturing techniques, food and drug processing techniques, and many types of experiments can be carried on. The space station will be available for just about any type of scientific application. Its facilities will be made available to many nations. What would you think of living in space?

TRANSPORTATION VEHICLES OF THE FUTURE

Considering our goals for the future (safety, energy conservation, and environmental protection), we must realize that the types of vehicles we produce will be a direct outcome of our goals. Modern cars, especially, will take advantage of fuel-saving devices. These will become more widely used as automotive technology progresses. Most vehicles will still use gasoline. Others will use propulsion systems that rely on alternate energy sources. The farther we look into the future, the more we see a need for less dependence on petroleum fuels. Can you name some reasons why?

Future Automobiles

Changes in automobile designs will come mainly in the form of body shape, guidance/control systems, and engine efficiency. Car bodies are now being tested in wind tunnels. Here, the car's wind resistance at high speeds can be studied while the vehicle remains still. Temperature and humidity levels are also controlled in the wind tunnel to test the car's operation under various conditions.

Wind resistance, for example, has a direct effect on horsepower needs at highway speeds. Such testing helps car builders design more fuel efficient vehicles.

Guidance systems on future automobiles will rely heavily on computer systems. Fig. 23-7 shows a type of video screen that will be mounted on the dashboards of automobiles. The screen will show a map of the area where the car is traveling. Onboard computer systems will determine the position of the car by sending and receiving satellite information. The computer will then pinpoint the car's location on the video map.

In the future, computers will also have more control over vehicles. A radar-type device will monitor objects and vehicles in front of a car. When another vehicle or structure is too close, the computer systems will automatically trigger warning lights or buzzers. Some models may be hooked up to automatic braking systems like those discussed in Chapter 22.

Fig. 23-7. The car in your future may have a video screen on the dash to help you find your way on unfamiliar roads. (General Motors Corp.)

Future automobiles may use solar energy for power. Look at Fig. 23-8. New designs are being tested, and much is being learned about battery capabilities. Solar powered cars could offer great benefits in conservation of energy and environmental protection. They burn no gas and no emissions would pollute the atmosphere.

FUTURE OF MARINE VEHICLES

The marine shipping industry has been plagued with problems of inefficiency. Costs are high; ships are slow and use too much energy. The future of the shipping industry will remain strong, but new vehicles must be developed if efficiency is to improve. Air cushion vehicles (hovercraft) and freight submarines may be the answer.

Fig. 23-8. Solar power is attracting many an engineer to the design of new land vehicles. (General Motors Corp.)

Air Cushion Vehicles

Air cushion vehicles have proven to be effective transport over water as well as on land. The size of these vehicles seems to be almost unlimited. Large hovercraft that can carry immense loads are already in the drafter's computer or her/his drawing board. The hovercraft will be faster than conventional ships while carrying the same amount of cargo. Because hovercraft can travel on water or land, there will be fewer loading and unloading operations.

Another use for large air cushion vehicles is passenger service. Huge, floating hotels that are able to propel themselves on a cushion of air may become popular.

Freight Submarines

Freight submarines may be another solution to the problems of ocean shipping. Large submersible ships would travel under the turbulent ocean surface. Here, wave stresses would not be as great as on the surface. Fuel economy would be increased since the shape of the vehicle would enable it to slip almost effortlessly through the water.

FUTURE OF AIR TRANSPORTATION

Aircraft enthusiasts and designers have been redesigning aircraft since the principles of flight were first discovered. New structures, materials, and shapes are continually being built and tested. Much of this work is being done for the armed services. However, a great deal of it is being adapted to the private sector. Only our imaginations will limit the possibilities in this area. See Fig. 23-9.

Fig. 23-9. VTOL (vertical takeoff and landing) planes are designed for landing in close quarters but fly longer distances than a helicopter, once in the air. (NASA)

One major advancement in future aircraft will be their ability to fly extremely high. Experiments and testing are under way on planes that can fly in the outer atmosphere where there is no oxygen. These vehicles are called **aerospace planes** because of this unique ability. Can you think of what propulsion system problems will have to be overcome? How about the inability of normal jet engines to operate in space?

Aerospace planes could be used for cargo and passenger transportation. Their advantage would be in their great speed. When needed, aerospace planes may even be able to carry cargo and supplies to manned space stations.

FUTURE OF INTERMODAL TRANSPORTATION

As you learned earlier, intermodal transportation involves the movement of containerized cargo on more than one type of vehicle. For industries that rely on the movement of freight, intermodal transportation is very efficient. Containerized cargo can be shipped through any medium, and easily switched to different vehicles.

The design of containers is very critical here. They must be made so that they can be easily loaded and unloaded onto a variety of vehicles. See Fig. 23-10. Future intermodal transportation containers may be the actual vehicles. For example, conventional ships that travel the seas may eventually be made so that they can be loaded onto large rail vehicles. The rail vehicles would be large enough to accommodate and secure the ship. The train would travel on tracks specially made to hold the combined massive weight.

The basic design of air cushion vehicles will benefit intermodal transportation companies. Because they can travel on land and water, there will be no need to transfer cargo containers. This

A

B

C

Fig. 23-10. In the future, intermodal transportation systems will require that containers for products and materials being shipped be easily transferred from one mode of transportation to another. A—A special crane delivers containers to and from ships at dockside. (Port of Long Beach) B—Lift trucks are capable of hoisting containerized shipping on and off trains and trucks. (Thrall Car Mfg. Co.) C—Containerized transport of liquids is possible with units such as this.

can make their operation more efficient thus saving money, fuel, and labor.

SUMMARY

The future of transportation promises to bring exciting changes. There will be changes to improvements to existing systems and totally new, innovative designs. Changes will update existing transportation systems, like the renovation of roads and bridges. Systems being developed and tested include magnetic levitation trains and air cushion vehicles.

Three goals that will help to shape the future of this technology are the improvement of safety, increased energy efficiency, and reduction of environmental hazards. In reaching these goals we can help save lives as well as improve the environment.

There will be greater use of computer systems in all aspects of transportation technology. They will be used in car guidance systems, and cargo handling to name two examples. Propulsion and control systems will be monitored by onboard computers. The computer systems can then automatically make adjustments to help the vehicle perform better.

Changes will occur in all aspects of transportation. The future will be exciting. Consider all the advancements we have made in the last 100 years. Then imagine what you will see in your lifetime!

KEY WORDS

All of the following words have been used in this chapter. Do you know their meaning?
Aerospace planes
Computer inventory systems
Electronic guidance systems
Freight submarines

TEST YOUR KNOWLEDGE

Write your answers on a separate sheet of paper. Do not write in this book.

Fill in the blank:

1. Three goals for the future of transportation technology are _____, _____, and _____.

2. Some states require _____ tests to reduce the amount of pollution given off by automobiles.

3. Most likely, future port facilities will be adapted to handle both _____ and _____.

4. _____ transportation reduces the number of vehicles by moving masses of commuters in or on one vehicle.

Matching:

5. __ Wind tunnels.
6. __ Air cushion vehicles.
7. __ Freight submarines.
8. __ Aerospace plane.
9. __ Intermodal transportation.
10. __ Computers.
11. __ Space station.

A. Underwater vehicle for carrying cargo.
B. Used for vehicle testing to decrease air resistance.
C. System that involves the movement of containers on more than one vehicle.
D. Aircraft that will be able to fly from our atmosphere into outer space.
E. Vehicle that will be used more by water transportation industries in the future.
F. Probable next goal for space travel.
G. Tools that will be relied upon more and more in transportation technology.

Short answer:

12. Describe the relationship between computer and robotic systems in cargo handling.
13. How will computers be used on cars?
14. Describe three ways current facilities will be adapted to meet future transportation needs.

ACTIVITIES

1. Research the school resource center for information on future technology. Using a computer, if possible, prepare a written report of the results of your research.
2. Imagine what transportation might be like in the year 2050 and write a scenario about traveling from one city to another 250 miles away.
3. Design a model of an air cushion vehicle and prepare sketches of it.

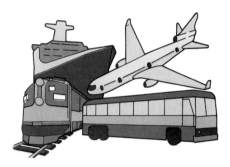

Chapter 24

YOU AND TRANSPORTATION

After studying this chapter, you will be able to:
- ☐ List and describe your interests, abilities, and aptitudes.
- ☐ Explain what qualities employers look for.
- ☐ Describe ways to find out more about career choices.
- ☐ List types of higher education that are available.
- ☐ List careers available in transportation technology.
- ☐ Describe the attributes and responsibilities of entrepreneurs.

The farthest thing from your mind right now may be deciding what type of career you want to follow. You are probably beginning to realize how important work is, however. Doing jobs you like can be a rewarding way to support yourself and a family. Even though a steady job is still some distance in the future you can think about it. You can consider what type of career path you want to take. It is never too early to anticipate the future.

Millions of people choose careers that are related to transportation. It is such a broad field that it can satisfy just about any type of interest.

This chapter will discuss some of the opportunities. More important, it will make you aware of the qualities and attitudes needed to be successfully employed.

Choosing a career can be difficult but it ought to begin with a look at your interests. Some people know what they want to do at an early age. They make their choices early and spend their lives doing work related to their interests. This is usually

a rewarding career that leads to high self-esteem and satisfaction. Other people are not so lucky. They have a difficult time deciding what they would like to do, and then often move from job to job. This can be stressful and devastating to one's self-confidence.

Do you fear that once you have made a decision you are locked into it forever? This is not the case. People frequently make career changes. Often the new career is radically different than the old one. The important thing is that you think about what you'd like and what you want to do.

LOOK AT YOURSELF

Within you is an unlimited source of energy, determination, and imagination. All you need to do is tap into it. This becomes easy when you find something you like to do. For example, if your mother asks you to sweep the floors, you might not want to do it right away. You probably are not interested in the job and will put it off. You will end up doing it and probably hate every minute of it. But if you are asked to fix a bicycle, or do any job that interests you, your attitude might be different, Fig. 24-1. You undertake that job with enthusiasm and determination. You will not stop until the job is done well. Here lies the most important consideration in choosing your career: your interests. *Interests* are things that you like to do. Your interests may include reading or writing, being outdoors, doing scientific experiments, or working on mechanical things.

Fig. 24-1. Your attitude improves when you are doing work that interests you.

Interests alone will not help you find comfortable employment. You should have aptitudes and abilities for the work you are doing. *Aptitude* refers to how quickly you are able to learn a particular skill or grasp an idea, Fig. 24-2. If you easily understand how mechanical things come apart and go back together, you have an aptitude in this area. *Abilities* are things that you can do well. Employers are not likely to hire someone just because they are interested in the work available. Companies need to see that a person is capable of doing the work before he or she is hired.

Now, while you are thinking about them, it might be a good time to list your interests, aptitudes, and abilities. Don't underestimate or underrate yourself, and don't take your abilities for granted. They can take you far in a career. List the things that you like to do, then the things you are able to do well. You will start to see a pattern. From this, you can start to choose a rewarding career.

Another thing that you must consider are your values. *Values* are things that you consider important. These must be considered above all else. If you make a career choice that disagrees with your values, you may become unhappy. For example, if you value time with your family and friends, you may not want to hold a job that keeps you away from them for long periods of time. If you value preserving the environment, you will not be happy working at something that is harmful to it. Values should be considered carefully because they are deeply rooted beliefs that are a part of you.

CHOOSING A CAREER

Once you have taken stock of your interests, aptitudes, abilities, and values, you are ready to explore career directions. How do you find information on careers? One way is to talk to your school guidance counselor, Fig. 24-3. This is probably the easiest and closest source of information that you have. He or she can lead you to all types of career information.

Other experiences at school are helpful in making career choices. The variety of elective courses available will help you to decide what you like, Fig. 24-4. More important, they will help you decide what you do not like! You obviously do not want to spend your life working at a career that you know you'll hate. Whatever electives you pursue, do not neglect the general requirements of an education. Reading, writing, math, and science skills will be important, no matter what career you choose.

Fig. 24-2. Your aptitude and abilities should match the job. (Mark Van Manen, BC Transit)

Fig. 24-3. Your guidance counselor can be a valuable source of information about careers.

Fig. 24-4. Elective classes can help you figure out what you like to do.

Fig. 24-5. Working in the transportation field will allow you to find out what you like to do. (Delta Airlines)

Part-time and summer employment can help you find work for which you are suited, Fig. 24-5. What is more important, this experience will open your eyes to the types and variety of work you may find interesting. Expect to start on the bottom of the employment ladder. You may find yourself doing dirty, tedious, and boring work at first. Don't be discouraged; everyone starts there.

Career Literature

Your library will have many books and other literature on careers. By researching these, you can learn much about your options, Fig. 24-6. The *Dictionary of Occupational Titles* and the *Occupational Outlook Handbook* are collections of hundreds of available careers. They list the responsibilities and duties of various careers. You will find information on benefits, wages, salaries, and the number of hours you will be expected to work. Types of education and training that are necessary will also be explained.

Talking to People

When you find a job that seems interesting, you can find out more about it by talking with people,

Fig. 24-6. Libraries have many sources of information on careers.

Fig. 24-7. Ask a person who is already working in that field questions about his or her job. Most people are willing to discuss their employment with interested young people. This is an excellent way to find out about job duties and responsibilities. Remember that these conversations help you gain an understanding of the job. Do not let the other person discourage you, because they may have different opinions and interests than you. Base your decisions on the facts available, not on other peoples' recommendations.

Fig. 24-7. Talking to people who work in the field you are interested in can be helpful in choosing your career.

CAREER DECISIONS AND YOUR FUTURE

It is not realistic to expect that you will make a career decision in school and stick with it for the rest of your life. Very few people are able to work at one job their whole life and be happy. It is normal to change jobs, many people do it. It is also important to remember that we live in a constantly changing, technological world. New jobs are always becoming available. You might find yourself working at a job 10 years from now that does not exist today. Look at Fig. 24-8.

It is for this reason that a solid foundation of basic skills are needed. More and more, employers

Fig. 24-8. New developments in technology will create jobs in the future that do not exist today. (Miller Electric Co.)

are looking for people who can communicate well. Reading and writing skills are essential. Teamwork is becoming very important in the workplace, and transportation industries are no different. These skills are essential, and will continue to be important in the future. Your ability to work in the field you choose may depend on your mastery of basic skills. It is very important to master these skills now, while you are in school. Giving yourself a good foundation of skills will not limit your future.

EDUCATION

It should be obvious to you by now that a good education is essential for a good future. Most employers need people with *at least* a high school education. The career path you choose will determine the amount of education you will need. Many transportation fields require more education than a high school diploma. In fact, any job you decide to undertake will require some form of training. The following are some of the types of education and training institutions available:
- College.
- Technical Institute.
- Industrial (on-the-job) training.
- Armed services.

College degrees are a must for many jobs related to the transportation and energy fields. There are basically four types of degrees offered by various institutions. An associate degree can be earned in two years. It means that the student has completed training in a specific field. A bachelor's degree normally requires four years of higher education. It combines a general education as well as advanced training in a specific area. Further education at the university level can result in a master's degree, then a doctoral degree.

Technical institutes across the nation offer up-to-date courses and training programs, Fig. 24-9. They are set up to provide specialized training for people who realize the need for technical education, but are unwilling or unable to go to college. Usually technical institute programs provide two years of study and/or training in a specific field. Hands-on training is a vital part of this experience. Companies are interested in hiring qualified individuals from these schools.

Many companies offer on-the-job training to everyone they hire. Because technology rapidly changes, industries need to constantly update equipment and techniques. This means, naturally, that employees need to update their skills fre-

Fig. 24-9. Technical institutes provide training for many people. (T.V. Vessel Photography)

quently. Industrial education is a necessity in today's workplace. This is why employers look for trainable people with good communication skills who are able to work as members of a team. Another quality employers look for is a positive attitude toward work and learning. They know that their industries will change, and their employes will need to change with them.

The armed services provide excellent training in many highly technical areas, Fig. 24-10. These areas include the transportation and energy fields. This training and experience can be used to advance in a military career, or it helps in getting rewarding employment in civilian life. Armed service training builds characteristics that many employers look for, including respect and discipline.

Fig. 24-10. By serving in the armed forces, you can receive valuable training. (U.S. Navy)

CAREERS AVAILABLE IN TRANSPORTATION

At the risk of repeating ourselves, there are numerous career options in the field of transportation. Every country in the world relies on transport services. Imagine your world with no transportation! Would it be the same? Definitely not!

Because of the number of jobs and careers available, it is not possible to discuss them all in this text. Only a sampling under various headings will be explored. These can be listed under four categories. They are: research and development, vehicle operation, support facility employment, and customer service.

To satisfy transportation needs of the future, research and development must take place today. There are many places for scientists, engineers, and technicians to carry out this type of work. Any new vehicle or support system must be thoroughly tested before a company will commit large sums of money to build it, Fig. 24-11.

The government alone has extensive research and development activities in space exploration. Many industries invest heavily in developing new products ideas.

People who work in the research and development field normally complete the requirements of a first-rate higher education program. They are most often creative and scientific people.

All vehicles need some type of operator. Some jobs in this area include taxi and bus drivers, truck drivers, aircraft and space shuttle pilots, ship captains, and train engineers. Fig. 24-12 shows some of these occupations. The amount and type of training required depends on the type of vehicle be-

Fig. 24-11. All vehicle designs must be tested before they are put into production. (General Dynamics)

Fig. 24-12. All vehicles require an operator. (BC Transit, NASA, UPS, Santa Fe)

ing operated. Pilots obviously must complete different requirements than truck drivers. However, each job is important and the training is rigorous. There are different regulations for each type of vehicle. Operators must be knowledgeable, qualified, and licensed to legally operate their vehicles.

There are so many types of support facilities that the number of types of jobs seems limitless. From baggage handlers and mechanics to cleaning crews and dock workers, the list goes on, Fig. 24-13.

Varying levels of education are required for different jobs. There are many opportunities for all types of people. Many times, construction workers are considered part of the transportation support team.

Customer service employees are an essential part of transportation industries. Jobs under this heading include ticket agents, flight attendants, travel agents, and salespeople. Look at Fig. 24-14. Varying degrees of training and education are necessary, and people who are good at these jobs have special traits. They must be friendly and knowledgeable so that customers feel comfortable dealing with them.

YOU COULD BE AN ENTREPRENEUR

Every year, numerous new businesses are started. Some grow and flourish in the economy, but many fail and go out of business. This does not discourage people from trying. There are many types of new businesses that can be successful and quite a few of these are related to transportation.

Entrepreneurs are bold people who start their own business or acquire an existing one. They are responsible for all aspects of that business. Entrepreneurs perform management as well as labor duties. To do this, a person must be dedicated to the success of the enterprise. There must be a great desire, as well as the ability to overcome obstacles. Entrepreneurs are people who see an idea and make it work for their benefit.

The qualities of an entrepreneur include great motivation, self-confidence, technical and management knowledge, and determination. The rewards can be many. Independence, status, and money are examples of what successful entrepreneurs receive. Long hours of work, personal and social sacrifices, and the possibility of failure are to be expected.

Fig. 24-13. The support services for transportation provide many different types of jobs. (Greyhound, Delta Airlines, United Airlines, U.S. Air Force)

Fig. 24-14. The people that work with the customers are one of the most important parts of any transportation system. (BC Transit/Mark Van Manen, Amtrak, United Airlines)

There are some basic steps that a person must follow to be successful in one's own business. The first step is to develop an idea. Entrepreneurs see something that people need. They are able to recognize a market. The time and location must also be right for such a business. If people are not ready for the goods or service, the business will not have any customers. If the entrepreneur chooses a bad location, nobody will find the business, or even be aware that it exists.

The next step in starting a business is to find money to finance the enterprise. Many entrepreneurs spend their entire savings, as well as borrow from banks, friends, and relatives. This money is known as capital, and is the major input. It is used to pay for building space, utilities, materials, employees, and advertising. If the entrepreneur can sell a business venture, he or she may be able to attract partners to help finance the venture. Partners may take an active role in the company, or may be silent, only providing money. The people involved must be willing to cooperate and should have something to offer the venture. People are the next step in organizing a successful business.

The number of owners, or people who provide capital will determine what type of ownership the business has. If one person finances and runs the whole operation, it is called a proprietorship. The proprietor is responsible for everything, and gets to keep all the profit.

Partnerships are formed when two or more people share the responsibilities of a business venture. Each partner contributes labor and money to the venture. Then the profits are split according to an agreement between the partners.

Corporations are formed when there are many owners. They are organized and governed according to laws. People buy into the venture by purchasing shares of stock. This way, large sums of capital can be accumulated. Usually no single person is responsible for running the company. A board of directors is responsible for making management decisions. When shares of the company are bought or sold, management is not usually affected. Management is affected only when large numbers of shares are sold or bought by one person.

The last step to ensure that any business will be a success is advertising. You see many advertisements everyday. They are on television and radio and in newspapers and magazines. Good advertising will let customers know that your business is ready to serve them. Your business will succeed only if you provide excellent service and superb products.

SUMMARY

Doing work that you like can be a rewarding way to earn a living. You can choose whatever you want to do. Getting a solid foundation of skills now will multiply your options. There are millions of jobs related to transportation. Reading this book has made you aware of many of them. If this subject interests you, maybe you will choose a career in the transportation field.

Before you can make a good choice, you need to know yourself. You need to understand your interests, aptitudes, abilities, and values. The career you choose should include a balance of all these. You can find more information about careers at your school and in your community. By doing research and talking to people you can know exactly what jobs offer and what they require.

If you do not wish to work for someone else your whole life, you may choose to become an entrepreneur. There are many benefits to starting your own business, but the work is hard and the risks are many. The steps that people follow when starting their own business are developing an idea, collecting money to invest, finding quality employees and then advertising. If you are a bold person, who likes to take risks, then your future might be in running your own business.

KEY WORDS

All of the following words have used in this chapter. Do you know their meaning?
Abilities
Aptitude
Entrepreneurs
Interests
Values

TEST YOUR KNOWLEDGE

Write your answers on a separate sheet of paper. Do not write in this book.
Fill in the blank:
1. _____ refer to how quickly you are able to learn a skill.
2. _____ are deeply rooted beliefs that you have.
3. Two references that list information about careers are _____ and _____.

4. _____ and _____ must be thoroughly carried out before investing heavily in a new vehicle.

5. _____ and _____ are two qualities of an entrepreneur.

Matching:

6. __ Entrepreneur.
7. __ Proprietor.
8. __ Ability.
9. __ Interest.
10. __ Guidance counselor.
11. __ Positive attitude.
12. __ Corporation.

A. Quality that employers seek in workers.
B. Something you like to do.
C. Business owned by many people.
D. Person who starts a business.
E. Something you can do.
F. One person who owns and operates a business.
G. School employee who can help you research career possibilities.

Short answer:

13. Make a list of your interests and abilities.
14. List possible jobs in the field of transportation in which you might be interested.
15. Explain why you will always have to be in training if you pursue a technological career.
16. What are the advantages and disadvantages of being an entrepreneur?

17. Describe three ways in which businesses can be funded and run.

ACTIVITIES

1. On a separate sheet of paper develop a chart like the one shown below. Fill in the chart by listing all of your interests and aptitudes. In the last column list careers that seem suited to your interests and aptitudes. Use your library as a resource for career tasks.

INTERESTS	APTITUDES	POSSIBLE CAREER

2. Interview someone whose job interests you. Prepare a report that describes: what the job is, the person's interests and hobbies, amount of education required, what skills are required, any influences that led them to that career.

3. As a class project, write away to trade associations in the transportation field for literature on careers available in that industry. You will need to:
   a. Develop a list of associations.
   b. Prepare a form letter. (This can be set up on a computer and printed out on a printer, if available.)
   c. Address envelopes and mail the letters.
   d. As information is received develop a booklet of career information. Make copies for all of the class.

Will you or someone you know be living in a space colony module like
this during your lifetime? It seems possible.　　(NASA)

DICTIONARY OF TECHNICAL TERMS

A

Abilities: Tasks one can do well.

Acceleration: Changing the speed of a vehicle so that it moves faster.

Actual mechanical advantage: The ratio of input to output power, including the losses from friction.

Actuators: Devices that convert fluid power to mechanical power in hydraulic and pneumatic systems.

Aeronautical charts: Maps made specifically for air navigation.

Aerospace planes: Aircraft that are able to travel both in the atmosphere and in outer space.

Air compressors: Pumps that convert the mechanical energy input into pneumatic power transmission.

Aircraft: A vehicle designed to travel in the air.

Air-cushion vehicles: Special all-terrain craft that move over water or land on a cushion of compressed air.

Airfoil: The shape of an airplane's wing that causes lift.

Airspeed indicators: Instruments that measure the difference between two pressures acting on an aircraft.

Air transportation: Transportation systems that operate in the air using various types of aircraft.

Airways: Paths or routes that airplanes follow in the air.

Airways: Paths or routes that airplanes follow.

Alternating current: Electron flow that moves back and forth alternately in opposite directions.

Alternators: Electrical generators that produce alternating current.

Ambient air: The air surrounding any area under discussion.

Amperage: The rate at which electrons flow through a conductor.

Apogee: Point in an earth orbit where the orbiting vehicle is farthest from the earth.

Aptitude: How quickly one is able to master a skill or grasp an idea.

Aquifers: Underground reservoirs so named because they hold in storage large quantities of water.

Articulated: A vehicle that is jointed somewhere along its chassis to negotiate turns better.

Atoms: The "building blocks" of all matter; the smallest particle of any element that contains all the characteristics of the element.

B

Ballast: Larger stone laid down on top of subballast.

Batch sequence: Different products sent through a pipeline in batches.

Bearings: Shaped parts designed to support shafts and reduce friction as the shafts rotate.

Belt and pulley systems: Devices that are used to control direction and speed of torque.

Bernoulli effect: As the speed of a fluid is increased, its pressure decreases.

Bilge keels: Downward extensions from the keel or centerline of a boat's hull. They provide lateral stability for the hull.

Blimps: Lighter-than-air vehicles that can be controlled both vertically and horizontally. Also called dirigibles.

Body: A part of a vehicle's structure that gives it shape and provides room for passengers or cargo.

Bottom dead center: The lowest point of piston travel in a reciprocating engine.

Boxcars: Rolling stock designed like a box with

sliding doors on each side and intended to haul a variety of cargo.

Bridges: Structures that span barriers such as rivers, gorges, etc., as part of a roadway or railway system.

British thermal unit: A measurement of the amount of heat energy. One Btu is the heat energy needed to raise the temperature of one pound of water one degree Fahrenheit.

Brushes: Carbon conductors that transfer current from the commutator of a DC generator to the circuit.

Bulkheads: Parts of the frame of a semimonocoque fuselage. They provide lateral stiffness.

Buoyancy: The upward force that water exerts on objects placed in it.

C

Camber: A tilting of a vehicle's wheel slightly off the vertical to improve steering action.

Canal: A channel dug to connect two bodies of water.

Capital: Those assets, such as buildings and vehicles, that are used to help operate a system.

Carbon-zinc cell: The most common primary cell.

Caster: A positioning of a steerable wheel so that the point of contact with the road is behind the centerline of the steering axis.

Cells: Devices that contain chemical energy that readily converts into electrical energy on demand.

Centrifugal force: The force that makes spinning objects want to move outward from the center.

Chart: In marine or air transportation, a term given to maps designed for navigation purposes.

Chassis: The frame of a vehicle which provides support for other systems of the vehicle as well as for the body.

Chemical energy: The energy produced by chemical changes such as burning of material.

Classification society: Maritime organizations that set and enforce ship construction standards.

Clutches: Mechanical devices that quickly connect and disconnect components of the drive system.

Coal: A solid form of fossil fuel comprised mainly of carbon.

Cockpit: Space in an airplane that houses the controls and navigational instruments and where the pilot sits.

COFC (Container on flatcar): Transport method that moves containerized products placed on railroad flatcars.

Commutator: Part of a DC generator that transfers generated current to the brushes.

Commuter service: Air transport that transports people from small airports to major airports.

Compasses: Instruments intended for indicating direction of travel.

Complex machines: Machines made up of a combination of two or more simple machines.

Compressibility: A measure of the amount of any matter that can be squeezed into a smaller space.

Compression-ignition engine: Another name for a diesel engine derived from the fact that it depends on the heat of compression to ignite the fuel.

Compression ratio: The difference in the volume of the combustion chamber when the piston is at bottom dead center compared to the volume at top dead center.

Computer inventory systems: Automatic methods of keeping track of materials and products by employing computers.

Conductors: Materials whose electrons transfer easily to other atoms.

Conning tower: A projection, usually in the center of a submarine, where the craft's periscope, radio antenna, and radar equipment is located. A snorkel tube is also located there.

Contact patch: The part of a tire that is actually touching the road as the tire rotates.

Containerization: Method of handling goods by packing many smaller packages in a large container.

Containerships: Ships designed to carry containerized shipping.

Control systems: Parts of vehicles used to change a vehicle's direction and speed.

Convertibles: Automobiles with a removable roof.

Crude oil: Petroleum in its natural state.

Current: Flow of electrons in a conductor.

Cuts: Excess earth that must be removed during construction of roadway.

Cyclical pitch: A method of direction control on helicopters achieved by changing the pitch of the rotor blades as they pass a certain point in their rotation.

D

DC generators: A generator type that produces direct current.

Dead reckoning: A method of navigation in which the position is determined by keeping track of speed and time lapse.

Deceleration: The slowing down or braking of a vehicle.

Deep mining: Use of underground passages to extract coal and other minerals from the ground.

Degrees of freedom: The degree of control over directions of travel of a vehicle. Some can only move forward or backward (one degree of freedom); others can also move up and down or left and right (three degrees of freedom).

Diesel engines: Internal combustion engines that use heat and pressure to ignite their fuel.

Direct current: Movement of electrons in only one direction in a conductor.

Dirigibles: Lighter-than-air vehicles that can be controlled vertically as well as horizontally. Also called blimps.

Disc brakes: Braking systems that apply friction devices, or pads, to a disc-shaped part also called a rotor.

Domestic airline service: Transport by air to and from major airports within a country.

Doppler effect: The apparent change in frequency of a wavelength as it travels toward or away from an observer; used in NAVSAT navigation.

Draft: How deep a hull sits in the water.

Drive system: Components needed to transmit and control power provided by the propulsion system.

Drum brakes: Braking systems that apply the friction devices, called shoes, to a drum.

Dry dock: A facility where a ship can be placed while out-of-the-water repairs are made or maintenance is done.

Dunnage: Straps, blocks, and special rigging used to secure freight to a rail vehicle.

E

Efficiency: In energy conversion, the amount of energy input compared to the energy output from the process.

Electric motors: Electrical devices that change electrical energy to mechanical energy.

Electrical circuit: The complete path of conductors and electrical devices through which current travels.

Electrical energy: The energy of electrons moving from one atom to another in a conductor.

Electrical systems: Those systems that perform their work using electrical energy.

Electrodes: The terminals of a cell or battery to which a circuit's conductors are attached.

Electrolyte: Chemical solution, either wet or dry, found in cells and batteries.

Electromagnet: Consists of a conductor wrapped around a core so that when current is introduced in the coil the core becomes magnetized.

Electromagnetic induction: The current produced in a wire when the wire is passed between the poles of a magnet, cutting the lines of force.

Electromagnetic levitation: Use of magnetism to support and propel a vehicle.

Electron theory: Theory that electrons move through a conductor from the negative to the positive terminal.

Electronic guidance systems: Cable systems buried in roadways for the purpose of guiding vehicles electronically.

Electrons: A particle of an atom having a negative charge.

Elevated train: A rail system running above city streets.

Empennage: Tail section of an airplane.

Energy: The ability to do work. Also, the input that provides power to operate a technological system.

Entrepreneurs: Persons who start and run a business enterprise.

Epitrochoidal curve: The special shape of the combustion chamber of the Wankel rotary engine. It is shaped somewhat like a figure "8."

Exosphere: A region of space extending from 500 to 1000 miles above the earth.

External combustion engines: Engines that burn fuel outside of the engine itself.

F

Feedback: Process of giving back information on how a system is working. A thermostat sending a signal to a furnace that more heat is needed is a type of feedback.

Ferries: Vessels designed to move people and land vehicles across narrow bodies of water.

Fills: The addition of rock and soil to build up low-lying sections of a roadway under construction.

Finance: Money that is needed to pay for other inputs (resources) of a system.

First-class lever: A lever having its fulcrum between the input force and the output force.

Fixed routes: Pathways for travel that are always the same; the vehicle must stay on the path. A railroad right-of-way is an example.

Flatcars: Rolling stock consisting basically of a platform on wheels; designed to carry heavy and cumbersome cargo.

Flow line: In oil pipelines, an above-ground line that carries the oil to storage tanks.

Fluid motors: Devices that convert fluid power into rotary mechanical motion.

Fluid power systems: Those systems that do work using the energy transferred to liquids or gases.

Flux: Lines of force found between the poles of a magnet.

Foils: Wings or planes on hydrofoils that lift the vessel from the water when underway.

Four-stroke cycle engine: An internal combustion engine that has one power stroke every fourth stroke of its piston or pistons.

Fractionating tower: A large tower in a refinery where heated crude oil is separated into various products.

Freight submarines: Submarines designed to haul cargo.

Freight train: A train designed to haul cargo.

Fulcrum: The fixed point upon which a lever rotates.

Fuselage: The main body of an aircraft that supports all other parts and cargo or passengers.

Fuses: Devices in an electrical circuit that open the circuit in case of overcurrent or overloads.

Fusion: The forcible joining of hydrogen atoms thereby releasing huge amounts of heat energy.

G

Gasohol: A mixture of unleaded gasoline and ethyl alcohol.

Gathering lines: In oil pipelines, lines that transport the oil into trunk lines.

Gear: A pulley or wheel whose rim is notched or toothed to mesh with other gears.

Gearsets: A combination of two or more gears consisting of a drive gear and a driven gear or gears.

Geothermal energy: Heat from the earth's interior.

Glider: An aircraft with no propulsion unit.

Globe: A spherical map of the world.

Goals: The purposes for which a system is created.

Gondolas: Rolling stock with low sides and no tops; designed for hauling loose material.

Gravitometer: A computerized control device that separates different products sent through a pipeline and directs them to their proper storage tanks.

Gravity: An attraction that tends to pull all matter earthward and keep it earthbound.

Guidance systems: Devices that provide information required by a vehicle to follow a particular path or perform certain operations.

Gyrocompasses: Compasses which depend on a rotating wheel to indicate direction of travel.

H

Heat engines: Engines that use combustion as the energy for moving mechanical power systems.

Hopper cars: Open-topped rolling stock with chutes beneath for quick unloading of loose material.

Horsepower: A standard unit of measurement for power. It is equal to the energy needed to lift 33,000 lb. 1 ft. in one minute.

Hot-air balloons: Nonsteerable lighter-than-air vehicles that depend on heating of the air they contain to keep them buoyant.

Hovercraft®: An air-cushion vehicle (rides on a cushion of compressed air).

Hull: The sides and bottom of a vessel.

Hydraulic braking system: Linking of a hydraulic system to devices that apply rotational friction to wheels for purpose of stopping the vehicle.

Hydraulic systems: Fluid power systems that use a liquid such as oil to transmit and control power.

Hydrofoils: Marine vehicles that use air-foil shapes to support them in the water.

I

Ideal mechanical advantage: Mechanical advantage minus the losses caused by friction.

Inclined planes: Mechanisms consisting of sloping surfaces used to elevate heavy loads without lifting them.

Induction motor: Electric motor that depends on a building/collapsing magnetic field for its operation.

Inland waterways: Water routes within land masses such as rivers and lakes.

Inputs: Resources needed to make a system operate.

Insulators: Materials made of atoms that do not readily transfer electrons.

Interests: Things one likes to do.

Intermodal transportation: Use of several transport modes in moving people or cargo.

Internal combustion engines: Engines that burn their fuel internally.

International airline service: Travel service between countries.

J

Jet pack: Device used by astronauts for maneuvering outside spacecraft while the vehicle is in orbit.

K

Kinetic energy: The energy of motion.

L

Land transportation: Any land transportation system that is supported by the land.

Launching pad: A supporting structure for launching space vehicles.

Lead-acid battery: A number of rechargeable cells forming one unit. This type of battery is usually found in automobiles.

Lever: A rigid bar that rotates on a fixed support called a fulcrum; its purpose is to multiply either force or speed of the input force.

Lift: The upward force exerted by air under an airplane's wings.

Light energy: A type of radiant energy given off by sources like the sun.

Light-emitting diodes: A semiconductor device that, when connected in a circuit a certain way, lights up.

Lines of force: Also called flux, invisible force field found in the space between the poles of a magnet.

Liquefied natural gas: Gas placed under such heavy pressure that it turns to a liquid.

Locks: Watertight chambers built in bodies of water to raise or lower ships from one level to another.

Logs: Speed indicators on marine vessels that measure speed by water pressure.

Longerons: Framework of aircraft running the length of the fuselage

Loran: A navigational system that uses a receiver to pick up signals transmitted by sending stations located at frequent intervals along coastal areas to guide ships and planes.

M

Machines: Devices that can change the size, direction, and speed of forces; used to manage mechanical power.

Magma: Molten rock located miles beneath the earth's surface.

Magnetic levitation: A suspension and propulsion system for trains, based upon the operational principles of a magnet.

Magnets: Materials that are attracted to any metal that contains iron.

Management: Activities or tasks necessary to keep people and cargo organized and on schedule.

Manned vehicles: Spacecraft with crew aboard.

Materials: In a transportation system the goods or raw material needed to operate the system.

Mechanical advantage: The increase in force provided by a machine; a multiplication of the input force as output force.

Mechanical energy: The energy of motion, also known as kinetic energy. The energy found in all moving objects.

Mechanical power: Mechanical energy converted to do work.

Mechanical systems: A basic type of power system that uses mechanical energy to do work.

Mesosphere: A region 50 miles above the earth that contains an ozone layer.

Methanol: A clean-burning liquid fuel that is a type of alcohol.

Military aviation: Air transport systems serving the armed forces of a country.

Mining: Removal of minerals, especially coal, from the ground.

Monorail: A railroad with only one rail; cars may ride on the rail or be suspended from it.

N

Natural gas: A gaseous form of fossil fuel.

Nautical charts: Maps that show routes for coastal waters, rivers, and other marine areas.

Navigation: The guidance given a vessel to keep it on course.

NAVSAT: An electronic navigational system set up by the Navy and utilizing signals from five satellites in earth orbit.

Neutrons: A particle of an atom having no charge.

Nonrenewable energy: Energy sources that cannot be replaced once they are used up.

Nuclear energy: The energy stored in atoms of certain fissile materials.

Nuclear fission: The splitting of nuclei (centers) of certain uranium isotopes, creating heat.

Nuclear power plant: A power station that uses nuclear fission to create steam for production of electric power .

Nucleus: The center of an atom which contains the protons and neutrons.

O

Ohmmeter: An instrument for measuring electrical resistance.

Oil shale: A rock that was formed millions of years ago from fossil materials that became mixed with clay.

Omega: Similar to the Loran navigational system but worldwide.

Orbit: The path taken by spacecraft circling the earth in space.

Outer space: Space that is around 10,000 miles above the earth.

Output: The end result of applying inputs and process in a system.

P

Parallel circuits: Electrical circuits in which electrical current (electron flow) can travel along more than one path as opposed to series circuits with one.

Perigee: Point during orbit when the orbiting vehicle is closest to earth.

Petroleum: A liquid form of fossil fuel comprised mainly of carbon and hydrogen.

Photons: Particles of light energy.

Photosynthesis: The process plants use to convert light energy into food for growth.

Photovoltaic cells: Also called solar cells, devices for collecting sunlight and converting it directly to electrical energy.

Pig: A barrel-shaped brush that is blown through pipelines to prevent or clear clogging.

Piggyback: The carrying of truck trailers on railroad flatcars.

Pneumatic systems: Fluid power systems that use a gas, such as air, as a transfer medium to control and transmit power.

Pneumatic tires: Tires that are filled with air to provide support.

Pneumatics: Systems that use gases to control and transmit energy.

Polarity: The type of charge, negative or positive, that an atom has.

Potential energy: Energy that is at rest but has the capability of motion.

Power: The amount of work done over a period of time.

Power brakes: A braking system that uses vacuum to apply pressure to the hydraulics.

Power systems: In the harnessing of energy sources, the machines used to convert energy into motion.

Primary cells: Cells that cannot be recharged once the chemicals in them have become exhausted.

Primary coil: The coil of a transformer attached to the input side of the circuit.

Process: The action part of a total technological system; the use of inputs to produce an output (desired result).

Production:. The "action" part of the system, usually called the process. Also, the technological systems comprising manufacturing and construction.

Propulsion system: The components of a vehicle's system of motion.

Protons: A particle of an atom having a positive charge.

Pulleys: A circular lever with its fulcrum at its center.

R

Radar: A system for detecting the presence and distance of other marine vehicles in the vicinity (stands for **ra**dio **d**etection **a**nd **r**anging).

Radials: The radio beams used by VOR stations for aerial navigation.

Radiant energy: A form of energy found in the movement of molecules as in heat and light from the sun.

Radio sextant: Electronic instruments that pick up radio signals given off by the sun to determine the location of marine craft.

Radioactivity: The giving off of radiation as a result of decay of radioactive particles.

Railroads: Permanent roadways made usually of a double line of tracks fixed to wood or concrete ties.

Rails: Ribbons of steel placed on a railway bed to support and control a train's direction of travel.

Random-route mode: Vehicular travel that allows the operator to take any route of choice.

Reaction engines: Jet and rocket engines (so called because they operate on the principle that for every action there is an opposite and equal reaction).

Reactor: A strong containment where nuclear fission takes place.

Regional airline service: Airline service involving transport from small airports within a specific region.

Renewable energy resources: Those energy sources that can be replaced as needed; examples are plant and animal life. The basic renewable resources are food, wood, animals, and alcohol.

Resistance: The opposition to current in a conductor.

Roadbed: The base of a roadway.

Rolling stock: Railroad cars that are pulled by a locomotive.

Rotor: Another name for the disc in a disc brake.

Rotor blades: Rotating wings used on a helicopter that provide lift.

Rudders: A vane or fanlike piece intended to help steer vehicles traveling in a fluid medium.

Runways: Paths used by airplanes for takeoff and landing.

S

Schematic drawings: A drawing of an electrical circuit and its devices on paper.

Screw: A mechanism consisting of an inclined plane wrapped around a cylinder or shaft.

Sea lanes: Routes that vessels travel at sea.

Secondary cell: Cells that can be discharged and recharged any number of times.

Secondary coil: The coil of a transformer attached to the output side of the circuit.

Second-class levers: Levers having the load between the input force and the fulcrum.

Semiconductors: Materials that neither conduct nor insulate well.

Series circuits: Circuits in which loads are connected one after the other along a single electrical path.

Series-parallel circuits: A combination of a series and a parallel circuit.

Shock absorber: A device for controlling spring oscillation.

Simple machines: The basic machines that control application of power. They are the lever, pulley, wheel and axle, inclined plane, screw, and wedge.

Skylab: A space satellite built by NASA to support scientific experiments and studies.

Slurry: Solid material that has been mixed with a liquid before being sent through a pipeline.

Solar energy: Energy of the sun given off as heat and light.

Solar panels: Panels used to collect solar energy and transfer it as heat to air or water.

Solid rocket boosters: Additional propulsion units found on space vehicles to help "boost" them into orbiting speed.

Sonar: Detection and ranging system similar to radar but depending on sound and echoes.

Space transportation: Transportation systems that operate in space above the atmosphere.

Spacecraft: Vehicles that travel beyond the earth's atmosphere.

Speedometers: Instruments that measure ground speed of land vehicles.

Spring oscillation: The tendency of a spring to compress and rebound repeatedly (bounce).

Springs: Devices that support heavy weights by storing the potential energy in the weight.

Staging: A series of propulsion systems placed one on top of the other in space vehicles. As each stage exhausts its fuel, it is separated and dropped to earth.

Stationary route: A route, such as a pipeline, that remains unmoving.

Steam turbines: A type of external combustion engine that can produce power continuously.

Step-down transformer: A transformer that reduces line voltage.

Step-up transformer: A transformer that increases line voltage.

Storage batteries: Common devices for storing and providing electrical energy for operating motors and other devices.

Stratosphere: A region ranging from 7 to 22 miles above the earth.

Structural systems: Parts of the vehicle that determine its shape. They include the frame as well as the covering that protects the other systems, passengers, and cargo.

Subballast: The first layer of crushed stone in a rail bed.

Submarines: Underwater vehicles that depend on increase and decrease of buoyancy to submerge or travel on the water's surface.

Subway: A train that runs on rails beneath the ground.

Support systems: All of the external operations that maintain transportation systems. These include maintenance, life support, economic support, and legal support.

Surface mining: Mining of coal that is close to the surface, also known as strip mining. Done with the use of huge shovels and bulldozers.

Suspension systems: Parts of a vehicle that support or suspend it in its environment.

T

Tail assembly: Surfaces at the back of the plane that help control it. Includes horizontal and vertical stabilizers as well as the rudder.

Tank cars: Rolling stock consisting of tanks on wheels designed for carrying liquids.

Tar sands: Fossils that became mixed with sand millions of years ago.

Technological system: A human-built system designed to make life better while using technical means in an efficient manner.

Technology: The application of knowledge and creative thinking that changes resources to meet human needs.

Terminals: A structure, usually sheltered, to provide needed service and shelter for travelers and cargo.

Thermosphere: A region of space from 50 to 300 miles above earth.

Third-class levers: Levers having their fulcrums closer to the input force than to the load. They are distance multipliers.

Thrust: A force that produces motion in a body. The force produced by a plane's propulsion system.

Top dead center: The highest point of piston travel in a reciprocating engine.

Torque converters: Devices that use fluid pressure to connect and disconnect moving parts.

Towboat: A boat designed to push barges.

Transformers: Electrical devices that change voltage.

Transmission systems: Devices that provide for multiplying, dividing, or reversing the mechanical power developed by the propulsion system.

Transocean: Traveling across oceans.

Transport cars: Rolling stock with side rails, often with an upper and a lower platform.

Transportation: Moving products or people from one place to another.

Transportation systems: Systems set up to relocate cargo and people.

Troposphere: Space that is about six miles above the earth.

Trunk lines: In oil pipelines, the lines that carry the oil from gathering lines to the refinery.

Tugboats: Boats designed to pull barges.

Turbine: A bladed wheel that captures the kinetic energy of fluids as the fluids strike the blades.

Two-stroke cycle engine: An internal combustion engine having a power stroke every two cycles.

U

Unibody construction: A vehicle structure in which the body and frame are one integral unit.

Universal electric motor: An electric motor that can operate on either AC or DC current.

Universal joints: Devices that allow a change of direction between two shafts rotating on different planes.

Unmanned vehicle: Any type of spacecraft with no crew aboard.

Uranium: A nuclear fuel in its natural state thought to have originated in volcanic ash.

V

Valence ring: The outermost ring of an atom containing one or more orbiting electrons.

Values: Things that one considers important.

Vehicular system: A collection of systems that allow the vehicle to move through its environment safely and efficiently. These systems are usually part of the vehicle itself but may be separate from it.

Voltage: The pressure that pushes the current through a conductor.

Voltmeter: Instrument that measure voltage.

W

Water transportation: Transportation through and supported by water. This includes ships, sailboats, rafts, barges, tugboats, and submarines.

Waterways: Routes that water vessels travel.

Wedges: Mechanisms consisting of two inclined planes placed back to back. Hatchets, knives, and nails are examples.

Weightlessness: A condition that occurs when the force of gravity and other counterforces are equal.

Wheels and axles: Machines that are based on the lever and able to change either force or distance when force is applied to them.

Wind turbines: Wheels that are designed to capture the energy of wind and use it to operate electric generators.

Work: The application of force applied to move an object.

INDEX

R